PACIFIC VOYAGES
AND EXPLORATION

PACIFIC VOYAGES AND EXPLORATION

FROM THE CARLSMITH COLLECTION
AND OTHER SOURCES

ANNE
McCORMICK **HORDERN HOUSE** DEREK
McDONNELL
RARE BOOKS • MANUSCRIPTS • PAINTINGS • PRINTS

HORDERN HOUSE
77 VICTORIA STREET • POTTS POINT • SYDNEY NSW 2011 • AUSTRALIA
TELEPHONE 356 4411 • TELEX AA75374 • FAX (02) 357 3635

For Leo Keyes
1914-1987

Anne McCormick & Derek McDonnell
Hordern House
77 Victoria Street
Potts Point Sydney 2011 Australia

First published in 1987 by Hordern House Pty. Ltd.
Copyright © Hordern House Pty. Ltd.

National Library of Australia
Cataloguing-in-publication data.

Hordern House.
The Carlsmith collection of Pacific Voyages and Exploration.

Bibliography.
Includes index.
ISBN 0 9588478 6 X.

1. Carlsmith, Wendell, 1904-1982 — Library — Catalogs.
2. Carlsmith, Donn — Library — Catalogs.
3. Pacific Area — Discovery and exploration — Bibliography — Catalogs.

I. McCormick, Anne. II. McDonnell, Derek. III. Title.

016.919'04

Photography by David Liddle
Printed by Bridge Printery Sales Pty Ltd. Rosebery 2018.

CONTENTS

INTRODUCTION

The Carlsmith family collection of Pacific voyages was carefully assembled over a 40 year period, beginning in the 1940s. Wendell Carlsmith was a man of the Pacific; born in Hawaii in 1904 he was educated at Stanford University. After graduating from Stanford Law School he joined his father in his Hilo law firm. By the time of his death in 1982 the firm employed 70 lawyers, with offices in Guam, Hilo, Kona and Honolulu.

In the course of the firm's expansion Wendell, who was in time joined by his son Donn, travelled widely; they became regular visitors to the leading booksellers of San Francisco, London and Paris. Together they built an outstanding library of voyage and travel books, always with an emphasis on fine condition.

Both father and son had the discerning eye of the collector, and this was further enriched in both by the deep knowledge that they possessed of their books. They were fascinated by the history of the early discovery and settlement of the Hawaiian islands; as a result the collection centres around the voyages of Cook and those of the early French, English and Russian explorers, but it is also set in a more general context of wider Pacific exploration.

When Wendell Carlsmith died, the Honolulu Star Bulletin reported that "he was internationally known for having assembled one of the nation's finest collections of rare books and maps dealing with the early voyages and discoveries in the Pacific . . .". Donn Carlsmith continued to add to the collection, but in 1986 decided that it was time that the pleasure he and his father had derived from building the collection should be shared with collectors around the world.

The Hawaiian islands are roughly at the centre of the Pacific; one of the boundaries — increasingly one of the most important boundaries — of the great ocean is Australia. The early history of the exploration of the Pacific coincides with the identification, exploration and ultimate settlement of the Australian continent, a facet of its history amply demonstrated by the Carlsmith collection. We are particularly pleased as Australian dealers to have been the successful purchasers of the collection, and to be offering it for sale on the eve of the Australian bicentenary.

This catalogue details the Carlsmith family collection of Pacific voyages, with some additions from other sources where appropriate. We are particularly grateful to David Forbes, of Honolulu and San Francisco, for his knowledgeable help with the compilation of the catalogue.

Anne McCormick
Derek McDonnell

Sydney, 1987.

I
Pacific Voyages before 1770, including collections

Pacific discovery began in the 16th century with the Spanish voyagers; the first to continue across the great ocean was Ferdinand Magellan, a Portuguese in the service of Spain. It was Magellan who named the ocean that would inspire navigators for several centuries the "Pacific".

The Portuguese and the Spanish searched tirelessly for a Southern Continent, while the Dutch looked to the East Indies and beyond to expand their trading empire. In 1606 William Jansz landed on Cape York Peninsula and in the following decades parts of the west, north and southern shoreline of an unknown continent were touched.

By the 18th century both the French and the English nations were systematically exploring the Pacific with a view to colonization. It was these great maritime and scientific powers which made the most distinctive contribution to the mapping of the Pacific. They did this with growing rivalry as both nations vied for honours, seeking to lead the scientific world.

Even by the time that most of the main island groups had been visited, there remained the "Terra Australis" mystery; the quest for a southern continent, and the gradual establishment of the outlines of Australia, represent the recurring theme of the early history of Pacific exploration. Not until the arrival of the Englishman James Cook were those questions to be solved.

BELOW:
2: ANSON. *Title vignette from the Dutch edition of Anson's voyage incorporating a portrait of Anson.*

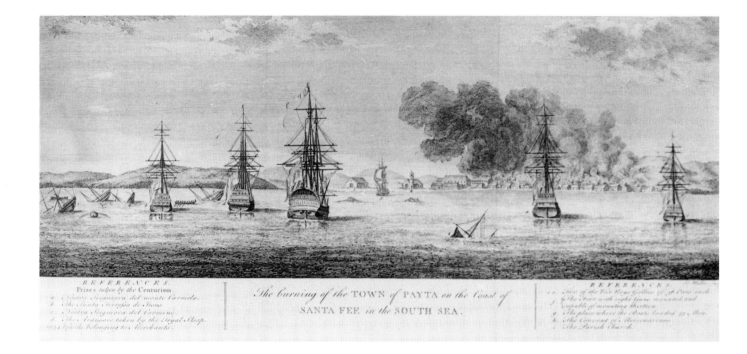

REFERENCES.
Prizes taken by the Centurion
a Nostra Segniora del monte Carmelo.
b The Santa Terrosa de Sesus.
c Nostra Segniora del Carmeno.
d The Transou taken by the Royal Sloop.
Ships belonging to Merchants.

The burning of the TOWN of PAYTA on the Coast of
SANTA FEE in the SOUTH SEA.

REFERENCES.
one of the First Rings Gollen of 80 Oars each
The Ships with eight Guns mounted and
capable of mounting thirteen
The place where the Boats landed 31 Men
The Convent of Missionaries
The Parish Church

THE FIRST EDITION OF ANSON'S VOYAGE

[1] ANSON, George. WALTER, Richard, *compiler*. A
VOYAGE ROUND THE WORLD, in the Years MDCCXL,
I, II, III, IV. By George Anson, Esq; Commander in
Chief of a Squadron of His Majesty's Ships, sent upon
an Expedition to the South-Seas . . . *Quarto, with 42
folding engraved plates and maps; a few tears to folds and one
map worn at outer margin; overall a good, fresh copy with
strong impressions of the plates, in contemporary mottled calf,
joints worn, later label.* London: Printed for the Author,
by John & Paul Knapton, 1748.

First and best edition of the official account of
Anson's voyage, with excellent impressions of the
many fine plates, which in later editions become
worn. Based on Anson's own journal, this narrative
had an enormous popular success: although the voyage
itself, while a success in terms of ships plundered and
treasure captured, was otherwise a disaster (of the six
ships and 1,955 men that set out in 1740, only one
ship and 904 men returned), for the mid-eighteenth
century reader, Anson's account was the epitome of
adventure. It was translated into several European
languages and stayed in print through numerous
editions for many years.

With the early ownership inscription of James
Whitehall. *Hill, pp. 317-18; Sabin, 1625.*

[2] ANSON, George. WALTER, Richard, *compiler*.
REIZE RONDSOM DE WERRELD, Gedaan in de Jaaren
1740 tot 1744, door den heere George Anson,
opperbevelhebber over een esquader engelsche
schepen op een expeditie naar den zuidzee. *Quarto, title
printed in red and black, with engraved vignettes on title and
dedication pp., and 34 engraved maps, charts and plates (most
folding); modern quarter calf antique, slight dampstaining to
margins only of part of text, small hole and dark stain to last*

few pages of text; a good copy. Te Amsterdam, By Isaak
Tition, 1749.

Second Dutch edition, and typographically one of
the most attractive editions of the voyage. The
handsome cartouche portrait on the dedication leaf is
of Gustaaf Willem, Baron van Imhoff, Governor
General of the Dutch East Indies, and the title vignette
(opposite) showing Anson and his ships does not
appear in any English edition.

THE FIRST FRENCH CIRCUMNAVIGATION

[3] BOUGAINVILLE, Louis Antoine de. VOYAGE
AUTOUR DU MONDE, par la frégate du Roi, La
Boudeuse, et la Flûte l'Etoile; en 1766, 1767, 1768 &
1769. *Quarto, with 20 engraved charts (including 18
folding) and 3 plates of boats; contemporary calf, rebacked,
small hole to last blank leaves, not affecting text, occasional
light spotting; a very good copy; with the armorial bookplate
of the Earl of Suffolk and Berkshire.* Paris, Chez Saillant &
Nyon, 1771.

First edition: the first French circumnavigation of
the globe. Bougainville sailed from Nantes in
November 1766 to the Falkland Islands. They picked
up a supply ship, the *Etoile*, and both ships passed
through the Straits of Magellan in January 1768, spent
time looking for the mythical "Davis Land", said to
be off the Chilean coast, and then started on a direct
route across the Pacific. Bougainville discovered the
Tuamotus, and in April sighted and thought he had
discovered Tahiti, not knowing that Wallis had been
there the previous year. He visited Samoa, sailed
through Melanesia, sighted the Great Barrier Reef,
passed through the Solomons, and New Britain, to
Batavia.

His lengthy account of Tahiti is an interesting

1: ANSON. *Anson's Fleet sacking
the town of Payta; an engraving from
the official account of the voyage.*

7: BOUGAINVILLE. *Louis Antoine de Bougainville, the first French circumnavigator.*

6: BOUGAINVILLE & MAGRA. *The two earliest works on Tahiti.*

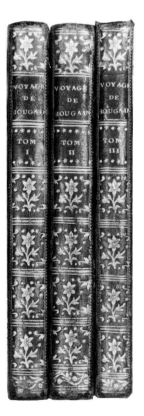

counterpart to Wallis' account, and the vocabulary of 300 words is the first to be printed of any Polynesian language. Bougainville's account of his travels in the Pacific created enormous interest in France, and was largely responsible for building up the romantic vision of a South Sea paradise where Rousseau's noble savage lived in a state of blissful innocence. *Hill, p. 31; Kroepelien, 109; O'Reilly-Reitman, 283.*

FIRST EDITION OF BOUGAINVILLE IN ENGLISH

[4] BOUGAINVILLE, Louis Antoine de. A VOYAGE ROUND THE WORLD. Performed by Order of His most Christian Majesty, in the Years 1766, 1767, 1768, and 1769 . . . in the Frigate La Boudeuse, and the store-ship L'Etoile. *Quarto, with five folding maps and a folding plate of canoes; contemporary speckled calf, gilt diaper patterned spine, red label (neatly rebacked), slight spotting of text, but a fine copy in an attractive contemporary binding; with the bookplate of Sir Stafford H. Northcote, Bt.* London, Printed for J. Nourse . . . and T. Davies . . . 1772.

First English edition. Translated and with an introduction by Johann Reinhold Forster, who calls the voyage "a work written by a learned, intelligent, and judicious traveller, which abounds with remarkable events and curious observations . . .". Forster says he has edited "and partially vindicated the

British nation where we thought the author had been unjustly partial". The discourse on the language having been found "imperfect and defective" has here been omitted. *Hill, p. 32; Kroepelien, 113; O'Reilly-Reitman, 285.*

[5] [BOUGAINVILLE] FESCHE, Charles Felix Pierre. LA NOUVELLE CYTHERE (TAHITI). Journal de navigation inedit, écrit à bord de la fregate du Roy la Boudeuse, commandée par M. le Chevalier de Bougainville. Avant-propos de Jean Dorsenne. *Octavo, with 2 colour illustrations, chart and plate of a canoe; original orange wrappers, yellow label on upper cover, spine and edges slightly darkened; a very good copy.* Paris, Editions Duchartre, [1929].

A description of Tahiti by one of the sailors on Bougainville's ship the *Boudeuse*, transcribed from the original manuscript in the Museum d'histoire Naturelle, Paris. *Hill, p. 420; O'Reilly-Reitman, 304.*

THE TWO EARLIEST WORKS ON TAHITI

[6] [BOUGAINVILLE and MAGRA] VOYAGE AUTOUR DU MONDE, par la Frégate du Roi La Boudeuse, et la Flûte l'Etoile, en 1766, 1767, 1768 & 1769. [With, as Volume III] Supplément au Voyage de M. De Bougainville, ou Journal d'un Voyage Autour du Monde, fait par MM. Banks & Solander, Anglois, en 1768, 1769, 1770, 1771. Traduit de l'Anglois, par M. de Freville. *3 volumes, octavo; contemporary tortoiseshell calf, gilt floral compartmented spines, red and green labels; slight wear to joints and spinal extremities, but a fine set.* Neuchatel, de l'Imprimerie de la Société Typographique, 1773.

Early and attractive editions of the two earliest works on Tahiti, and one of the earliest continental sources for the knowledge of the eastern coast of Australia. The Bougainville account is a reprint of the first (Paris) edition of 1771, and the Magra account, though the title reads "supplément", is complete in itself. This second work by John Magra is the second French edition of the anonymously published account of Cook's first voyage (see item 49), and was printed only a year after the first Paris edition. It contains a French-Tahitian vocabulary and letters from Commerson on Madagascar; from "M. le B. de G." on the North West Passage (1771); and Condamine's "Observations" on Tahiti. *Beddie, 700; Kroepelien, 112 (note); O'Reilly-Reitman, 290 & 363 (note).*

[7] BOUGAINVILLE, BELLIARD, S. LOUIS ANTOINE DE BOUGAINVILLE. *Coloured lithograph portrait, 255 x 215 mm., in good condition; mounted.* Paris, Lith. de Delpech, circa 1830.

A good portrait of the navigator, facing front, wearing wig and flounced shirt. *Nan Kivell & Spence, p. 37.*

[8] DE BROSSES, Charles. HISTOIRE DES NAVIGATIONS AUX TERRES AUSTRALES. Contenant ce que l'on scait des moeurs & des productions des Contrées decouvertes jusqu'à ce jour; & ou il est traité de l'utilité d'y faire de plus amples découvertes, & des moyens d'y former un établissement. *2 volumes,*

quarto, with 7 folding maps, original cloth; a good modern facsimile. Paris, Chez Durand, 1756. [Amsterdam, Nico Israel, 1967].

One of the most important general works dealing with early voyages to the Pacific, which aimed to stimulate French discovery and colonisation of the South Seas. It contains an account of all voyages to the south, beginning with the second Vespucci expedition of 1502 and going up up to 1747, including the voyages of Magellan, Drake, Schouten, Tasman and others.

THE FIRST PACIFIC VOYAGE PRINTED IN AMERICA

[9] BULKELEY, John and John CUMMINS. A VOYAGE TO THE SOUTH SEAS, in the years 1740-1. Containing a faithful Narrative of the Loss of His Majesty's Ship the Wager on a desolate island in the lattitude of 47 south, longitude 81 west: with the proceedings and conduct of the officers and crew . . . with many things not published in the first edition. *Duodecimo, xxxii, 306 pp.; modern half calf, chips to title, text browned as usual, corners slightly shaved; despite defects, a good copy.* London, Printed, Philadelphia, Reprinted by James Chattin, for the author, 1757.

First American edition, and very rare: the first Pacific voyage to be printed in America. This renowned account describes the wreck of the *Wager*, one of Anson's fleet, off the coast of Chile, the survivors' life on shore, and their subsequent voyage in a long boat through the Straits of Magellan to Rio de Janeiro.

Bulkeley, who had emigrated to America, dedicated this edition to William Denny, Lieutenant Governor of Pennsylvania, and the list of some 1162 subscribers, accounting for 1216 copies of the work, reads like an early eighteenth century Who's Who of America. Despite the large number of copies subscribed, very few copies have survived. The narrative of Isaac Morris, one of the crew of the *Wager* (pp. 244-303), does not appear in any English edition. *Hill, p. 39.*

[10] [BULKELEY, John and John CUMMINS.] REIZE NAER DE ZUIDZEE, met het schip de Wager, onder het opzicht van den Heere George Anson. Ondernomen in den jaere 1740. *Quarto, title printed in red and black, with engraved vignette on title and 8 engraved plates (4 folding); modern quarter calf, a good copy.* Te Leyden en Amsterdam, By Johannes Le Mair, Stephanus Jacobus Baalde, Cornelis van Hoogeveen, Junior, 1766.

First Dutch edition of this important supplementary account of Anson's voyage; the Mitchell Library catalogue indicates that it was "composed rather than directly translated from the French 1756 edition". The finely engraved plates by Kuipers give this edition particular distinction.

"CONTAINING PRACTICALLY EVERYTHING OF IMPORTANCE"

[11] BURNEY, James. A CHRONOLOGICAL HISTORY OF THE DISCOVERIES IN THE SOUTH SEA OR PACIFIC OCEAN. *5 volumes, quarto, with 28 engraved maps*

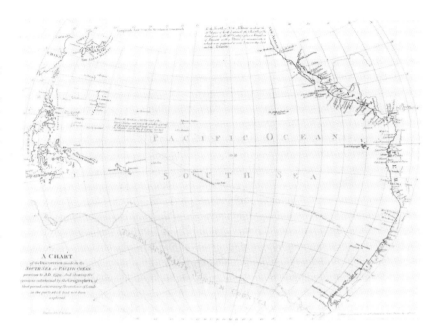

11: BURNEY. *"A Chart of the Discoveries made in the South Sea"; engraved map from Burney's Chronological History.*

(including 16 folding), 13 plates and 6 text woodcuts; contemporary full russia, neatly rebacked, all edges gilt; occasional light browning of end leaves, but a very good set. London, Printed by Luke Hansard . . . and Sold by G. and A. Nicol, booksellers to His Majesty, 1803-1807.

First edition. "The most important general history of early South Sea discoveries containing practically everything of importance on the subject" (Hill). Burney covers in an orderly and erudite fashion more than 250 years of Pacific exploration prior to that of Cook, including Spanish, Dutch, French and English voyages, with a general *History of the Buccaneers of America*, and concludes with Bougainville's voyage to Tahiti.

Burney, who had sailed with Cook as lieutenant during the last two voyages, received encouragement from Sir Joseph Banks (to whom the work is dedicated) and enjoyed free access both to Banks' magnificent library of books and manuscripts, and to Dalrymple's collection of scarcer Spanish books. Whenever possible, he relied on manuscript accounts, generally comparing them with printed narratives for purposes of style. The collection contains much that is nowhere else accessible, and will always remain one of the chief authorities for the history of the geographical exploration and discovery of the Pacific.

Burney himself explains (in volume 5) that "the termination of this present work is adapted to the commencement of voyages in another collection [i.e. that of Hawkesworth] which with the addition of M. de Bougainville's voyage round the world, follows as an immediate sequel, without any chasm being left, to the Discoveries here related" *Davidson, p. 37; Hill, p. 40.*

THE LOSS OF THE WAGER

[12] BYRON, John. THE NARRATIVE OF THE HONOURABLE JOHN BYRON . . . containing An Account of the Great Distresses suffered by himself and his companions on the Coast of Patagonia, from the year 1740, till their arrival in England, 1746. With a

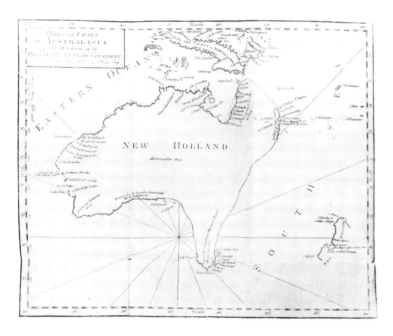

14: CALLANDER. *Callander's chart of Australasia shows the gaps in contemporary knowledge of the continent.*

description of St. Jago de Chile . . . also a relation of the loss of the Wager Man of War, one of Admiral Anson's Squadron. *Octavo, with a frontispiece; calf antique, spine gilt, red label; a very good clean copy.* London, Printed for S. Baker and G. Leigh, 1768.

First edition. "Admiral Byron's narrative of the loss of the Wager is one of the most thrilling accounts in the language, and supplied his illustrious descendant with many particulars for the shipwreck in Don Juan" (Sabin). The author, later a noted Pacific explorer and known as "foul weather Jack", was a midshipman aboard the *Wager* and his narrative provides a notable supplement to the main account of Anson's voyage. *Hill, pp. 41-2.*

[13] BYRON, John. THE NARRATIVE OF THE HONOURABLE JOHN BYRON . . . containing An Account of the Great Distresses suffered by himself and his companions on the Coast of Patagonia, from the year 1740, till their arrival in England, 1746. With a description of St. Jago de Chile . . . also a relation of the loss of the Wager Man of War, one of Admiral Anson's Squadron. *Octavo, with a frontispiece; old quarter calf rebacked, preserving original spine, red label, extremities of boards worn, title-page and plate browned, with contemporary ms. annotations throughout.* London, Printed for S. Baker and G. Leigh, 1768.

First edition. *Hill, pp. 41-2.*

[BYRON]-see also items 50-53 (Hawkesworth).

VOYAGES TO THE SOUTHERN HEMISPHERE

[14] CALLANDER, John. TERRA AUSTRALIS COGNITA; OR, VOYAGES TO THE TERRA AUSTRALIS, OR SOUTHERN HEMISPHERE, during the Sixteenth, Seventeenth, and Eighteenth Centuries. Containing an account of the manners of the people, and the productions of the countries, hitherto found in the southern latitudes; the advantages that may result from further discoveries, and the methods of establishing colonies there, to the advantage of Great Britain. *3*

volumes, octavo, with 3 folding maps; neat repairs (clear of text) to defects in upper margins of several early leaves; the general map in volume 2 backed on tissue and repaired; overall an excellent copy in contemporary calf, spines gilt, double leather labels (one chipped). Edinburgh, Printed by A. Donaldson, 1766 [-1768].

First edition: the scarce issue (only recently identified — see Quaritch *Bulletin 22*, item 25), with the variant dedication to Sir Laurence Dundas in volume 1, replacing the dedication to Charles Townshend who died in 1767. With the contemporary ownership inscriptions of John Campbell; bound without the advertisement leaf in volume 1.

Based on the De Brosses account which had appeared ten years earlier, Callander's collection contains forty one narratives, some of which appear here for the first time in English, generally prefaced by a general summation and short biography of the narrator. Included are the voyages of Magellan, Drake, Sarimento, Cavendish, de Quiros, Schouten, Narborough, Dampier, Funnell, Woodes Rogers, Shelvocke, Roggewein and others.

Callander also promotes the idea of a penal settlement in the Pacific, but at New Britain, to support the further exploration and settlement of New Holland, and claims the inevitability of English occupation of that continent by her superior sea power. His book represents the fundamental proposal for the first European settlement of the 'Southern Continent'. *Hill, p. 367.*

[15] CAMPBELL, Alexander. THE SEQUEL TO BULKELEY AND CUMMINS' VOYAGE TO THE SOUTH-SEAS: or, The Adventures of Capt. Cheap, the Hon. Mr. Byron, Lieut. Hamilton, Alexander Campbell, and others, late of His Majesty's Ship the Wager, which was wreck'd on a desolate island in lat. 47. S. long. 81.40 W. in the South-Seas, anno 1741. *Duodecimo; contemporary calf, rebacked, gilt spine, green label; a few pages trimmed to running title, not affecting text.* Dublin, Printed by J. Kinnier, 1747.

First Dublin edition, published the same year as the London edition. The author sailed aboard the *Wager*, part of Anson's fleet. The ship was wrecked off the southern coast of Chile after passing through the Strait of Magellan, and the account includes a general description of that country. Campbell's account contains the defence of his conduct during the voyage, and the unjust treatment of Captain Cheap, who had claimed that Campbell had gone into the Spanish service, thus depriving him of further employment. The author claimed the work "devoid of art, malice, or misrepresentation". *See Hill, p. 44, for London edition.*

[CARTERET]-see also items 50-53 (Hawkesworth).

THE CHURCHILLS' COLLECTION

[16] CHURCHILL, Awnsham & John (comp.). A COLLECTION OF VOYAGES AND TRAVELS, some now first printed from original manuscripts, others now first published in English . . . with a general Preface,

giving an account of the progress of navigation, from its first beginning. Illustrated with a great number of useful Maps and Cuts, curiously engraved. *6 volumes, folio, with list of subscribers including leaf of engraved arms of subscribers (some of which do not appear on the list), with 714 engraved maps, plates and views (many folding); contemporary speckled panelled calf, neatly rebacked, corners expertly repaired; slight soiling to blank end leaves, text very clean and fresh; with the armorial bookplate of James Plunkett, Earl of Fingal.* London, Printed by Assignment from Messrs. Churchill, for John Walthoe [& 6 others], 1732.

This compilation of voyages by two ambitious and successful English bookseller brothers, which anticipates the dawning age of navigation and discovery, enjoyed a well deserved popularity. John Locke, the philosopher, their intimate friend, had much to do with the production of this work (DNB) and there is some evidence to suggest that he wrote the preliminary essay on navigation. The "Political and Moral Sentences . . . of Confucius" in the first volume may well have been added at his suggestion.

There are three voyages to China, and travels to Formosa and Japan, Korea, the Solomon Islands, India, South East Asia and the Philippines. Baldaeus's description of Malabar, the Coromandel Coast and Ceylon contains 13 engraved plates. The African accounts include visits to the Cape of Good Hope, the Congo, Ethiopia, and North and South Guinea (with 50 plates and maps).

The American narratives include descriptions of Chile, Paraguay, the "Caribee Islands", Nieuhoff's visit to Brazil and the East Indies (with 70 plates and maps), and the travels of John Smith in Europe, Asia, Africa and America. Munck's account of his voyage to Greenland in 1619-20, contains the 5 important whaling plates.

The two supplemental volumes, generally known as the "Harleian Voyages", were published later and are not present here. *Hill, pp. 52-53 (listing the 3rd edition).*

PRE-COOK DISCOVERY OF AUSTRALIA

[17] COLLINGRIDGE, George. THE DISCOVERY OF AUSTRALIA. A Critical, Documentary and Historic Investigation Concerning the Priority of Discovery in Australasia by Europeans before the arrival of Lieut. James Cook, in the "Endeavour", in the year 1770. *Quarto, with numerous maps (some folding), plates and text illustrations; full plum cloth, gilt vignette on upper cover, brown endpapers; small splits to extremities of spine; a good sound copy.* Sydney, Hayes Brothers, 1895.

An important nineteenth century contribution to the history of Australia and the pre-Cook discovery of the continent, this is also the first serious attempt at a geographical history of the continent. Although outmoded, it is a standard and basic work for the collector; Collingridge was able to claim "I believe I can truly say that I have read every book, and examined every map of real importance to the question, which has been produced in English, French, Spanish, Portugese, Italian and Dutch". Rodney Davidson, in *A Book Collector's Notes* (Melbourne, 1970) calls it "a sought after item". *Ferguson, 4865.*

AN

HISTORICAL COLLECTION

OF THE SEVERAL

VOYAGES AND DISCOVERIES

IN THE

SOUTH PACIFIC OCEAN.

VOL. I.

Being chiefly a LITERAL TRANSLATION from the SPANISH WRITERS.

By ALEXANDER DALRYMPLE, ESQ.

LOOKING FOR A GREAT SOUTHERN CONTINENT

[18] DALRYMPLE, Alexander. AN HISTORICAL COLLECTION OF THE SEVERAL VOYAGES AND DISCOVERIES IN THE SOUTH PACIFIC OCEAN. *2 volumes (in 1), quarto, with 2 maps (1 folding), a chart & 12 engraved plates; contemporary calf, rebacked, blue label, corners neatly repaired; occasional spotting mostly confined to front and back leaves; a very good copy, with the bookplate of Augustin Kramer.* London, Printed for the Author; and sold by J. Nourse . . . and P. Elmsley, 1770, 1771.

An important collection of Spanish and Dutch voyages, announcing the dawn of the golden age of Pacific exploration. Beginning with Magellan's voyage of 1519, the Spanish accounts include Mendana's voyage to the Solomon Islands in 1595, and that of de Quiros in 1606. The Dutch accounts include those of Le Maire, Schouten, Tasman and Roggewein. Dalrymple's long introduction on trade and his "investigation of what may be farther expected in the South Sea" expound his belief in the existence of a "Great Southern Continent", a theory firmly laid to rest when Cook later sailed right over a substantial portion of it.

Dalrymple (1737-1808), the great hydrographer, who had made his career in the East India Company, was offered the command of the expedition to observe the transit of Venus, but partly because of his insistence on being given an Admiralty commission, the command went to Cook. His disappointment is hinted at in the remarkable "undedications" of this

18: DALRYMPLE. *Dalrymple's* Historical Collection *summarised European knowledge of the Pacific before Captain Cook.*

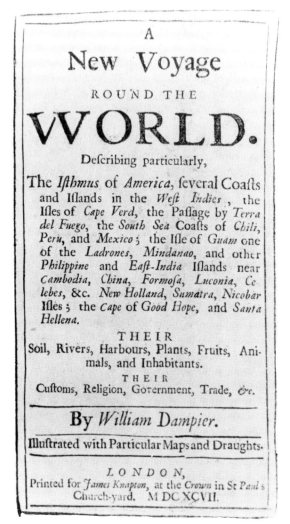

A
New Voyage
ROUND THE
WORLD.

Deſcribing particularly,

The *Iſthmus* of *America*, ſeveral Coaſts and Iſlands in the *Weſt Indies*, the Iſles of *Cape Verd*, the Paſſage by *Terra del Fuego*, the *South Sea* Coaſts of *Chili*, *Peru*, and *Mexico*; the Iſle of *Guam* one of the *Ladrones*, *Mindanao*, and other *Philippine* and *Eaſt-India* Iſlands near *Cambodia*, *China*, *Formoſa*, *Luconia*, *Celebes*, &c. *New Holland*, *Sumatra*, *Nicobar* Iſles; the *Cape* of *Good Hope*, and *Santa Hellena*.

THEIR
Soil, Rivers, Harbours, Plants, Fruits, Animals, and Inhabitants.
THEIR
Cuſtoms, Religion, Government, Trade, &c.

By *William Dampier*.

Illuſtrated with Particular Maps and Draughts.

LONDON,
Printed for *James Knapton*, at the *Crown* in St *Pauls* Church-yard. MDCXCVII.

20: DAMPIER. *The first edition of Dampier's* New Voyage Round the World, *describing the first English visit to Australia. This copy of the famous buccaneering narrative belonged to a Lord of the Admiralty (below).*

work: to Byron "who discovered scarcely anything but Patagonians" and to Banks who "infatuated with female blandishments forgot for what he went abroad and hastened back to amuse the European world with stories of enchantments . . .". *Hill, p. 71; Kroepelien, 245.*

THE SOUTH PACIFICK

[19] DALRYMPLE, Alexander. CHART OF THE SOUTH PACIFICK OCEAN, Pointing out the Discoveries made therein previous to 1764. *Engraved map, 305 x 515 mm, in excellent condition, mounted.* London, Publish'd according to Act of Parliament, October 1767.

Dalrymple's famous map of the South Pacific — from his *Historical Collection of the Several Voyages and Discoveries in the South Pacific Ocean* — gives perhaps the neatest summary of European knowledge of the South Sea just before Cook's first voyage. Dalrymple was in fact passed over by the Admiralty in favour of Cook for the command of the *Endeavour* voyage.

THE FIRST ENGLISH LANDING IN AUSTRALIA

[20] DAMPIER, William. A NEW VOYAGE ROUND THE WORLD. Describing particularly the Isthmus of America, several Coasts and Islands in the West Indies, the Isles of Cape Verd, the Passage by Terra del Fuego,

the South Sea Coasts of Chile, Peru and Mexico; the Isle of Guam one of the Ladrones, Mindanao, and other Philippine and East-India Islands . . . New Holland, Sumatra, Nicobar Isles; the Cape of Good Hope, and Santa Helena . . . Illustrated with particular maps and draughts. *Octavo, with 5 engraved maps (4 folding); contemporary speckled calf, rebacked, preserving the original gilt panelled spine, red label; marginal defect to one leaf neatly repaired; a fine crisp copy with the engraved bookplate of Thomas Earl of Strafford on verso of title-page.* London, Printed for James Knapton, 1697.

First edition: the first account of the first landing in Australia by an Englishman. From the library of Thomas Wentworth, Earl of Strafford, who as Baron Raby was ambassador-extraordinary to The Hague. He succeeded to the title of third Earl of Strafford in 1711, and the bookplate used here was printed in 1712, the year of his appointment as Lord of the Admiralty. Dampier was perhaps England's most famous buccaneer, and it is particularly appealing to see that this fine copy of the first edition of his adventures came from the library of a senior member of the naval establishment.

Dampier's descriptions of his wide-ranging buccaneering travels include the account of the first English visit to Australia, when in 1688, "being now clear of all the Islands, we stood off South, intending to touch at New Holland, a part of Terra Australis Incognita, to see what the country would afford us . . . New Holland is a very large tract of Land. It is not yet determined whether it is an Island or a main Continent; but I am certain that it joyns neither to Asia, Africa, nor America . . .".

Dampier describes the appearance of the country and its natural produce, and includes a long description of the native inhabitants, to whom he was not attracted — "the miserablest people in the world . . .". The folding "Map of the East Indies" shows a large proportion of the north west coast of Australia and marks the point (present-day Dampier Land) where the expedition stopped before turning back to the East Indies.

Publication of Dampier's works at the end of the 17th and beginning of the 18th century presents a muddled picture to bibliographers. The genuine first edition of the *New Voyage round the World* — which is relatively scarce, not being held in the Hill Collection, for example — may be distinguished from later issues by a number of points, a schedule of which is available on request. *Hill, p. 75 (later editions); Wing, D161.*

[21] DAMPIER, William. A NEW VOYAGE ROUND THE WORLD. Describing particularly the Isthmus of America, several Coasts and Islands in the West Indies, the Isles of Cape Verd, the Passage by Terra del Fuego, the South Sea Coasts of Chile, Peru and Mexico; the Isle of Guam one of the Ladrones, Mindanao, and other Philippine and East-India Islands . . . New Holland . . . *Octavo, with 5 engraved maps, contemporary calf, somewhat worn, spine repaired and front inner hinge strengthened.* London, Printed for James Knapton, 1697 [-1699].

The first account of the first landing in Australia by an Englishman. Although appearing to be the first

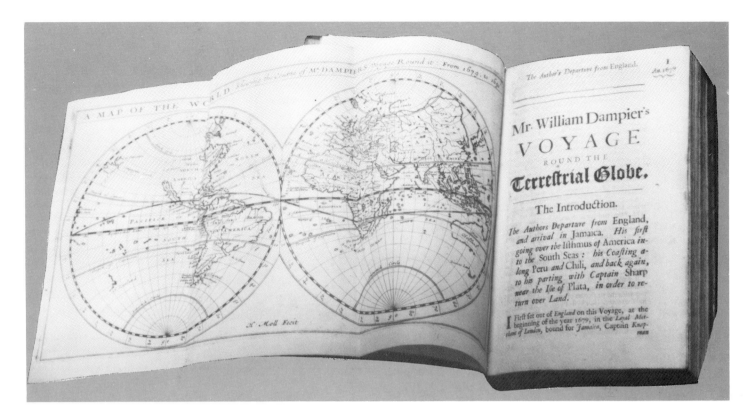

edition, at least some leaves in this copy are from the fourth edition of 1699, and the final leaves are of the issue without errata; whether this represents a contemporary compilation or not is open to question. *Hill, p. 75; Wing D161/164.*

THE FOUR-VOLUME DAMPIER

[22] DAMPIER, William. A COLLECTION OF VOYAGES. In Four Volumes. Containing:

I. Captain William Dampier's Voyages round the World: Describing particularly the Coasts and Islands in the East and West-Indies. The South-sea Coasts of Chile, Peru and Mexico. The Countries of Tonquin, Achin and Malacca. The Cape of Good Hope, New Holland &c.

II. The Voyages of Lionel Wafer; giving an account of his being left on the Isthmus of America . . . with a particular Description of the Country . . .

III. A Voyage round the World: containing an Account of Capt. Dampier's Expedition into the South Seas in the ship St. George . . . By W. Funnell, Mate to Capt. Dampier.

IV. Capt. Cowley's Voyage round the Globe.

V. Capt. Sharp's Journey over the isthmus of Darien, and expedition into the South-Seas.

VI. Capt. Wood's Voyage through the streights of Magellan.

VII. Mr. Roberts' Adventures and Sufferings amongst the Corsairs of the Levant . . .

4 volumes, octavo, with many engraved plates and maps; two folding maps worn at outer margins; contemporary calf, spines gilt; neat repairs to spines, preserved in two folding boxes. London, Printed for James and John Knapton, 1729.

A fine set of the collected edition of Dampier's works, which by 1729 had reached a total of 3 volumes, with a fourth volume added by the publishers containing Funnell's account of the Dampier voyage (see also 27 below) as well as the accounts of Cowley, Sharp, Wood and Roberts (parts III-VII in the list of contents given on the general title-page reproduced above).

Dampier's publishers Knapton used the latest editions of each of the four volumes with a new general title-page to produce the collected edition as it appears here; thus the first volume is in its "seventh edition, corrected" form, while the others are represented by third or fourth edition texts.

Dampier's complete works represent a major body of Pacific description, and are of considerable importance for any study of the discovery and colonisation of the Pacific. As James A. Williamson wrote in his introduction to the Argonaut Press's 1939 edition of the *Voyage to New Holland*, "Dampier's permanent service to his countrymen was to arouse their interest in the exploration of the Pacific. He did it so effectively that in the eighteenth century they took the lead in revealing the tropical islands and the coasts of Australia and New Zealand and two dominions of the British Commonwealth are . . . the outcome of that enterprise. His third and last book, the Voyage to New Holland, concentrated attention more particularly on the western and southern Pacific. It might have been more aptly described as a voyage to New Britain and a project for Eastern Australia, for there essentially lay the focus of his interest . . .".

The "four-volume Dampier" is generally considered the best edition of the various works, and

22: DAMPIER. *The fullest edition of Dampier's Voyages.*

20-22: DAMPIER. *The Western Australian aborigines struck Dampier as "the miserablest people in the world".*

The poor winking People of New Holland,

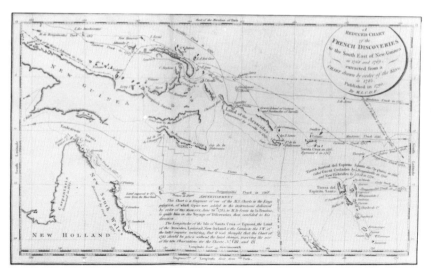

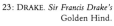
25: FLEURIEU. *Fleurieu used the accounts of numerous voyages to produce charts of New Guinea and Northern Australia.*

is surprisingly scarce today. This fine set is from the library of the Duke of Leeds, with his bookplate in each volume. *Hill, pp. 77-78.*

THE GOLDEN HIND

[23] DRAKE, Sir Francis. WOODCUT EMBLEM OF THE GOLDEN HIND and poem addressed to Richard Drake in praise of Sir Francis Drake [from Whitney, Choice of Emblemes]. *Single leaf, measuring 8 x 6 ins., woodcut emblem within typographical border, 20-line poem below.* Leiden, Plantin Press, 1586.

A very early illustration of Drake's great ship, the *Golden Hind*; this is a single leaf from the rare first English emblem book, Geoffrey Whitney's *Choice of Emblemes.*

23: DRAKE. *Sir Francis Drake's Golden Hind.*

The poem honours Drake who "Throughe scorchinge heate, throughe coulde, in stormes, and tempests force,/by ragged rocks, by shelfes, & sandes: this knighte did keepe his course . . ." and invites the reader "And you, that live at home, and can not brooke the flood,/give praise to them, that passe the waves, to doe their countrie good./Before which sorte, as chiefe: in tempeste, and in calme,/Francis Drake, by due deserte, may weare the goulden palme." *S.T.C., 25438.*

NEW UNIVERSAL COLLECTION

[24] DRAKE, Edward Cavendish. A NEW UNIVERSAL COLLECTION of Authentic and Entertaining Voyages and Travels . . . *Folio, numerous engraved maps and plates; a very good copy in contemporary straight-grained purple roan, gilt, joints neatly repaired.* London, Printed for J. Cooke, 1768.

A good mid-18th century compendium of voyages collected from most European languages. The frontispiece shows Anson giving King George II an account of his voyage around the world.

FLEURIEU: UNCUT IN ORIGINAL BOARDS

[25] FLEURIEU, Charles Pierre Claret de. DISCOVERIES OF THE FRENCH IN 1768 AND 1769, TO THE SOUTH-EAST OF NEW GUINEA, with the subsequent visits to the same lands by English Navigators, who

gave them new names . . . To which is prefixed, an historical abridgement of the voyages and discoveries of the Spaniards in the same seas. *Quarto, with 12 folding plates (including 9 maps); original blue-grey boards, spine renewed, with original label; contemporary signature "Christine Renira Reede Ginckell 1806" on title; a very fine, completely uncut copy in choice original condition.* London, Printed for John Stockdale, 1791.

First English edition of the great work on the French discovery of the Solomon Islands, and a direct result of the "First Fleet" voyage to Australia in 1788.

With the publication of Phillip's *Voyage to Botany Bay* in 1790, appeared the journal of Lt. Shortland on his return voyage in the *Alexander* transport from Botany Bay to England, during which he coasted along a group of large islands, which he named "New Georgia". Fleurieu, writing in a period of intense international rivalry over Pacific discoveries, denies that discovery and promotes those of Louis de Bougainville and Jean de Surville. He draws on unpublished manuscripts as well as the printed narratives of Cook, Bougainville, Phillip, Mendana, Quiros and others.

The Surville voyage was then hardly known, "and, perhaps if Mr. Shortland had not endeavoured to appropriate to himself a discovery which he only improved . . . the expedition of the French navigator would have remained in a manner forgotten. But injustice rouses indolence . . . the desire of restoring to the French nation its own discoveries, which an emulous and jealous neighbour has endeavoured to appropriate to herself, induced us to connect in one view, all those that we have made towards the south-east coast of New Guinea . . .". To this, the translator announces, "We now offer to the world, a voluntary sacrifice to truth . . .".

There are also interesting comments on the La Pérouse voyage. Fleurieu announces the receipt of journals from as far as Botany Bay, and in discussing the *Great Ocean Chart* (a fragment of which is published here), says publication is to be delayed until his later discoveries can be inserted. The translator of this edition notes that the explorer had still not turned up and "the apprehension for his loss increases daily". *Ferguson, 105; Hill, p. 105; Beddie, 1302.*

SCARCE COLLECTION

[26] FORSTER, R. P. A COLLECTION OF THE MOST CELEBRATED VOYAGES AND TRAVELS, from the Discovery of America to the Present time. Arranged in systematic order . . . the whole exhibiting a faithful and lively delineation of the world. *4 volumes, quarto, with 5 maps and 33 engraved plates; contemporary diced calf, occasional light spotting, but a very good copy.* Newcastle upon Tyne, Printed and published by Mackenzie and Dent, 1816-1818.

A popular collection, now surprisingly scarce. The compiler includes "such a selection as might amuse without fatiguing . . . even to the humblest class of society", and modestly states that "several writers of great celebrity" had published voluminous and expensive collections, but that the "stale digressions with which they are frequently interlarded, render

De Stadt Bantam

them unfit for general use . . .". Beginning with Columbus, the voyages include Cortes, Pizarro, Drake, De Lesseps, Bligh, Phipps to the North Pole, Barrow's China, Anson and Wilson's voyage of the *Duff*. Cook's three voyages are omitted. The *Duff* voyage contains curious asides on other parts of Polynesia, including Hawaii, where in 1802 he states "some Englishmen who escaped from Botany Bay . . . have been extremely useful to these ingenious and industrious people".

His adaptation of Collins' *History of New South Wales*, combined with later information derived from Hunter's *Voyage* and remarks of Captain M'Konochie, carries the narrative to 1810 and is illustrated with 2 plates and a map. *Ferguson supplement, 638a (recording a single copy).*

[27] FUNNELL, William. A Voyage Round the World. Containing an Account of Captain Dampier's Expedition into the South-Seas in the ship St. George, in the years 1703 and 1704 . . . Together with the author's voyage from Amapalla on the west-coast of Mexico, to East India. *Octavo, with 5 folding maps & 10 plates; original cloth; a good modern facsimile.* London, printed by W. Botham for James Knapton, 1707. [Amsterdam, Nico Israel, 1969].

Funnell sailed on the *St. George* as Dampier's mate, and although Dampier went only as far as the South Seas, Funnell completed the circumnavigation, arrived

back in England before his captain and was the first into print. Dampier, disapproving of this account, published his own in which he disputed many of the statements contained here, but the Funnell narrative was later rehabilitated and appeared in the fourth volume of Dampier's collected voyages (see 22 above).

HOUTMAN AND DIRCKSZ IN THE EAST INDIES

[28] HOUTMAN, Cornelis. Eerste Schip-Vaert der Hollanders naer Oost-Indien, met vier Schepen onder 't beleyde van Cornelis Houtman van Alckmaer, uyt Texel t'zeylgegaen, Anno 1595. *Small quarto, [ii], 102 pp., with an engraved vignette on the title and 7 engravings in the text, small stain on last few leaves, basically an excellent copy in 19th century half calf, spine worn.* Amsterdam, Voor Ioost Hartgers, 1650.

Rare: an account of the Dutch voyage of 1595 to the East Indies, under the command of Cornelis van Houtman and Pieter Dircksz, who sailed to Bantam and around Java, returning with three of their original four ships to the Netherlands in 1597. They had lost two-thirds of the men, and the return cargo was insignificant, but it was one of the first of a series of Dutch voyages into the Pacific which aimed at the colonisation of the East Indies.

With the release stamp of the Lenox Library, New York. *Not in the catalogue of the Hill collection; not listed by Robert.*

28: HOUTMAN. *The town of Bantam, visited by Cornelis van Houtman in 1595.*

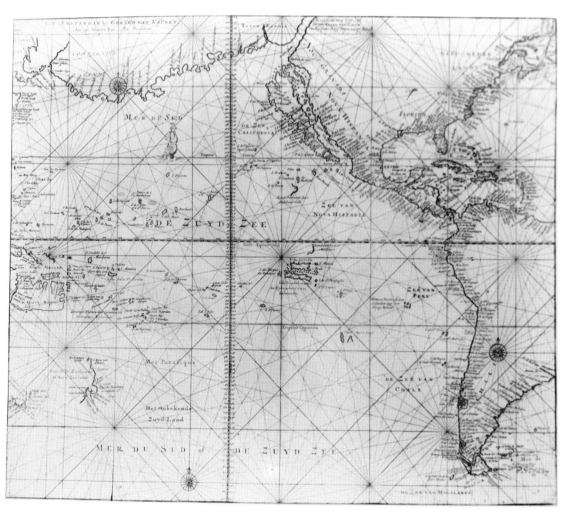

QUIRI REGIO

[29] KEULEN, Gerard van. SEA CHART OF THE PACIFIC. *Engraved map, 510 x 590 mm, in fine condition, framed and glazed.* Amsterdam, Gerard van Keulen Aan de Nieuwe brug met privilegio, circa 1720.

A most impressive and rare sea chart of the Pacific Ocean, based by Gerard van Keulen on his father's "Pascaert Vande Zuyd Zee" which had been published some years earlier. This issue of the map shows for the first time a land mass named "Quiri Regio" which corresponds roughly to parts of Arnhem Land and the Gulf of Carpentaria.

The chart shows the Pacific coast of America from the Strait of Anian (Hudsons Bay) to Cape Horn, and is bounded on the left by parts of the Dutch East Indies in the north, the Ladrones Islands, New Guinea and the embryonic Northern Australia at the centre, and Van Diemen's Land and a tentative outline for New Zealand in the south. The Northern Australian section presents an unusual configuration: it shows inlets on the northern coast and a list of Dutch names down the west coast: R. van Spult, R. Batavia, R. Coen, Bereenichde Riv., Waterplaets, E. Nassau, Staten R., and van Diemen R. The whole west coast is named Carpentaria, and the land mass is "Quiri Regio" — still following the Quiros myth.

Gerard van Keulen took over the management of his father Joannes' successful chart publishing business in 1704. The family firm was noted for the production of the *Zee-Atlas* and *Zee-Fakkel*, which were "the largest and finest marine atlases in Holland" (Koeman). *Koeman, IV, p. 395; Tooley, Mapping of America, p. 131, Mapping of Australia, p. 106.*

THE POCKET NAVIGATOR

[30] LEMOINE, Ann & J. ROE. THE POCKET NAVIGATOR; consisting of a collection of the most select voyages . . . *4 volumes, duodecimo, engraved and printed titles; binder's cloth.* London, Printed by T. Maiden for Ann Lemoine and J. Roe, 1806 [-1807].

A particularly interesting small collection of voyages. A number of the articles were issued in separate chapbooks — including the 58-page 1807 edition of Phillip's *Voyage to Botany Bay*, which "constitutes one of the earliest, if abbreviated, contemporary accounts of Governor King's New South Wales . . ." (Wantrup).

The fourth volume deals exclusively with Cook's voyages while the others include accounts of Columbus, Cortes, Pizarro, Drake, Raleigh, Cowley, Dampier, Rogers, Middleton, James, Ellis, Shelvocke, Anson, Byron, Wallis, Carteret and Wilson. *Not in the catalogue of the Hill collection; Ferguson, 450 (part); Wantrup, 31 (part).*

THE NASSAU FLEET AND QUIROS

[31] L'HERMITE, Jacques. JOURNAEL VAN DE NASSAUSCHE VLOOT, ofte Beschrijvingh van de

JOURNAEL
VANDE
Naſſauſche Vloot/
OFTE
Beſchrijvingh van de Voyagie om den gantſchen Aert-
Kloot, Gedaen met elf Schepen:
Onder 't beleydt van den Admirael
Iaques l'Heremite, ende Vice-Admirael Gheen Huy-
gen Schapenham, inde Iaren 1623.1624.1625. en 1626.
Noch is hier by gevoegt een Beſchrijvinge vande Regeeringe van Peru, door
Pedro de Madriga gebojen tot Lima, Als mede een verhael van Pedro
Fernandez de Quir, aengaende de ontderlinge van 't on-
bekent Auſtralia, ſijn grooten ſijckdom ende
vjuchtbaerheyt.
Oock mede eenige Diſcourſen de Ooſt-Indiſche Vaert en de Coopmanſchap betreffende.

t'AMSTELREDAM,
Door Jooſt Hartgertſz. Boeckverkooper / woonende inde Gaſt-Huys-
ſteegh naeſt het Stadt-huys/inde Boeck-winckel, Anno 1648.

The Iſle of PINES,
DISCOVERED
Near to the Coaſt of *Terra Auſtralis Incognita*, by *Henry Cornelius Van Sloetten*, in
a Letter to a friend in *London*, declaring
the truth of his Voyage to the Eaſt
Indies.

SIR,

I Received your Letter of this ſecond inſtant, wherein
you deſire me to give you a further account concerning
the Land of *Pines*, on which we were driven by diſtreſs
of Weather the laſt Summer, I alſo peruſed the Printed
Book thereof you ſent me, the Copy of which was ſur-
reptiouſly taken out of my hands, elſe ſhould I have given
you a more fuller account upon what accaſion we came
thither, how we were entertained, with some other circum-
A 3   ſtances

Voyagie om den gantschen Aert-Kloot, Gedaun met elf Schepen: Onder 't beleydt van den Admirael Jacques l'Hermite . . . Noch is hier by gevoegt een Beschrijvinge van de Regeeringe van Peru, door Pedro Fernandez de Quir . . . oock mede eenige Discoursen de Oost-Indische vaert en de Coopmanschap betreffende . . . *Small quarto, [viii], 76 pp., with an engraved vignette on the title; a little staining, wormhole in outer margins clear of text, a sound copy in old vellum.* Amsterdam, Voor Joost Hartgertsz, 1648.

Very scarce account of the circumnavigation made by the Dutch in the "Nassau Fleet", of which l'Hermite was the Admiral, between 1623 and 1626. In this edition, an 8-page section deals with Quiros and Peru. The account of the expedition had first appeared in 1626, with a second edition in 1631; in 1643 it had reappeared with the addition of the Quiros material, which format was used again here. A number of subsequent editions followed, but all are rare. *Robert, 552; Tiele, 667; not in the catalogue of the Hill collection.*

MAVOR'S VOYAGES

[32] MAVOR, William [Fordyce]. HISTORICAL ACCOUNT OF THE MOST CELEBRATED VOYAGES, TRAVELS, AND DISCOVERIES, from the time of Columbus to the present period. *20 volumes, duodecimo; contemporary tree calf, gilt spines with urn and bird ornaments, red and black labels; an attractive set.* London, Printed for E. Newbery, 1796-1797.

A popular and often reprinted work. The author, a prolific "compiler of educational works" (DNB XII, 108) greatly expanded this during publication, and includes separate indices in volumes 10 and 20. The Pacific voyages, many of which contain an engraved plate, include those of Magellan, Drake, Cavendish,

Dampier, Woodes Rogers, Shelvocke, Roggewein, Anson, Wallis, Carteret, Bougainville, Cook's three voyages, Sparrman, Portlock, Dixon, Wilson, Governor Phillip, Shortland, Bligh and John Byron. *Beddie, 57; Hill, pp. 195 (note), 493.*

ON THE ISLE OF PINES FOR 100 YEARS: FECUNDITY

[33] [NEVILLE, Henry]. THE ISLE OF PINES, OR, A LATE DISCOVERY OF A FOURTH ISLAND NEAR TERRA AUSTRALIS, INCOGNITA BY HENRY CORNELIUS VAN SLOETTEN. Wherein is Contained, A True Relation of certain English persons, who in Queen Elizabeth's time, making a Voyage to the East Indies were cast away, and wrecked near to the Coast of Terra Australis, Incognita, and all drowned, except one Man and four Women. And now lately Anno. Dom. 1667, a Dutch Ship making a Voyage to the East Indies, driven by foul weather there, by chance have found their Posterity, (speaking good English) to amount (as they suppose) to ten or twelve thousand persons. The whole Relation (written, and left by the Man himself a little before his death, and delivered to the Dutch by his Grandchild) is here annexed with the Longitude and Latitude of the Island, and the situation and felicity thereof, with other matter observable . . . *Small quarto, [ii], 31 pp.; old library stamp on title, slight fraying to upper margins, but a good copy in quarter morocco.* London, Printed for Allen Banks and Charles Harper next door to the three Squerrills in Fleet-Street, over against St. Dunstans Church, 1668.

First complete edition of a fascinating text, a rare imaginary voyage and a precursor of Robinson Crusoe. Neville's text represents the continuing obsession with and search for the fabled temperate southern continent — a search which was laid to rest

31: L'HERMITE. *The Nassau Fleet made its circumnavigation under Jacques l'Hermite in 1623-1626.*

33: NEVILLE. *A rare imaginary voyage — the discovery of an island utopia.*

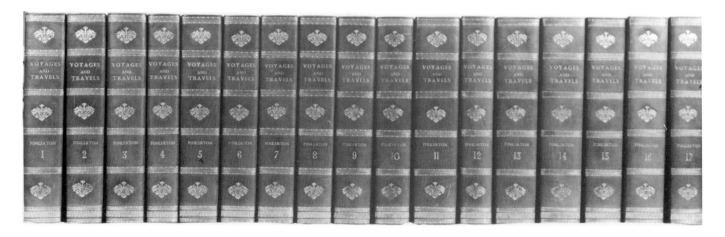

34: PINKERTON. An extensive collection of voyages and travels in 17 volumes.

only after Cook's second voyage.

This fictitious account of an island utopia located off the coast of Terra Australis appeared in a very much slimmer version a month before this (licensed on June 27th 1668 while the present edition was licensed on July 27). It evidently enjoyed some success, as a continuation soon appeared, which must have been published at practically the same time as this version. Here the whole text appears — the supposed narrative by Pine himself, which constituted the first edition, and the long 'letter' from the discoverer Van Sloetten, to a friend in England describing the island, its inhabitants, code of law, climate, etc. The island is populated by the massive and sudden progeny of George Pine and the four women with whom he is supposed to have been shipwrecked 100 years earlier. By the time of Van Sloetten's accidental visit the population has reached 12,000, and a model society has developed — a lush paradise inhabited by a community where all speak good English and are raised according to the precepts of the Bible; there is even a bagpipe-player to entertain them.

The bibliographies show considerable confusion in dealing with the two editions of 1668; copies of the present edition are known with a frontispiece (see, for example, McDonnell II/1), but neither the Mitchell Library nor the John Carter Brown Library copies have such a frontispiece; nor does Wing identify the fact that the present edition is an entirely separate printing from the other 1668 version. *JCB, III, pp. 172-3; Wing, N506; Sabin, 35255 (not calling for the frontispiece); see also Quaritch 1006/575 and 1017/244-247.*

ILLUMINATIONS DIFFUSED OVER AUSTRALIA

[34] PINKERTON, John. A GENERAL COLLECTION OF THE BEST AND MOST INTERESTING VOYAGES AND TRAVELS IN ALL PARTS OF THE WORLD; many of which are now first translated into English. Digested on a new plan. *17 volumes, quarto, with numerous engraved maps and plates; three-quarter calf antique, gilt compartmented spines, marbled boards; a very good and attractive set.* London, Printed for Longman, Hurst, Rees and Orme, 1808-1814.

An important and elaborate compilation "of great value for its texts" (Hill), Pinkerton's *General Collection* also contains one of the earliest

bibliographies on Australasia and the Pacific. This 255 page catalogue found in volume 17 lists voyages by geographical location, and includes sections on world voyages, Australasia, New Holland, and Polynesia; followed by an extremely detailed analytical index, certainly one of the most ambitious ever attempted, comprising in its 472 pages everything from Aa to Zwellendam.

The author's summation in the same volume discusses the achievements of Cook from a contemporary perspective: "The Voyages of Cook may therefore be regarded as forming an illustrious epoch . . . the old catalogues of pictures and statues, with trifling adventures by sea and land, which were called books of travels, have sunk into obscurity before the new and important works". Pinkerton concluded his remarks on Cook with the note that ". . . an English colony was sent to Australia, which will infallibly diffuse illuminations over that remote quarter of the world" (p. xxxi). *Beddie, 77; Hill, p. 236.*

NEW DISCOVERIE IN THE SOUTH SEA

[35] QUIROS, Pedro Fernandez de. RELATION OF THE NEW DISCOVERIE IN THE SOUTH SEA made by Pedro Fernandez Giros Portuguez 1609. With his Petitions to the King, one Englished, another in Spanish. [*with*] A note of Australia del Espiritu Santo. Written by Master Hakluyt. *Folio; good modern binding of half morocco, spine lettered in gilt; fine condition.* London, William Stamsby, 1625.

Second edition in English of the Quiros Memorial, extracted from Purchas' great 1625 collection of voyage accounts, *Hakluytus Posthumus, or Purchas his Pilgrimes.* This is realistically the earliest available edition in English, since the first English edition of 1617 is notoriously rare.

Quiros, the last of the great Spanish discoverers, sailed on the Mendana expedition across the Pacific in 1595, and then commanded his own expedition of 1605-06 in search of the 'Terra Australis', actually discovering Tahiti and other Pacific Islands, and reaching the New Hebrides. His second-in-command, Luis Vaez de Torres, took one of the expedition's ships through the consequently named Torres Strait, and probably sighted Cape York.

The remainder of Quiros' life was spent

petitioning the King for an expedition with settlers to Terra Australis, without success; his secret 'Memorial' to the Spanish Court, which gradually became leaked through Europe in editions such as this, provoked the search for a southern continent that was not finished until Cook's expedition 150 years later.

In the Memorial, Quiros compares Terra Australis favourably with America and Asia in regard to size, natural wealth and the possibilities for successful settlement; and though he had actually discovered the New Hebrides, Columbus thought that he had discovered Cathay, and the Quiros Memorial in its importance to Australia may be compared with the celebrated Columbus Letter in its various printings at the end of the fifteenth century in its importance to America. As Dalrymple later wrote, "the discovery of the Southern Continent, whenever and by whomsoever it may have been completely effected, is in justice due to his immortal name . . .". *See Dunn, F.M. 'A Catalogue of Memorials by Pedro Fernandez de Quiros . . . in the Dixson and Mitchell Libraries', p. 23; Sanz, C. 'Australia su descubrimien to y denominacion', no. 21, pp. 237-8 and passim.*

EARLY PRINTING OF THE QUIROS MEMORIAL

[36] QUIROS, Pedro Fernandez de. REQUESTE PRESENTEE AU ROY D'ESPAGNE . . . sur la descouverte de la 5 Partie du Monde appellée la Terre Australe incogneue . . . [On pp. 163-179 of Mercure Francois, volume V, for the period 1617-1619]. *Octavo, 3 parts in 1 volume, contemporary limp vellum.* Paris, chez Estienne Richer, 1620.

An early printing of the Quiros memorial in French; 2 other articles of Pacific interest are contained in this Parisian periodical — *Des Terres Australes, et des Voyages faicts tant par les Hollandois, que par les Espagnols pour les descouvrir* (pp. 145-148), and *Voyage de Isaac le Maire et Guillaume Chouten allans chercher un autre destroict que celuy de Magellan . . . dans l'Australe ou Pacifique . . .* (pp. 148-163).

DISCOVERY OF TORRES STRAIT

[37] [QUIROS] STEVENS, Henry N. & George F. BARWICK. NEW LIGHT ON THE DISCOVERY OF AUSTRALIA, as revealed by the Journal of Captain Don Diego de Prado y Tovar . . . *Octavo, 2 folding maps in a pocket at the end; a fine copy in the original blue cloth.* London, Printed for the Hakluyt Society, 1930.

The first account in English of the discovery of Torres Strait and northernmost Australia, based on Don Diego de Prado's *Relacion*, the manuscript of which was discovered this century.

The account sheds new light on the Quiros voyage; Prado and Torres continued on to Manila from Espiritu Santo when Quiros returned to America.

[QUIROS]-see also 31 (L'Hermite)

BUCCANEERING CLASSIC

[38] ROGERS, Woodes. A CRUISING VOYAGE ROUND THE WORLD: First to the South-Seas, thence to the East-Indies, and homewards by the Cape of Good

39: SCHENK. *Schenk's 1710 map of the world shows a variety of different projections.*

Hope. Begun in 1708 and finish'd in 1711. *Octavo, with 5 folding maps; original cloth; a good modern facsimile.* London, Printed for A. Bell . . . and B. Lintot, 1712 [Amsterdam, Nico Israel, 1969].

A buccaneering classic. William Dampier was the pilot on this privateering expedition which crossed the Pacific to Asia, captured the Manila galleon at Puerto Seguro, and rescued Alexander Selkirk — the prototype for Robinson Crusoe — from Juan Fernandez Island.

Rogers' account went through four editions, and also appears in the 1729 Dampier (see item 22); the first edition is scarce.

QUIROS LAND

[39] SCHENK, Pieter. DIVERSA ORBIS TERRAE VISU INCEDENTE PER COLUROS TROPICIORUM . . . *Engraved map, 50 x 57 cms., contemporary colouring to landmasses; minor stain to cartouche, otherwise in fine condition; framed.* Amsterdam, circa 1710.

A fine early eighteenth century Dutch world map with good Pacific and Australian detail. Schenk's map is also a good example of the movement away from the use of allegorical and imaginary images in cartography towards the use of scientific sources for decoration.

The borders are filled with several illustrations on the use of projection. Schenk shows north and south polar projections, a pair of oblique projections centred on Amsterdam and its antipodes, and a pair of optica projections. Two small globes show the Ancient and New Worlds, while four diagrams illustrate cartographic ideas. The twin hemispheres and twelve accompanying globes are highlighted by a dramatic use of dark cross-hatching for the background.

The map contains good Australian detail, naming much of the west, north-west and south-west coasts as well as Van Dieman's Land. There is still a "Quiros

36: QUIROS. *An early appearance of the Quiros Memorial, in French.*

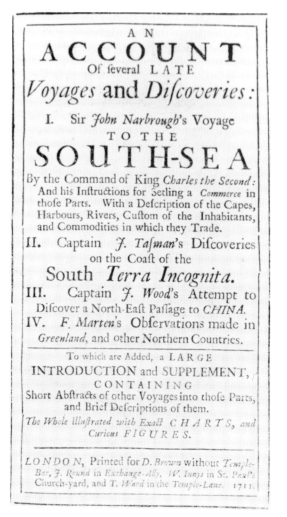

AN
ACCOUNT
Of feveral LATE
Voyages and *Difcoveries* :

I. Sir *John* Narbrough's Voyage
TO THE
SOUTH-SEA
By the Command of King *Charles the Second* :
And his Inftructions for Setling a *Commerce* in
thofe Parts. With a Defcription of the Capes,
Harbours, Rivers, Cuftom of the Inhabitants,
and Commodities in which they Trade.

II. Captain *J.* Tafman's Difcoveries
on the Coaft of the
South *Terra Incognita.*

III. Captain *J.* Wood's Attempt to
Difcover a North-Eaft Paffage to *CHINA.*

IV. *F. Marten's* Obfervations made in
Greenland, and other Northern Countries.

To which are Added, a LARGE
INTRODUCTION and SUPPLEMENT,
CONTAINING
Short Abftracts of other Voyages into thofe Parts,
and Brief Defcriptions of them.
The Whole Illuftrated with Exact CHARTS, *and
Curious* FIGURES.

LONDON, Printed for *D. Brown* without *Temple-
Bar, J. Round* in *Exchange-Ally, W. Innys* in *St. Paul's*
Church-yard, and *T. Ward* in the *Temple-Lane.* 1711.

43: TASMAN. *Tasman's narrative in
one of its earliest English versions.*

Government, Commerce, and Natural History of
most Nations in the Known World. *7 volumes,
duodecimo, with 26 maps and plans (19 folding), 17 views
(6 folding) & 4 portraits; contemporary speckled calf, raised
spines, gilt with garlands, vines and stars, red and green
labels; very slight spotting, one or two clean tears to the
maps; a very fine copy in a most attractive contemporary
binding.* London, Printed for W. Strahan and others,
1766.

Second edition of a popular collection of voyages,
edited by Tobias George Smollett (1721-1771) the
novelist, author of *Roderick Random* and *Humphrey
Clinker.* Known for his "literary adroitness", he was
employed in times of improvidence by Dodsley and
other London publishers as an editor. The voyages in
the collection include those of Columbus, Vasco da
Gama, Cortes, Pizarro, Magellan, Drake, Raleigh,
Nieuhof, Dampier, Woodes Rogers and Anson.
Smollett, who had himself sailed as a Surgeon's mate
on the Cartagena Expedition (1741-1743) includes his
account of the voyage in the fifth volume. *Hill, p. 576
(first edition).*

EARLIEST EXPLORATION OF POLYNESIA

[42] STENBACK, Jonas. POLYNESIA DETECTA,
DISSERTATIO HISTORICA, Quam, Consent. Ampliss.
Ord. Philos. Praeside Nic. Henry Sjoborg ... Pro
Gradu Magisterii modeste exhibet Jonas Stenback.
*Small quarto, 20 pp., original blue wrappers removed; fine
copy.* Lund, Literis Berlingianis, 1807.

First edition, very rare. A dissertation on the
exploration of Polynesia and Australasia from the
earliest times to 1791, presented for the baccalaureat at
the University of Lund, and evidence of Sweden's
continuing interest in Pacific exploration. *Ferguson,
452; not in Hill; Kroepelien, 1193.*

Land", however, and California is shown as an island,
while the Mississippi flows through Texas. *Koeman,
III, p. 119.*

SOURCE OF THE ANCIENT MARINER

[40] SHELVOCKE, George. A VOYAGE ROUND THE
WORLD BY WAY OF THE GREAT SOUTH SEA, perform'd
in the years 1719, 20, 21, 22, in the Speedwell of
London ... till she was cast away on the Island of
Juan Fernandes, in May 1720; and afterwards
continu'd in the Recovery, the Jesus Maria and Sacra
Familia, &c. *Octavo, with folding world map & 3 plates (2
folding); white and blue cloth as issued; a good modern
facsimile.* London, Printed for J. Senex, 1726.
[Amsterdam, Nico Israel, 1971].

A controversial narrative written by the buccaneer
Shelvocke to defend himself against charges of piracy
and embezzlement. This is also the direct source for
Coleridge's *Rime of the Ancient Mariner:* Wordsworth
found and pointed out to Coleridge the anecdote of a
sailor killing an albatross, and thus condemning the
ship to a terrible polar passage. *Hill, pp. 272-3.*

SMOLLETT'S VOYAGES

[41] [SMOLLETT, Tobias, *editor*]. A COMPENDIUM OF
AUTHENTIC AND ENTERTAINING VOYAGES, Digested in
a Chronological Series. The whole exhibiting a clear
View of the Customs, Manners, Religion,

"TIS THE DISCOVERY OF A NEW WORLD,
NOT YET KNOWN TO THE ENGLISH"

[43] [TASMAN, Abel Janszoon]. AN ACCOUNT OF
SEVERAL LATE VOYAGES AND DISCOVERIES; I. Sir John
Narbrough's Voyage to the South Sea, by the
command of King Charles the Second ... II. Captain
J. Tasman's Discoveries on the Coast of the South
Terra Incognita. III. Captain J. Wood's Attempt to
Discover a North-East Passage to China. IV. F.
Marten's Observations made in Greenland ... To
which are added, a large introduction and supplement,
containing short abstracts of other voyages into those
parts. *Octavo, with folding frontispiece "Chart of the
western and southern oceans", folding chart of Terra del
Fuego, a polar map and 19 engraved views of Marten's
voyage to Spitzbergen and Greenland; old calf rebacked,
spine gilt, red label, extremities a little rubbed, joints a little
tender, internally a very clean copy; armorial bookplate of
James Smith; boxed.* London, Printed for D. Brown
without Temple Bar, 1711.

Second edition, with the additional chart of the
western and southern oceans not appearing earlier.
"Of the greatest importance to an Australian
collection" (Hill), this compendium of early voyages
contains an early account in English of Tasman's

The Introduction.

'*Tis probable by Abel Janfen Tafman's Navigation, that New Guinea, New Carpentaria, and
New Holland, are a vaft prodigious Ifland, which
he feems to have encompafs'd in his Voyage, fetting
out from Batavia to Maurice Ifle, Eaft of Mada-
gafcar ; from whence bearing away South to 49 deg.
of South Lat. and then Eaft and by North to Lat. 42
and 44, he fell upon thofe new Trads of Land call'd
Van Diemen's, and afterwards upon New Zealand ;
to the South Eaft of New Holland ; returning to
Batavia through part of the South Sea (wherein he
Difcover'd new Iflands) and fo Northwards of
New Guinea to the Molucco's, and Java.
III. Captain Wood was a moft excellent Navigator : He, together with Sir Cloudfly Shovel,

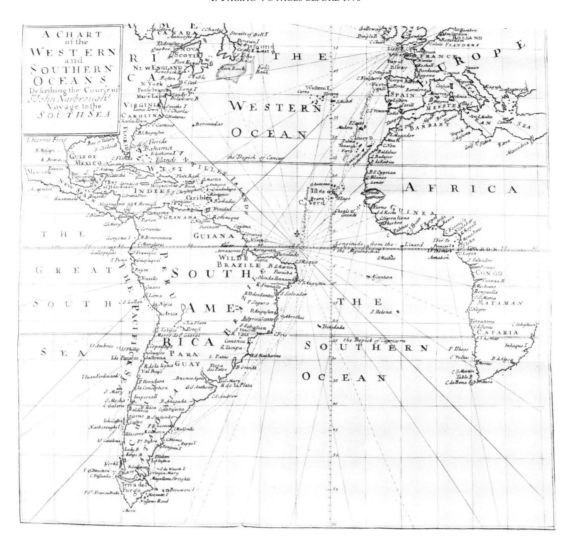

celebrated voyage of 1642 from Batavia, on which he discovered Tasmania, New Zealand and part of Tonga, and visited new Guinea and the Solomon Islands. It is based on the account of Dirk Rembrantse published in Holland in 1674. The Narbrough voyage in the *Batchelour* through the Strait of Magellan and into the Pacific was widely read by later navigators including the survivors of the *Wager* (part of Anson's fleet), who used this account for their own navigation through the passage.

Edited by Tancred Robinson, the introduction contains a resumé of voyages to date, including those of Quiros, Drake and Magellan, and a plea for scientific exploration of the globe; lamenting "that the English nation have not sent with their Navigators, some skilful Painters, Naturalists, and Merchanists, under publick Stipends and Encouragement as the Dutch and French have done ...". Of Tasman's voyage he exclaims: "tis the Discovery of a new World, not yet known to the English, 'Tis probable by Abel Jansen Tasman's Navigation, that New Guinea, New Carpentaria, and New Holland, are a vast prodigious Island, which he seems to have encompass'd in his Voyage ...". *Hill, p. 1-2 (first edition)*..

TASMAN'S JOURNAL

[44] TASMAN, Abel Janszoon. ABEL JANSZOON

TASMAN'S JOURNAL of his discovery of Van Diemen's Land and New Zealand in 1642, with documents relating to his exploration of Australia in 1644 ... *Thick folio, facsimile of the original manuscript, 5 folding maps in a pocket at end; a fine copy in the original cloth, dust jacket slightly soiled.* Los Angeles, N. A. Kovach, 1965.

Limited edition: one of only 200 copies for sale. Photolithographic facsimile of the original manuscript of Tasman's Journal held in the colonial archives at The Hague, with a biography of Tasman, and cartographical notes by Dr. W. van Beemelen.

EARLY ACCOUNT OF THE CENTURION VOYAGE

[45] THOMAS, Pascoe. A TRUE AND IMPARTIAL JOURNAL OF A VOYAGE TO THE SOUTH-SEAS, and round the globe, in His Majesty's Ship the Centurion, under the command of Commodore George Anson. Wherein all the material incidents during the said voyage, from its commencement in the year 1740 to its conclusion in 1744, are fully and faithfully related. *Octavo, half calf antique, brown label, a very good copy.* London, Printed, and Sold by S. Birt, J. Newbery, J. Collyer, 1745.

First edition. A popular account of Anson's voyage by the "teacher of mathematicks on board the Centurion". Thomas' account, taken from his diary,

43: TASMAN. *Engraved map from the 1711 Account of Several Late Voyages and Discoveries, showing the track of Narbrough's voyage.*

45: THOMAS. *Pascoe Thomas, who sailed on the* Centurion, *wrote an alternative account of the Anson expedition.*

A TRUE and IMPARTIAL
JOURNAL
OF A
VOYAGE
TO THE
SOUTH-SEAS,
AND
ROUND the GLOBE,
In His MAJESTY's Ship the *Centurion*,
Under the COMMAND of
Commodore *George Anson*.

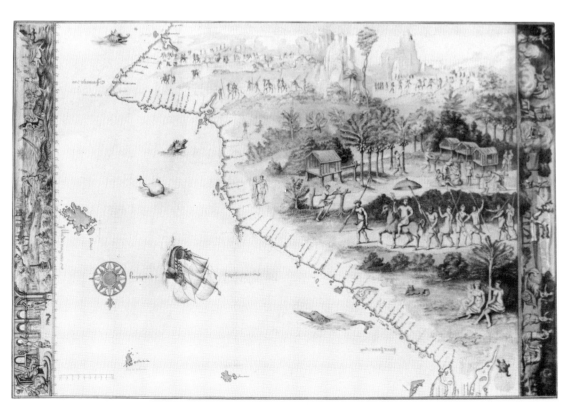

47: VALLARD. *Nicholas Vallard's highly decorative chart, one of the "Dieppe Maps" which demonstrate an early knowledge of the Australian coasts.*

preceded Lord Anson's official account by three years. The appendix contains a table of longitudes and latitudes, including one by Sr. Prieto 'Professor of Arts in Peru' and an account of the treasure taken from the *Nuestra Signora del Buono Carmella*. The list of subscribers (accounting for 397 copies) includes a good many fellow voyagers, whose names and professions are duly noted, and demonstrates a singular lack of any noble patronage. *Hill, p. 291.*

TUCKEY'S MARITIME GEOGRAPHY

[46] TUCKEY, James H. MARITIME GEOGRAPHY AND STATISTICS, or, A Description of the Ocean and its Coasts, Maritime Commerce, Navigation &c. &c. &c. *Four volumes, octavo; somewhat spotted, but an excellent uncut and partly unopened copy in modern half morocco, the cloth sides rather marked.* London, Printed for Black Parry & Co., Booksellers to the Hon. East India Company, 1815.

A wide ranging work on maritime geography in all its aspects, which describes the principal voyages round the world, including those of Cook, La Perouse, Broughton, and Vancouver. It also contains sections on America, New Spain (including California), the Northwest coast, Polynesia, New South Wales and Van Diemen's Land.

The author is probably better known for his *Account of a Voyage to Establish a Colony at Port Phillip* published in 1805 in which he described the attempt at settlement in Victoria after the voyage in the *Calcutta. Ferguson, 628; not in the Hill collection.*

DIEPPE MAP

[47] VALLARD, Nicholas. MAP OF THE EAST COAST OF AUSTRALIA. *376 x 553 mm., map chromolithographed on card, mounted; in excellent condition.* Middle Hill Press,

for Sir Thomas Phillips, 1856.

The only early printing of any of the so called "Dieppe maps". This map by the celebrated cartographer Nicholas Vallard was reproduced from the manuscript atlas (now in the Huntington Library in California) in the possession of Sir Thomas Phillips, the extraordinary collector of manuscripts and books.

The present map has an important place in the cartographic history of the Pacific as it points to an early unidentified voyage of discovery along the east coast of Australia. It was printed in a limited edition of probably only 60 copies.

Together with the recently produced Rotz *Boke of Idrography*, this is one of few available specimens of the Dieppe School of cartography, whose surviving maps all display a more extensive 16th century knowledge of the Pacific and Australia than had been supposed. All eleven of the manuscript atlases which survive are held in major libraries in Europe and America.

THE DOLPHIN'S BARBER

[48] [WALLIS] RICHARDSON, R. A POETICAL ESSAY ON THE DOLPHIN Sailing round the World in the years 1766, 1767, 1768, by R. Richardson, Barber of the said Ship, with an introduction by Miss Phyllis Mander-Jones. *Octavo, printed in the Japanese style on alternate rectos and versos with edges unopened, English text on the left in Roman letter and French text on the right in Italic, with an original (unsigned) etching; original wrappers with paper label, marbled slipcase.* Paris, Bibliophiles de la Société des Oceanistes, 1965.

The first printing of a long narrative poem written by the barber aboard the *Dolphin* on Wallis's voyage into the South Pacific. The manuscript of the poem is held by the Mitchell Library; this printing was limited to 125 copies.

II
Cook's First Voyage

Captain James Cook's voyage in the Endeavour *was one of the most successful Pacific voyages ever made; it was also politically the most important of his three voyages — effectively carving up the South Pacific into the political configuration that we know today.*

The publicly stated object of the expedition was to observe the Transit of Venus across the sun, but the secret purpose was the search for the mythical "Great Southern Continent" supposed to lie somewhere between Australia and South America. The Endeavour *left Plymouth on the 25th August, 1768; among those aboard were Joseph Banks, the naturalist Daniel Solander, and the artist Sydney Parkinson. After completing observations at Tahiti, during which Borabora, Huaheine and Raiatea were discovered, they sailed westward. On the 8th October, 1769, Cook became the first European to set foot on New Zealand.*

They continued to the west and on the 19th April, 1770, the east coast of New Holland came into European view for the first time, thus determining the limits of the Pacific basin. Cook named the land New South Wales.

Anson and other pre-Cook explorers had enormously excited public curiosity, but it was not until Cook's first voyage that a tradition of exhaustive publication began, which was to continue throughout the age of exploration. Both official and "surreptitious" narratives were eagerly bought by the public; narrative accounts, maps and engravings brought the stories of Pacific exploration directly to the European reader.

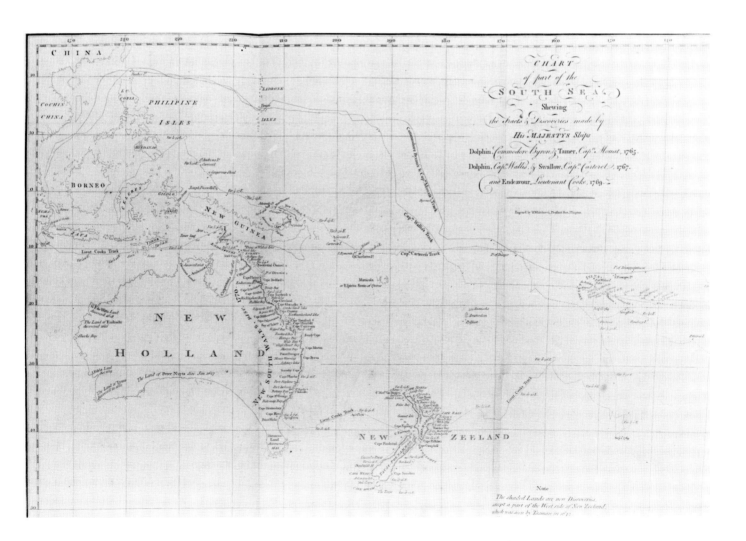

THE FIRST ACCOUNT OF THE FIRST VOYAGE

[49] [MAGRA, James, *attributed to*]. A Journal of a Voyage round the World in His Majesty's Ship Endeavour, in the years 1768, 1769, 1770 and 1771; Undertaken in Pursuit of Natural Knowledge, at the Desire of the Royal Society: containing All the various Occurrences of the Voyage, with Descriptions of several new discovered Countries in the Southern Hemisphere; and Accounts of their Soil and Productions; and of many Singularities in the Structure, Apparel, Customs, Manners, Policy, Manufactures, &c. of their Inhabitants. *Quarto, modern quarter calf; title-page dust soiled, portion of lower margin torn at an early date and neatly repaired, occasional spotting of text, but an excellent copy with the very rare dedication leaf.* London, Printed for T. Becket and P. A. De Hondt, 1771.

First edition, first issue: very rare. The earliest published account of Cook's first voyage to the Pacific, containing the first printed account of the east coast of Australia. Its publication predates the naming of Botany Bay, here called Sting-ray Bay as it was originally christened by Captain Cook. Published anonymously some two months after the return of the *Endeavour* and nearly two years before Hawkesworth's official account, its author remains unknown, though the great Cook scholar Beaglehole has demonstrated that the sailor James Magra is the likeliest candidate. (*Journals*, I, pp. cclvi-lcclxiv).

Two issues of the book were published; this is the first, and scarcer of the two, with a leaf of dedication to Banks and Solander, quickly withdrawn after their objections to this spurious authentication of an unauthorised publication. Most copies known are of the second issue, with the dedication leaf removed. *Beddie, 693; Hill, p. 158 (the second issue); Holmes, 3.*

[MAGRA]-see also item 6 (Bougainville and Magra).

A FINE SET OF THE OFFICIAL ACCOUNT

[50] HAWKESWORTH, John. An Account of the Voyages undertaken by the Order of His present Majesty for making Discoveries in the Southern Hemisphere, and successively performed by Commodore Byron, Captain Wallis, Captain Carteret, and Captain Cook, in the Dolphin, the Swallow, and the Endeavour. *3 volumes, quarto, with 52 engraved charts and plates (most folding); contemporary full diced russia, gilt raised spines with urn and vine motifs, carefully rebacked preserving all original spines; corners bumped and partially repaired, very slight spotting of text, a few leaves lightly dampstained, but generally a fine and clean set.* London, Printed for W. Strahan, and T. Cadell in the Strand, 1773.

The official account of Cook's first voyage, edited from his journals by the professional writer Hawkesworth. Cook's voyage occupies volumes 2 and 3; the first volume contains the official accounts of the voyages of Byron, Wallis and Carteret, with the result that Hawkesworth's compendium actually contains the cream of English exploring voyages of the mid-18th century.

This is the second and best edition, published in

JOURNAL

OF A

VOYAGE round the WORLD.

IN the beginning of the year 1768, the British ambaſſador at Madrid applied to the court of Spain for the grant of a paſſport to a ſhip deſigned for California, to obſerve the tranſit of Venus, which was promiſed, with a proviſion that the aſtronomer ſhould be a member of the Romiſh church, and an Italian gentleman was conſequently engaged for the undertaking; but the paſſport when demanded was refuſed by the Spaniſh miniſtry, who alledged that it was repugnant to the policy of government to admit foreigners into their American ports, unleſs driven there by neceſſity; but eſpecially thoſe who by their profeſſion would be fitted to make ſuch obſervations as might facilitate the approaches and deſcents of their enemies at any future war with Great Britain.

the same year as the first edition, but containing the chart of the Straits of Magellan, and the preface to the second edition in which Hawkesworth replies to the charge of poor editing made against him by Dalrymple. *Beddie, 650; Hill, pp. 139-1140.*

[51] [HAWKESWORTH, John.] An Account of the Voyages undertaken by the order of His present Majesty for making Discoveries in the Southern Hemisphere, and successively performed by Commodore Byron, Captain Wallis, Captain Carteret, and Captain Cook, in the Dolphin, the Swallow, and the Endeavour. *4 volumes, octavo, with 2 folding maps, 9 engraved folding plates; modern half calf; slight browning to a few leaves, the occasional spot, but an attractive copy.* London, Printed for W. Strahan, and T. Cadell, 1785.

Third London edition, and the first octavo issue, having a wider popular circulation than the quarto editions. *Beddie, 665.*

WITH PORTUGUESE MANUSCRIPT NOTES ON TAHITI

[52] [HAWKESWORTH, John]. Viagem do Capitao Cook. A roda do mundo no navio de sua magestade, a diligencia. *Duodecimo; original blue paper wrappers, manuscript title label on spine, with contemporary owner's inscription on front end paper, and two pages of manuscript notes on Tahiti at the end of the text, followed by later notes on the voyage of Captain Perry, 1822, added at the end; a very fine copy enclosed in a modern half tan morocco bookform box.* Lisboa, a Typografia Rollandiana, 1819.

A rare edition of Hawkesworth's narrative which, though greatly abridged, shows the tremendous continuing interest in this voyage. Pages 193-195 contain a short Tahitian-Portuguese vocabulary. *Beddie, 678.*

[53] [HAWKESWORTH, John] FREVILLE, A.F.J. de. Histoire des Nouvelles Decouvertes faites dans la mer du Sud en 1767, 1768, 1769 and 1770, redigée d'apres les dernières relations. *2 volumes,*

49: MAGRA. The Journal of a Voyage Round the World is the first printed description of Cook's first voyage.

52: HAWKESWORTH. Portuguese account of Cook's first voyage.

VIAGEM

DO

CAPITAÓ

COOK

A RODA DO MUNDO NO NAVIO DE SUA
MAGESTADE, A DILIGENCIA.

LISBOA,
NA TYPOGRAFIA ROLLANDIANA.
1819.
*Com licença da Meza do Desembargo
do Paço.*
*Vende-se em Caza do Editor F. B. O. de M
Machos na Largo do Cacz do Sodré, N. 3. A.*

octavo, with two engraved folding maps; modern maroon morocco, a fine and entirely uncut copy. Paris, chez de Hansy le jeune, 1774.

An important French compilation and the first to include Hawkesworth's collected voyages to Tahiti, New Zealand and the east coast of Australia. De Freville, who acquired much of his knowledge while translating Cook's first voyage into French, here gives a concise view of geographical and ethnographic knowledge of Oceania including Australia and New Zealand. He was later to translate the second voyage.

The chart, prepared by Vaugondy, the King's geographer, shows the tracks of Byron, Wallis and Carteret in the Pacific, and that of Cook through the Society Islands, New Zealand and along the east coast of Australia. More than 250 pages are devoted to New Zealand, and 70 pages to New Holland. *Beddie, 720; O'Reilly-Reitman, 100.*

THE COOK FLORILEGIUM

[54] BANKS, Sir Joseph & Daniel SOLANDER. CAPTAIN COOK'S FLORILEGIUM. A Selection of Engravings from the Drawings of Plants collected by Joseph Banks and Daniel Solander on Captain Cook's first Voyage to the Islands of the Pacific, with Accounts of the Voyage by W. Blunt and of the Botanical Explorations and Prints by W. T. Stearn. *Large folio, with 30 engravings; a fine copy, specially bound by Zaehnsdorf in black Nigerian goatskin and Japanese silk, housed in a protective buckram case.* The Lion and Unicorn Press [London, Royal College of Art], 1973.

One of the finest botanical productions of all time. The Royal College of Art's printing of these original eighteenth century copper-plates appeared in an edition of only 100 copies, on a specially hand made paper, which were presented in a specially designed binding by Zaehnsdorf of London; the edition was fully subscribed long before it was completed. Copies now change hands only infrequently.

When Cook set out on his first voyage, Joseph Banks travelled with him, as did another great naturalist, Daniel Solander, as well as the talented botanical artist Sydney Parkinson, who was to die on the voyage. The original botanical drawings from the expedition with the collection of actual specimens, were made into detailed and accurate paintings under Banks' supervision when the expedition returned to London. Following this they were engraved, and we know that Banks intended to oversee full publication of the collection of engravings. In fact only a proof impression was made and the undertaking abandoned. The British Museum (Natural History) holds the original copper-engraved plates, as well as the drawings and specimens themselves, and a set of the proof impressions made from the copper-engravings.

Between 1900 and 1905 lithographic copies were made of 318 of these proof impressions, and published as *Illustrations of Australian Plants collected in 1770*. The copper-plates themselves remained unused, until in 1960 it was decided that the Royal College of Art should print a selection of the most beautiful. The result, after thirteen years of planning, was this splendid production, which for the first time showed the extraordinary strength of the images. Perfectly printed, rich impressions in strong black ink, they show the important botany of the Cook voyage to great advantage, and at the same time make it a matter for great regret that no eighteenth century edition ever appeared. These very pure images present a more austere and quite as beautiful an interpretation of Banks' magnum opus as the massive project now in progress, the printing in colours by Alecto Historical Editions from all the plates.

BANKS IN THE GOSSIP COLUMNS

[55] [BANKS]. ANONYMOUS. HISTORIES OF THE TETE-A-TETE ANNEXED; or Memoirs of the Circumnavigator and Miss B------n. Extract from The Town and Country Magazine. *Octavo, 3 pp., and engraved portraits of Miss B------n. and 'The Circumnavigator', tipped onto a card.* September, 1773.

A little known eighteenth century "thrilling" account of the private life of Sir Joseph Banks, both before and after his voyage with Cook, and with many references throughout to the voyage.

Banks was a favourite target of the satirists and gossip-mongers of the period. The story here is his relationship with a Miss B., a ladies companion, and daughter of an insolvent 'gentleman of fortune', whom he is said to have met on a tete-a-tete party to Hampton Court, soon establishing her as his mistress.

[56] KING, Philip Gidley, the younger. COMMENTS ON COOK'S LOG (H.M.S. Endeavour, 1770) with extracts, charts, and sketches. *Quarto, with 22 maps and plates (some folding); original mauve pebbled cloth, spine a little faded, endleaves browned as usual, joints a little weak; a good copy.* Sydney, Charles Potter, Government Printer, 1892.

Interest in Cook was greatly increased by the sale in 1890 of the "Corner Journal". Philip Gidley King here attempts to use entries from the Log held in the Public Record Office, London, to produce a continuous narrative of the voyage, because "It has lately been noticed that in one instance at least Dr. Hawkesworth has ignored matter in Cook's journal that might well have been given to the world, and it is with a view to bringing to light the most important nautical incidents connected with his exploration of the Coasts of New South Wales, as recorded in the log of his ship . . . that the following pages have been put together".

Some of the illustrations to the "comments" that King uses were reproduced from sketches made by his father, Philip Parker King, on his surveying voyage of 1818-1821. *Beddie, 4784.*

55: BANKS. *Highly imaginative portraits of Sir Joseph Banks and his mistress.*

OPPOSITE:
54: BANKS. *Captain Cook's* Florilegium *was published in this magnificent form by the Royal College of Art, who printed a selection of the botanical plates from the original eighteenth century engravings.*

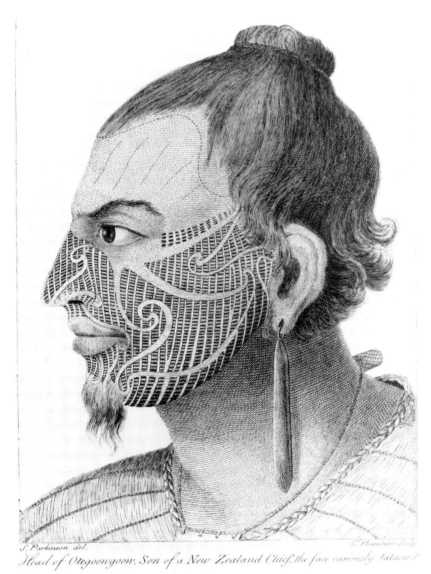

S. Parkinson del.   *T. Chambers Sculp.*

Head of Otegoongoon, Son of a New Zealand Chief, the face curiously tattowed.

57: PARKINSON. *Otegoongoon, the son of a New Zealand chief, as engraved from an original drawing by Sydney Parkinson.*

THE NAMING OF THE KANGAROO

[57] PARKINSON, Sydney. A JOURNAL OF A VOYAGE TO THE SOUTH SEAS, IN HIS MAJESTY'S SHIP, THE ENDEAVOUR ... Embellished with Views and Designs, delineated by the Author, and engraved by capital Artists. *Quarto, with frontispiece portrait, 1 map and 26 plates; contemporary marbled calf, rebacked, raised bands, dark blue label; some foxing of text and plates, frontispiece portrait browned and with slight offsetting to title; a good tall copy, with the armorial bookplates of Robert Shafto of Benwell and William Adair.* London, Printed for Stanfield Parkinson, the Editor, 1773.

First edition. The most handsome of the unofficial accounts of Cook's first voyage; it contains extensive accounts of New Zealand and Australia, is the first work to identify the Kangaroo by name, and contains splendid engravings by the expedition's official artist — and incidentally the first professional artist to set foot on Australian soil.

Parkinson, the son of a Quaker brewer of Edinburgh, was apprenticed to a draper when his ability for drawing "flowers, fruits and other objects of natural history" first attracted the attention of Sir

Joseph Banks. Banks engaged him as botanical artist on the first voyage, during which he produced an enormous number of magnificent botanical and natural history drawings of Tahiti, New Zealand and Australia. At the end of the voyage, enroute from Batavia to the Cape of Good Hope, Parkinson died of a fever.

Parkinson's manuscripts and drawings became a matter of dispute and considerable acrimony. Banks considered that they were his, while Parkinson's brother Stanfield claimed them under the provisions of his brother's will. When Hawkesworth learned of the impending publication of this work, he obtained an injunction to prevent it appearing until some time after the official account. Hawkesworth further retaliated by deliberately omitting Parkinson's name from his account and even the botanical illustrations in his publication lack their proper credit.

Parkinson's journal of the voyage is plain and unaffected, and in the words of its editor " . . . its only ornament is truth, and its best recommendation characteristic of himself, its genuine simplicity".

Curiously, as the botanical drawings were retained by Banks, none of his botanical drawings appear in his own account, and not until recent years has the world at large learned of Parkinson's genius as a botanical artist. *Beddie, 712; Davidson, pp. 54-56; Hill, pp. 223-225; Holmes, 7.*

FIRST VOYAGE DRAWINGS

[58-60] ANONYMOUS ARTIST, after Cipriani, Parkinson, Barralet and others.

The following 12 items form a series of late eighteenth century drawings relating to Cook's first voyage, and the *Endeavour*'s visit to Tierra del Fuego and her stays in the Society Islands and New Zealand.

The drawings are unsigned, mostly captioned in a flowing 18th century hand; four of them have (undated) Whatman watermarks. All 12 of the drawings relate to engravings published in Hawkesworth (*An Account of the Voyages undertaken by the order of His Present Majesty for making Discoveries in the Southern Hemisphere*, 3 volumes, London, 1773, the second and third volumes of which contain the official account of Cook's first voyage — see item 50).

Full reference is made below to Rudiger Joppien's and Bernard Smith's authoritative *The Art of Captain Cook's Voyages: Volume 1. The Voyage of the Endeavour 1768-1771:t (Melbourne, 1985)*.

The drawings are offered for sale in three groups: the first drawing, no. 58, which relates to the *Endeavour*'s visit to Tierra del Fuego in January 1769; drawings 59A to 59G, which derive from the *Endeavour*'s stay in Tahiti and the other Society Islands from April to August 1769; drawings 60A to 60D, which deal with the stay in New Zealand, from October 1769 to March 1770.

[58] After Giovanni Battista Cipriani. "A VIEW OF THE INDIANS OF TERRA DEL FUEGO IN THEIR HUT." *238 x 280 mm., pen and ink on paper.*

The Tierra del Fuego hut was first drawn by Parkinson, but there are several later versions: John

James Barralet made a version of the Parkinson drawing, probably for engraving for use in the Hawkesworth account, but which was not actually used; a version by Alexander Buchan, in the British Library, was exhibited at the Australian Museum in 1970; a version by Giovanni Battista Cipriani is held in the Dixson Library in a collection of third voyage watercolours by Webber; plate 1 in Hawkesworth, (volume II, p. 55) is engraved by Bartolozzi after the Cipriani version.

The only major changes here from the Cipriani/Bartolozzi version are the addition of clothing to the figures on extreme left and right and a change of both clothing and posture to the figure directly behind the fire. *Hawkesworth, plate I (Vol. II, p. 55); Joppien and Smith, 1.6A-B (see also 1.5).*

[59A] After Sydney Parkinson and John James Barralet. "A VIEW OF MATAVIAN[*SIC*] BAY IN ŌTAHEITE TAKEN FROM ONE TREE HILL, and the Tree is a new species of the Erythrina." *247 x 250 mm., pen and ink on paper.*

The view shows the *Endeavour*'s watering-place at Matavai Bay in Tahiti; the *Endeavour* is at anchor, and Fort Venus, Cook's encampment, can be seen across the bay.

Parkinson's original drawing is held in the British Library; two versions by Barralet (respectively Dixson Library and British Library) gradually turn the standing figures from the Europeans who appear in Parkinson's drawing to the Tahitians who are seen towards the left of the present drawing. *Hawkesworth, plate II (Vol. II, p. 80); Joppien and Smith, 1.29 and 1.29A-lC.*

[59B] After John Frederick Miller. "A FLY-FLAP OF THE ISLAND OHITEROO." *235 x 183 mm., pen and ink on paper.*

Joppien and Smith have identified an early drawing for the engraving in Hawkesworth by J.F. Miller, dated 1771 (i.e. after the return of the voyage). It could have been based on a voyage drawing, perhaps by Parkinson, although Adrienne Kaeppler (*Artificial Curiosities*, 1978, 160.5) has identified the image as that of a fly-whisk now in the British Museum. The published engraving also has two further figures, one on each side, of handles of a similar instrument. *Hawkesworth, plate XII (Vol. II, p. 185); Joppien and Smith, 1.94 and 1.94A.*

[59C] After John Frederick Miller. [TOOLS FROM THE SOCIETY ISLANDS]. *203 x 162 mm., pen and ink on paper.*

Joppien and Smith have identified several drawings by Miller of Society Islands artefacts; one drawing in particular is reversed, but otherwise identical. The engraving based on it was made by Record; the present drawing has captions under each artefact which do not exactly correspond to any of the other versions. *Hawkesworth, plate X (Vol. II, p. 191); Joppien and Smith, 1.98 and 1.98A.*

[59D] After Sydney Parkinson and John James Barralet. "A VIEW IN THE ISLAND OF OTAHEITE WITH THE HOUSE CALLED TUPAPOW, under which the Dead are deposited, & a representation of the Person who performs the principal part in the funeral Ceremony in his peculiar Dress; with a man climbing the Bread Fruit Tree to get out of his way." *252 x 330 mm., pen and ink on paper, margins extended with blank paper.*

Parkinson's original drawing of this scene (described in his *Journal*, p. 26) is held by the British Library, while a drawing by Barralet based on it is in the Dixson Library. Barralet made a number of changes for the engraving, to which the present drawing corresponds. *Hawkesworth, plate V (Vol. II, p. 234); Joppien and Smith, 1.45 and 1.45A-B.*

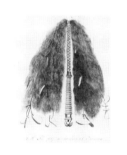

59E-60D: ANONYMOUS ARTIST. *Drawings of the Society Islands and New Zealand, completing the series of first voyage images by an unknown artist.*

[59E] After Sydney Parkinson and John James Barralet. "A VIEW IN THE ISLAND OF HUAHEINE; with the House of Prayer, a small Altar with its Offering; and a Tree called Owharra with which the Houses are Thatched". *247 x 368 mm., pen and ink on paper.*

Various drawings by Sydney Parkinson of the altar and the tree separately were used as sources by Barralet for a drawing — now in the Dixson Library — on which was based the engraving by William Woollett. *Hawkesworth, plate VI (Vol. II, p. 252); Joppien and Smith, 1.70A-C (see also 1.32 and 1.70).*

[59F] After Sydney Parkinson. [A VIEW OF THE ISLAND OF ULIETEA, with a double canoe and a boathouse]. *203 x 445 mm., pen and ink on paper.*

This image is based on two sets of drawings by Parkinson, one of the boathouse and the other of the double canoe. As Joppien and Smith point out in discussing the engraving, however, "there are no known sources for the [central group of] figures, which are probably neo-classical inventions". *Hawkesworth, plate III (Vol. II, p. 258); Joppien and Smith, 1.78A, and see 1.75, 1.76 and 1.76A, 1.77 and 1.78*

[59G] After Giovanni Battista Cipriani. "A VIEW OF THE INSIDE OF A HOUSE IN THE ISLAND OF ULIETEA, with the representation of a Dance to the Music of the Country." *247 x 327 mm., pen and ink on paper, lower margin extended.*

This inside view of a Tahitian house was developed by Cipriani from several Parkinson drawings (see Joppien and Smith 1.83-1.85) although the source for the details of internal construction of the house is not known. Cipriani's drawing is held in the Dixson Library. A highly romantic painting of the same subject (see Joppien and Smith 1.87C) is at Goodwood House. *Hawkesworth, plate VII (Vol. II, p. 265); Joppien and Smith, 1.87A and 1.87B.*

[60A] After Herman Diedrich Sporing and John James Barralet. "A VIEW OF A PERFORATED ROCK IN TOLAGA BAY IN NEW ZEALAND". *221 x 252 mm., pen and ink on paper.*

Sporing's original drawing of this scene, which shows the *Endeavour's* pinnace on the water through

the arched rock, is in the British Library. It was probably Banks who lent the Sporing drawing to Barralet: his drawing, which is in the Knatchbull Collection, has added English and native figues at left and in the foreground. *Hawkesworth, plate XVII (Vol. II, p. 318); Joppien and Smith, 1.111, 1.113A and 1.113B.*

[60B] After Herman Diedrich Sporing and John James Barralet. "A FORTIFIED TOWN CALLED A HIPPAH, built on a perforated Rock in Tolaga Bay New Zealand". *221 x 252 mm., pen and ink on paper.*

Sporing's original drawing, probably made on the spot on 12 November 1769, is in the British Library; again it was probably Banks who arranged its loan to Barralet, whose version, which introduces the English and native boats, is in the Knatchbull Collection.

Another view of the same rock (which collapsed towards the end of the 19th century) appears as plate XXIV in Parkinson's Journal, but Parkinson's original drawing for it is not known. *Hawkesworth, plate XVIII (Vol. II, p. 341); Joppien and Smith, 1.121, 1.122A and 1.122B.*

[60C] After R. Ralph (?and John Frederick Miller). "A CHEST OF NEW ZEALAND, or a specimen of the carving of that Country". *282 x 214 mm., pen and ink on paper.*

Two drawings of the same subject are recorded by Joppien and Smith, both now in the British Library. The engraving in Hawkesworth and the present drawing both follow the drawing by R. Ralph (1.164), but it is possible that the Ralph drawing was in turn based on the Miller version (1.163). *Hawkesworth, plate XV (Vol. III, p. 59); Joppien and Smith, 1.163 and 1.164.*

[60D] After John Frederick Miller. [PATOO PATOOS or bludgeons from New Zealand]. *166 x 204 mm., pen and ink on paper.*

The drawing of this subject by Miller is in the British Library; it relates to two other drawings of objects reproduced by Joppien and Smith (1.154 and 1.156). Record's engraving of the subject for use in Hawkesworth was in reverse, as is the present drawing. *Hawkesworth, plate XIV (Vol. III, p. 62); Joppien and Smith, 1.155 and 1.155A.*

III
Cook's Second Voyage

Cook's second voyage to the Pacific, aided by new and improved methods of determining longitude and latitude, refined his discoveries in the South Pacific. The search for the Southern Continent continued, and Cook determined for once and for all that it did not exist.

The Resolution *and the* Adventure *sailed from Plymouth on 13th July, 1772. The complement included the two Forsters, and the artist William Hodges; Anders Sparrman, a Swede, was taken on at the Cape of Good Hope. In January 1773, Cook made the first crossing of the Antarctic Circle. March to June 1773 were spent in New Zealand waters, then they worked variously north and east to Tahiti. At Huaheine, Omai was taken aboard the* Adventure *and accompanied them back to England. In 1774 Cook made a second sweep through the Pacific from New Zealand, stopping at Easter Island, the Marquesas, Tahiti and the Tuamotus. Further discoveries included southern islands of the New Hebrides, New Caledonia, and Norfolk Island.*

The voyage of three years and eighteen days was remarkable for the preservation of the health of officers and crew. Only one succumbed to a "lingering illness, without any mixture of scurvy" and three others died as a result of shipboard accidents. The improved dietary and sanitary conditions, rigidly enforced by Cook, earned him a permanent place in medical history and the coveted medal of the Royal Society.

FIRST ACCOUNT OF THE SECOND VOYAGE

[61] MARRA, John. JOURNAL OF THE RESOLUTION'S VOYAGE, in 1772, 1773, 1774, and 1775. On Discovery to the Southern Hemisphere, by which the Non Existence of an Undiscovered Continent . . . is demonstratively proved. Also a Journal of the Adventure's Voyage, in the years 1772, 1773, and 1774. With an Account of the Separation of the two Ships. *Octavo, with folding map and 5 plates; contemporary tree calf, rebacked, preserving original gilt spine with floral and anchor ornaments, red labels; bookplate of Joseph Whittuck and date 1789; with occasional contemporary annotations; a fine copy in a most attractive contemporary binding.* London, Printed for E. Newbery, 1775.

First edition. The first full account of Cook's second voyage to be published, preceding the official account by at least eighteen months.

Though published anonymously, due to the strict injunction against private publications, its authorship was soon known. It seems to have been prepared for the press by David Henry, editor of the *Gentleman's Magazine*, who to disguise the author could not resist commenting that the work "appears to have been hastily written, and hastily printed". "Correspondence between Cook and the Admiralty shows that the author was John Marra, one of the gunners' mates in the Resolution. He was an Irishman whom Cook had picked up at Batavia during the first voyage. He made an abortive attempt to desert at Tahiti on May 14th, 1774, an escapade of which Cook took so lenient a view that he says — "I know not if he might have obtained my consent, if he had applied for it in proper time". This did not, however, as Marra states at p. 241, prevent his being put in irons . . ." (Holmes).

Whittuck, of whom nothing is known, seems to have been a Cook enthusiast. Beside the mention of the commemorative medals struck off by Mathew Boulton for Joseph Banks, he notes that he owns one of the few silver examples, and a blank leaf at the end of the present volume contains his manuscript obituaries of both J.R. Forster and William Wales. *Beaglehole, II, pp. cliii-clv; Beddie, 1270; Hill, p. 60; Holmes, 16; Kroepelien, 809.*

COOK'S ACCOUNT OF THE VOYAGE

[62] COOK, Captain James. A VOYAGE TOWARDS THE SOUTH POLE, AND ROUND THE WORLD. Performed in His Majesty's Ships the Resolution and Adventure, in the years 1772, 1773, 1774, and 1775. Written by James Cook, Commander of the Resolution. In which is included, Captain Furneaux's Narrative of his proceedings in the Adventure during the separation of the ships. *2 volumes, quarto, with frontispiece portrait and 63 engraved charts, portraits and plates; half calf antique, red and black labels, original marbled boards; some browning and offsetting of plates, but a very good and tall copy, completely uncut.* London, Printed for W. Strahan, and T. Cadell in the Strand, 1777.

First edition: the official account of Cook's great second voyage, which he prepared for publication himself, dissatisfied with Hawkesworth's treatment of the first voyage.

This was historically the most important of Cook's three voyages. For the first time the Antarctic circle was crossed when, at the beginning of the voyage, Cook cruised as far south as possible, round the edge of the Antarctic ice. His belief in the existence of a land-mass in the southern ice ring was eventually

61: MARRA. *The first published view of the Antarctic landscape.*

61: MARRA. *Marra's Journal was the first description of Cook's second voyage to be published.*

38. BARRINGTONIA.

a

b

64: FORSTER. *Although the Forsters were ridiculed for their engravings of small plants on large sheets of paper, their book remains an important source for our early knowledge of the botany of Australasia and Polynesia.*

proved by the nineteenth century explorers. In the Pacific, he visited New Zealand again, and either discovered or revisited many of the islands, including New Caledonia, Palmerston and Norfolk Islands, Easter Island, the Marquesas, New Hebrides, Tonga, the South Sandwich Islands and South Georgia. *Holmes, 24; Beddie, 1216; Hill, p. 61; Printing and the Mind of Man, 223.*

MINIATURE ATLAS

[63] COOK, Captain James. ATLAS DU SECOND VOYAGE de James Cook. *Oblong octavo, with title, 8 text pp., folding map, portrait of Cook and 26 plates on 22 sheets; original green printed wrappers, light dampstaining not affecting images; very scarce.* Paris, Chez la veuve Le Petit, 1804.

A charming miniature atlas, part of the collected *Bibliotheque portative des Voyages*, but complete in itself, and evidence of continuing French interest in Cook's voyages. The map shows the route of the *Resolution* among the New Hebrides and the coast of New Caledonia. *Beddie, 87.*

THE BOTANICAL DISCOVERIES

[64] FORSTER, Johann Reinhold. CHARACTERES GENERUM PLANTARUM, quas in itinere ad insulas australis, collegerunt, descripserunt, delinearunt, annis 1772-1775. *Quarto, with 78 engraved plates (numbered 1-76 and including 38 a & b, & 51 a); contemporary tortoise calf, gilt spine, black label; joints a little tender, some scuffing of extremities, occasional spotting and browning of text, but a good copy.* Londini, Prostant apud B. White, 1776.

First edition: one of two contemporary issues, probably the first, with the longer dedication to George III. The book is a Linnean classification of botanical discoveries made during the voyage; the descriptions are by Anders Sparrman and the engravings are after drawings by the younger Forster.

The Forsters, father and son, travelled as scientists on the second voyage. Their intellectual arrogance earned them considerable ridicule — including some mockery for the present work "owing to the minute scale on which the plants were drawn as compared with the size of the paper" (Holmes). Scientifically, the work was not of major importance; in Beaglehole's words (II, p. cliiin) "the botanists speak despitefully" of both this and the *Florulae* which George Forster published some ten years later in Gottingen. Nevertheless the book is one of the earliest sources for our knowledge of the plants of Australasia and Polynesia, has considerable significance for the history of the second voyage, and is one of a perhaps surprisingly small number of monuments to the major scientific achievements of the three voyages.

The *Characteres* is one of the earliest publications resulting from the second voyage; the previous year Marra's surreptitious narrative had been published, while in 1776 only this and the anonymous *Second Voyage round the World* appeared. In 1777 both the Forsters' narrative and the official account by Cook were published, along with Wales and Bayly's *Astronomical Observations*, while a year later came the Forsters' *Observations*. The rush to get it into print should probably be seen in the light of the quarrel with the Admiralty over the Forsters' claims to publishing rights for the official account of the voyage. This pre-emptive scientific publication may well have been intended to show the strength of the Forster camp. *Beddie, 1385; Hill, p. 422-423; Holmes, 17.*

THE FORSTERS' ALTERNATIVE ACCOUNT

[65] FORSTER, George. A VOYAGE ROUND THE WORLD, IN HIS BRITANNIC MAJESTY'S SLOOP RESOLUTION, commanded by Capt. James Cook, during the years 1772, 3, 4, and 5. *2 volumes, quarto, with large folding map and errata list at end of vol. I; contemporary calf, rebacked, old gilt spines, red and black labels; slight browning to first and last leaves, occasional light spotting to text, but an extremely good copy.* London, Printed for B. White, 1777.

First edition of this alternative account of the second voyage. "When the Admiralty decided to allow the elder Forster to take no part in the official account of the voyage, the Forsters set to work to forestall it with an account of their own, and succeeded in doing so by about six weeks. George Forster in the preface states that he wrote the account himself but consulted his father's journal. Wales the astronomer roundly accused him of being author in name only, the real author being his father. This George Forster roundly denied. But whatever the respective shares of father and son in the composition of this book, it is pertinent to observe that no acknowledgement is made of the assistance derived from Cook's journal, the proof-sheets of which had in accordance with the agreement signed at the Admiralty on April 13th, 1776, been placed at the elder Forster's disposal" (Holmes). *Beddie, 1247; Hill, p. 108; Holmes, 23.*

UNRECORDED PRE-PUBLICATION ISSUE

[66] FORSTER, John Reinhold. OBSERVATIONS MADE DURING A VOYAGE ROUND THE WORLD, on Physical Geography, Natural History and Ethic Philosophy. *Quarto, with folding table, lacking the map and 4 pp. "contents" but with no indication that they were ever present; with list of subscribers following the text; contemporary diced russia, compartmented spine with ship ornaments in gilt, slight spotting to text, but overall a particularly fine copy.* London, Printed for G. Robinson, 1778.

A pre-publication issue, of which no other copy seems to be recorded. Forster, who was anxious for recognition after his rejection by the Admiralty, began sending out copies of this, his most important work, before its completion. In July copies were forwarded to the King of Sweden and to the Royal Swedish Academy of Sciences, but the final sheets were not sent out until August. Both the 4 pp. "contents" and the folding map (which appears to have been an after-thought) are absent here, with no indication that they were ever present. They would have been the last parts to be completed.

The first signature including the title-page, printed on thinner paper, has a defect to the fold and last leaf which would not have passed inspection by the printer or binder, but would have been acceptable if the work was being sent out by Forster himself. The fine diced russia binding is also perhaps further evidence of the special issue.

The *Observations* is a pioneer work on the anthropology of the Pacific, by a naturalist aboard the *Resolution*. It was originally intended to be a part of the official narrative, but when it was rejected by the Earl of Sandwich, Forster had it printed on his own account. His "Remarks on the Human Species", accounting for two thirds of the text, and its most important part, is primarily concerned with the South Sea Islanders, with inquiries into their "progress toward civilisation", principles of happiness, health and diseases, religion, morals, manners, arts and sciences, with a comparative table of languages from the Society Islands to New Holland. Forster carefully interviewed the natives (identifying his informants) in all aspects of their culture, and includes an account of Tahitian knowledge of geography and navigation. There is a long chapter on preserving the health of mariners. The list of subscribers, mostly Oxford

academics, accounts for only 91 copies.

See Hoare, Michael, *The Tactless Philosopher,* Melbourne, 1976, pp. 182-183 for a discussion of the publication of this work. *Beddie, 1261; Hill, p. 109; Holmes, 29.*

THE NOBLE SAVAGE

[67] [OMAI] BARTOLOZZI, F. after Nathaniel DANCE. OMAI, A NATIVE OF ULAIETEA. *Stipple engraving, 463 x 286 mm., trimmed to margins, uniformly lightly browned.* London, 1794.

A full-length portrait, based on the original drawing by Nathaniel Dance. Omai was the embodiment of Rousseau's noble savage when he arrived in the *Adventure* in England with Captain Cook in 1774. His natural grace captivated London society, and this fine portrait epitomises the eighteenth century ideal of the noble South Sea islander.

In 1776 Omai returned to the Pacific with presents of "every article known to be held a treasure in Tahiti", including a house; and landed at Huaheine in a breastplate and helmet decorated with large red

67: OMAI. Bartolozzi's portrait of Omai, after a drawing by Dance.

66: FORSTER. *Forster's* Observations, *in a special presentation version.*

69: SPARRMAN. *The botanist Sparrman was at the Cape of Good Hope when Cook's second expedition called there; he was engaged as assistant naturalist. His book discusses both his experiences at the Cape and the voyage itself.*

plumes. His subsequent history was unhappy and he died in obscurity. *Nan Kivell and Spence, p. 238.*

[68] [OMAI] CLARK, Thomas Blake. OMAI, FIRST POLYNESIAN AMBASSADOR TO ENGLAND. The true story of his voyage there in 1774 with Captain Cook; of how he was feted by Fanny Burney, approved of by Samuel Johnson, entertained by Mrs. Thrale and Lord Sandwich and painted by Sir Joshua Reynolds. *Octavo; original tan cloth spine, paper title label, patterned boards; slight browning of end papers and top edges, but a very good copy.* San Francisco, The Colt Press, 1941.

Second edition of this Pacific classic, produced at Jane Grabhorn's Colt Press. *Hill, p. 53.*

THE ASSISTANT NATURALIST'S ACCOUNT

[69] SPARRMAN, Anders. VOYAGE AU CAP DE BONNE-ESPERANCE, et Autour du Monde avec le Capitaine Cook, et principalement dans le pays des Hottentots et des Caffres. Traduit par M. Le Tourneur. *3 volumes, octavo, with folding map and 16 folding engraved plates; contemporary quarter calf, yellow glazed paper spine labels and boards, slight wear to extremities and tops of spines, slight spotting to half titles and part of text, some wear to plates where folded; a very good copy.* Paris, Chez Buisson, 1787.

First octavo edition in French, published simultaneously with the quarto edition. Sparrman, a professor of Zoology at Uppsala University, was in South Africa when the *Resolution* and *Adventure* called in 1772. John Reinhold Forster engaged him to accompany the expedition as assistant naturalist. Though most of the account is a narrative of Sparrmann's travels in Africa with emphasis on its flora and fauna and containing a remarkable series of plates on termites and their habitations, he includes an interesting account of his voyage with Cook in the first volume.

Sparrman published an expanded version of this voyage in 1802 (with a second volume in 1818), but this account which was widely read and translated, remains the only eighteenth century text by this member of the second voyage. *Beddie, 1280; not in Hill; Kroepelien, 1224.*

GOLDEN COCKEREL PRESS

[70] SPARRMAN, Anders. A VOYAGE ROUND THE WORLD WITH CAPTAIN JAMES COOK in H.M.S. Resolution ... Introduction and notes by Owen Rutter, wood engravings by Peter Barker-Mill. *Quarto; original olive glazed cloth; a fine copy.* London, Golden Cockerel Press, 1944.

First English translation of Sparrman's narrative published in Sweden in 1802-1818. His observant and well written account of the second voyage contains much that appears nowhere else, emphasising naturally Sparrman's interests in medicine, health and natural history.

One of 350 numbered copies. A handsomely produced and beautifully illustrated work, printed at a renowned private press, all the more remarkable in that it was issued during wartime. *Hill, p.279; Kroepelien, 1231; O'Reilly-Reitman, 409.*

TRANSLATED WITH ONE LEG AROUND THE TABLE

[71] [SPARRMAN] ROSEN VON ROSENSTEIN, Nils. THE DISEASES OF CHILDREN, and their Remedies. *Octavo; contemporary half calf, red and green labels, corners slightly worn, joints just cracking but firm, some spotting throughout, heavier on first and last leaves; old institutional stamp on title and a few leaves, book label inside front cover.* London, Printed for T. Cadell in the Strand, 1776.

A curious and important, if little known result of Cook's second voyage. Anders Sparrman, the great Swedish botanist and traveller, carried a copy of the recently published third and complete edition of Rosen von Rosenstein's paediatric classic when he travelled to South Africa in 1772, and retained it when he joined Cook on the *Resolution*. He was encouraged to translate the work into English by Georg and Johann Forster, under circumstances vividly described in his account of the voyage. It was "finished in our last year of cruising in the South Sea, mostly in the rougher climates, as I at that time was the least taken up with business of any kind, except that of writing; though even in this case I was not unfrequently obliged, on account of the stormy weather, to cling with my leg round the foot of the table, and hold myself fast with one hand, in order to be able to write with the other . . .".

Sparrman left the ship at the Cape, and the translation was taken to London by the Forsters, who there edited it and arranged for its publication. It is thus a shipboard collaboration between three of the most important European scientists to travel with Cook. It is also a pioneering work on paediatrics. The author "was the oldest practitioner of physic in Sweden ... being especially famous for his great knowledge of, and success in curing, the diseases of children" (Preface). For a full discussion, see B. Vahlquist *Anders Sparrman and his Translation of Rosen von Rosenstein's Textbook on Children's Diseases . . .* in Acta Paediatrica Scandinavica 676:269-272, 1977. *Not in Beddie.*

IV
Cook's Third
Voyage

Cook's third Pacific voyage was as important for the exploration of the North Pacific as the first two voyages had been for the South Pacific. It was also the best equipped both navigationally and scientifically, and resulted in the discovery of Hawaii which Cook himself regarded as his greatest Pacific discovery, and in the disproval of the existence of a navigable northern passage from the Atlantic to the Pacific.

The Resolution *sailed from Plymouth on 12th July 1776 with Cook, John Gore, Lieutenants James King and William Bligh. On the* Discovery, *which sailed on 1st August under Charles Clerke, were James Burney, George Vancouver and John Webber, the artist. All of these men were of the greatest importance to the history of the Pacific.*

First sailing south to check Kerguelen's Land in the Indian Ocean near the Antarctic, they called at Van Diemen's Land, and at Queen Charlotte Sound, New Zealand. In March 1777, the Island of Mangaia in the Cook group was sighted, then in May they discovered the Haapai section of the Tonga Islands, where an extensive investigation was made. The island of Tubuai was sighted on 8th August 1777. Sailing north from Borabora they discovered and named Christmas Island on that day, and on 18th January 1778 had their first sight of Hawaii (Waimea Kauai). Continuing on to California, they sighted the coast on 7th March, in the vicinity of Drake's New Albion. The ships worked their way up the American coast, passed through Bering Strait to latitude 70 degrees 40 minutes before ice made them turn back, surveyed a part of the Asiatic coast and the island of Oonalashka (Alaska).

Sailing south, on 26th November 1778 they discovered more of the Hawaiian chain (Maui) then worked their way round the coast of Hawaii to Kealakekua Bay, anchoring there on 17th January 1779. On 14th February, Cook was killed in a shoreline skirmish with the natives.

FIRST ACCOUNT OF THE THIRD VOYAGE

[72] RICKMAN, John. JOURNAL OF CAPTAIN COOK'S LAST VOYAGE TO THE PACIFIC OCEAN, ON DISCOVERY; performed in the years 1776, 1777, 1778, 1779, illustrated with cuts and a chart, shewing the tracts of the ships employed in this expedition. Faithfully narrated from the original Ms. *Octavo, with folding map and 5 engraved plates (1 folding); early 19th century gilt panelled calf, raised spines with gilt floral ornaments, green endpapers; armorial bookplate; with list of 6 errata in ten lines of text at end of advertisement leaf; extensively annotated in ink in an 18th century hand.* London, Printed for E. Newbery, 1781.

First edition. This scarce and important account of Cook's third voyage, though published anonymously, was conclusively shown by Judge Howay (*Zimmerman's Captain Cook*, Toronto, 1930) to be by John Rickman, a lieutenant on the voyage. The narrative, which predates the official account by three years, differs in many particulars — particularly regarding the death of Cook, for which this is a prime source.

The extensive contemporary annotations, corrections and underlinings by an unknown person, are obviously the work of someone well acquainted with the voyage and a number of the participants. Regarding the meeting of Omai with George III at Windsor "in a gracious manner", the owner of this copy has added "To ye King he said (having in ye amazement of such a high forgott all his lessons of a compliment or 2) only How d'ye do? How d'ye do?" The commentator seems to have been greatly interested in orthography: throughout the text indigenous names have been corrected or altered: King 'Oreo' to 'oraeo', 'Maw-lhee'(Island) to 'mawee' (p. 298) and 'indians' has been altered to 'men'. Regarding the word 'Preteanne' for Britain he notes "they can pronounce R. but soften ye B into P"; arabic and hebrew characters appear beside the Hawaiian word 'Matee' [make-to die or kill, p. 302]. The plate captioned "Ounalashkan Chief" has been altered to read "The Fashionable Headdress of an Ounalashkan Chief".

The annotator reveals a possible connection with the voyage at the point where Rickman observes stones being rolled down hill: he makes the comment that the "stones were part of their normal weapons" (p. 314) and identifies a father and mother of two girls on board ship by the names "Bolo and Kind" (p. 326).

The armorial bookplate is that of Kenneth Howard, first Earl of Effingham (1767-1845). *Beddie, 1607; Hill, p. 253; Holmes, 38; Lada-Mocarski, 32.*

THE OFFICIAL ACCOUNT

[73] COOK, James and James KING. A VOYAGE TO THE PACIFIC OCEAN. Undertaken by Command of his Majesty, for making Discoveries in the Northern Hemisphere. *3 volumes quarto and an atlas folio; with altogether 87 engraved plates and maps, of which 63 appear in the atlas volume; uniformly bound in modern quarter calf; the text volumes uncut.* London, Printed by W. and A. Strahan, for G. Nicol and T. Cadell, 1784.

First edition of the official account of Cook's last

Representation of the Murder of Capt Cook at O-Why-ee Island knocked down, had Stabb'd with a Pahooie thro' the Back. [woe]

voyage: a good clean set.

The full story of Cook's great third voyage, and his eventual murder while revisiting the Hawaiian Islands that he had discovered earlier during the voyage, was so eagerly awaited by the English public that the entire first edition was sold out, at the considerable price of four pounds fourteen shillings and sixpence, within three days and copies were soon changing hands at up to ten guineas.

Bligh, Burney, Colnett, Vancouver and Riou — all later to command important voyages of their own — were all members of the expedition, which set out to return Omai to Tahiti and to search for a northwest passage. They called at Kerguelen Island, Tasmania, the Cook, Tonga and Society Islands, turned north and discovered Christmas Island and the Hawaiian Islands and went on to chart the northwest coast of America from Northern California to 70° 44' where they were stopped by pack ice.

The official artist on the voyage was John Webber, and his romantic views of the islands of the Pacific published here remain the most evocative portrayals of the islands — helping to create the notion of an island paradise that so affected the European public eagerly reading the voyages of discovery being published in the eighteenth century. *Beddie, 1543; Holmes, 47.*

FIRST OCTAVO EDITION

[74] COOK, James. A VOYAGE TO THE PACIFIC OCEAN; undertaken by Command of His Majesty, for making Discoveries in the Northern Hemisphere; performed under the directions of Captains Cook, Clerke, and Gore, in the years 1776, 1777, 1778, 1779, and 1780. *4 volumes, octavo, with numerous engraved plates; contemporary speckled calf, rebacked, retaining all original spines, red labels; a very good set.* London, Printed for John Stockdale, Scatcherd and Whitaker, John Fielding, and John Hardy, 1784.

72: RICKMAN. The death of Cook was a particularly popular subject for eighteenth century illustrators.

72: RICKMAN. Rickman's Journal was the first published account of Cook's third voyage.

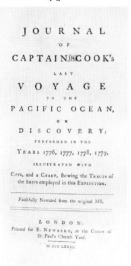

JOURNAL
OF
CAPTAIN COOK's
LAST
VOYAGE
TO THE
PACIFIC OCEAN,
ON
DISCOVERY;
PERFORMED IN THE
YEARS 1776, 1777, 1778, 1779,
ILLUSTRATED WITH
Cuts, and a CHART, shewing the TRACTS of
the Ships employed in this EXPEDITION.
Faithfully Narrated from the original MS.
LONDON:
Printed for E. NEWBERY, at the Corner of
St. Paul's Church Yard.
M DCC LXXXI.

76: COOK. *An unfamiliar portrait of the navigator.*

77A, 77C & 77D: CLEVELEY. *Aquatint views by Cleveley of the death of Cook in Hawaii; Huaheine; and Matavai Bay, Tahiti.*

First octavo edition, and the first to reach the general public. Appearing very soon after the full quarto edition, the text here has been abridged, omitting some of the technical details of navigation. The plates have been re-engraved in a smaller format. *Beddie, 1545.*

DUBLIN PIRATED EDITION

[75] COOK, James and James KING. A VOYAGE TO THE PACIFIC OCEAN. Undertaken by the command of His Majesty, for making Discoveries in the Northern Hemisphere ... Performed under the direction of Captains Cook, Clerke, and Gore, in His Majesty's Ships the Resolution, and Discovery. In the years 1776, 1777, 1778, 1779, and 1780. *3 volumes, octavo, with frontispiece portrait [with] Atlas volume, containing 26 folding maps, charts and elevations. Together 4 volumes, octavo, the text bound in contemporary tree calf, rebacked, corners expertly repaired, red and olive labels; the atlas, bound in half calf antique and original marbled boards, with matching labels; occasional spotting of text, generally confined to end leaves, some folding maps dampstained and a little browned; contemporary signature on title of volume I and small ownership labels throughout.* Dublin, Printed for H. Chamberlaine and others, 1784.

First Irish edition. Published in the same year as the official edition, this pirated account, the first to be published outside London, was particularly popular in America. This set is unusual in that the original owner has had the plates bound separately for ease of use. *Beddie, 1546; this edition not in Hill.*

SCARCE ABRIDGEMENT

[76] COOK, James and James KING. CAPTAIN

COOK'S THIRD AND LAST VOYAGE, TO THE PACIFIC OCEAN, in the years 1776, 1777, 1778, 1779 and 1780. Faithfully abridged from the Quarto Edition published by order of His Majesty. *Octavo, with frontispiece portrait of Cook after Dodd, engraved title and six engraved plates; contemporary tree calf, gilt spine with ship ornaments, red label, neatly rebacked preserving all original spine.* London, Printed for John Fielding, Pater Noster Row, and John Stockdale, Piccadilly, [1785].

A very attractive copy of a particularly scarce abridgement of the third voyage: the plates are all by Birrell or Cary after Dodd, and include a full-length portrait of Cook as frontispiece and a version of the death of Cook plate. *Beddie, 1555 (Mitchell and State Library of Victoria copies).*

CLEVELEY'S MAGNIFICENT PACIFIC AQUATINTS

[77] CLEVELEY, James. THE SERIES OF FOUR SEPARATELY ISSUED COLOURED AQUATINT VIEWS OF THE PACIFIC relating to Cook's Third Voyage.

[77A] VIEW OF OWHYHEE, one of the Sandwich Islands. *Uniformly browned and aged.*

This pictorial version of the tragic events of February 14th, 1779 is generally regarded as the most accurate.

[77B] VIEW OF MOREA, OR EIMO, one of the Society Islands. *A fine and fresh impression.*

Cook records in his journal the beauty of this island when visited in September 1777.

[77C] VIEW OF HUAHEINE, one of the Society Islands, showing the Resolution and Discovery at anchor in the magnificent harbour of O Wharre. *Uniformly browned and aged.*

[77D] VIEW OF CHARLOTTE SOUND in New Zealand. *Uniformly browned and aged with a small area of the upper left sky skilfully retouched.*

This view was mistitled by the artist and is actually Matavai Bay, Tahiti.

Aquatints, 440 x 600 mm., hand coloured. *All trimmed to plate margins, lacking captions; uniformly framed; a rare set.* London, 1787-1788. Drawn on the spot by James Cleveley. Painted by John Cleveley. Aquatints by Francis Jukes.

These fine aquatints, prepared from watercolours by John Cleveley, are probably the most magnificent Pacific marine prints issued. They show the *Resolution* and *Discovery*, Cook's ships on his third Pacific voyage, at anchor in both the Society and Sandwich Islands.

John Cleveley, a professional draughtsman, was not with Cook on this expedition, but his brother James was, in the position of ship's carpenter. After the voyage returned to England in October 1780, John worked up sketches made on the voyage by James, who although not formally trained, was a proficient artist. It was from these finished watercolours that in 1787-1788 the aquatints were prepared. In the process of preparing them for European eyes, the landscape has been tamed and the

islanders portrayed in a manner both dignified and classical. This cultivated serenity substantiates the notion that artists and engravers working in England in the late 18th century, in order to comprehend the unfamiliar and strange newly discovered Pacific, resorted to their Christian and classical heritage. *Beddie, 1752-1783.*

SURREPTITIOUS NARRATIVE BY THE ARTIST ELLIS

[78] ELLIS, William. An Authentic Narrative of a Voyage performed by Captain Cook and Captain Clerke, in His Majesty's Ships Resolution and Discovery during the years 1776, 1777, 1778, 1779 and 1780; in search of a North-West Passage between the Continents of Asia and America. Including a faithful account of all their discoveries, and the unfortunate death of Captain Cook. *2 volumes, octavo, with folding chart and 21 engraved plates; half calf antique over original marbled boards, red and black labels; early repairs to folding map, occasional spotting of text; a very good copy.* London, Printed for G. Robinson, J. Sewell and J. Debrett, 1782.

First edition. Ellis, a surgeon's mate and talented amateur artist, was first on the *Discovery* and later on the *Resolution.* Despite the prohibition by the Admiralty of the publication of any unauthorised account of the voyage, Ellis, who was in financial straits, sold his narrative to a London publisher for 50 guineas, thus earning the condemnation of Sir Joseph Banks, who wrote to him in January 1782 that "I fear it will not in future be in my power to do what it might have been, had you asked and followed my advice".

Ellis' narrative contains much valuable information on Alaska, the Northwest Coast and Hawaii, and the attractive engraved plates, after the author's drawings, include 8 of Hawaii, 2 of Alaska and 3 of the Northwest Coast. *Beddie, 1599; Holmes, 42; Lada-Mocarski, 35.*

[79] ELLIS, William. An Authentic Narrative of a Voyage performed by Captain Cook and Captain Clerke, in His Majesty's Ships Resolution and Discovery during the years 1776, 1777, 1778, 1779 and 1780; in search of a North-West Passage between the Continents of Asia and America. Including a faithful account of all their discoveries, and the unfortunate death of Captain Cook. *2 volumes, octavo, with folding chart and 21 engraved plates; contemporary calf, spines rubbed, joints cracked, upper cover of volume I detached, portion of one label chipped; internally a fine copy.* London, Printed for G. Robinson ... J. Sewell ... and J. Debrett, 1783.

The second edition of this important alternative account, published to satisfy public curiosity since it is basically unchanged from the first edition. It is surprisingly scarce today. *Beddie, 1600.*

RARE AMERICAN ACCOUNT

[80] LEDYARD, John. A Journal of Captain Cook's last Voyage to the Pacific Ocean, and in quest of a North-West Passage, between Asia and America; performed in the years 1776, 1777, 1778, and 1779 ... Faithfully narrated from the original ms. of Mr. John Ledyard. *Octavo; contemporary calf, lacking the map (as in almost all copies known); some spotting, as in all copies; contemporary calf, somewhat worn, joints repaired.* Hartford, Printed and sold by Nathaniel Patten, 1783.

An extremely scarce surreptitious narrative of the voyage: a better than average copy. Ledyard, one of several Americans on Cook's third voyage, and the

77B: CLEVELEY. *The fine aquatint view of Morea, one of the Society Islands.*

only one to publish an account of the expedition, sailed as a corporal of marines. It is generally acknowledged that he obtained a copy of Rickman's narrative from which he compiled this account after his return to America. He himself describes the sealing of all diaries, drawings, memorandums and charts of all officers and crew aboard ship at Canton (p. 198). However, the narrative contains considerable information not available elsewhere, including a description (the first published) of the Russian presence on Unalaska, the first permanent Russian settlement in Northwest America — only Ledyard, Samwell and Edgar visited the settlement. The map, which is an almost direct copy of Rickman map, is missing in almost every copy, and in keeping with erratic nature of American eighteenth century publishing was almost certainly not generally issued.

The account of his stay at Hawaii, his expedition inland and the death of Cook occupies 64 pp. of the text. The account of New Zealand and Australia is short but includes his observation that "the island of New-Holland (for its boundaries are now ascertained) is by much the largest known, and most eligibly situated on the map of nature . . . even the Empress of Russia might be gratified with such a portion". *Beddie, 1603; Hill, p. 176; Holmes, 45. See also Svet, Y.M. & S.G. Fedorova, "Captain Cook and the Russians", in Pacific Studies, Vol II, No 1, 1978.*

DANIEL WEBSTER'S COPY

[81] [LEDYARD] SPARKS, Jared. THE LIFE OF JOHN LEDYARD, the American Traveller; comprising selections from his Journals and Correspondence. *Octavo, original boards, cloth spine neatly renewed preserving original paper label; uncut, untrimmed, a fine tall copy; signature of Chas. A. Townley, 1892, on title and book plate of Daniel Webster.* Cambridge, Published by Hilliard and Brown, 1828.

First edition. Soon after Ledyard's death in Egypt in 1789, his cousin Dr. Isaac Ledyard of New York, began collecting materials for a biography. The project was abandoned, but the material was preserved and ultimately turned over to Sparks. A substantial portion of the text relates to Cook's third voyage, and contains critical comments on Ledyard's narrative found nowhere else.

Sparks, a noted American historian, owner and editor of the *North American Review*, and later President of Harvard (1849-1853) added "important original letters" and his compilation remains one of the great American biographies. This copy is from the library of the great lexicographer Daniel Webster. *Beddie, 4524; Holmes, 85.*

[82] [LEDYARD] SPARKS, Jared. THE LIFE OF JOHN LEDYARD, the American Traveller; comprising selections from his Journals and Correspondence. *Octavo, cloth spine, original boards, printed paper label; uncut, untrimmed; book label neatly removed from inside front cover; occasional light spotting as usual; a fine, tall copy enclosed in a blue quarter morocco bookform box.* Cambridge, Published by Hilliard and Brown, 1828.

First edition. A fine copy. *Beddie, 4524; Holmes, 85.*

[83] [SAMWELL] DAVIES, Sir William Llewelyn. DAVID SAMWELL, 1751-1798, surgeon of the Discovery, London-Welshman and poet. *Octavo, pp. 70-133 with portrait of Samwell and numerous plates; modern speckled calf, gilt, red label.* An extract from the Society of Cymrodorion-Transactions, 1926-27.

The most complete biography to date of David Samwell, surgeon on the *Discovery* during Cook's third voyage, and very scarce. The author, first assistant librarian at the National Library of Wales, uses Welsh sources not otherwise available. *Beddie, 4623; not in Hill.*

WEBBER'S VIEWS IN THE SOUTH SEAS

[84] WEBBER, John. VIEWS IN THE SOUTH SEAS, FROM DRAWINGS BY THE LATE JAMES WEBBER, DRAFTSMAN ON BOARD THE RESOLUTION, Captain James Cooke, from the year 1776 to 1780. With letter-press, descriptive of the various scenery, &c . . . The drawings are in the possession of the Board of Admiralty. *Folio, with 16 hand coloured aquatint plates; modern green morocco spine and corners sympathetic to the original, over original marbled boards; a few spots to title-page, not affecting the frontispiece, and a few spots to text; all plates bright and beautifully coloured; a remarkably attractive copy.* London, Published by Boydell and Co., 1808.

The most beautiful English colour plate book of the Pacific, the only colour plate book relating to Cook's third voyage, and the last of the great Cook publications. The 16 aquatints, after Webber's drawings, and produced by the artist himself, together form one of the finest visual statements of the South Seas as a romantic Eden.

John Webber first issued these views in sepia (and very rarely in colour) between 1788 and 1792, but this is their first collected publication. The work has always been a bibliographical curiosity. Despite the date on the title-page, it is evident that it was not issued until 1820. The plates are dated April 1, 1809, and watermarks dated variously between 1805 and 1820. This copy agrees in nearly all points with copies we have examined (with slight variations in watermark dates) and agrees in all points with the noted Abbey copy. The work is also curious in that both the artist's name and that of Captain Cook have been misspelled on the title-page.

The magnificently coloured views include five of Tahiti, two each of Kamschatka and Macao, one of New Zealand and one of Tongan interest. The views

of vegetation on Cracatoa and Pulu Condore are among the most beautiful aquatints of tropical foliage ever issued. *Abbey, Travel, 595; Beddie, 1872; Hill, p. 611; Holmes, 79.*

EARLY SEPIA ISSUES OF WEBBER'S VIEWS

[85] WEBBER, John. SEPARATELY ISSUED SEPIA ENGRAVINGS from the *Views in the South Seas* series.

[85A] VIEW IN THE ISLAND OF CRACATOA. *Sepia aquatint, mounted, 310 x 420 mm., a repaired tear in sky at centre, but basically in sound condition.* London, Published July 1, 1789 by J. Webber, No. 312 Oxford Street.

[85B] WAHEIADOOA, CHIEF OF OHEITEPEHA, lying in State. *Sepia aquatint, mounted, 317 x 443 mm., in fine condition.* London, Published July 1, 1789 by J. Webber, No. 312 Oxford Street.

The sepia issues of the plates, which are considerably earlier and very much scarcer than their coloured versions, have a particularly austere appeal. *Beddie, 1869-1871.*

SEPARATE COLOURED PLATES FROM WEBBER'S VIEWS

[86] WEBBER, John. SEPARATE COLOURED AQUATINT PLATES from the *Views in the South Seas* series.

[86A] VIEW IN THE ISLAND OF CRACATOA. *Hand coloured aquatint, mounted, 330 x 450 mm.* London, Boydell & Co., April 1st, 1809.

[86B] BALAGUNS OR SUMMER HABITATIONS, with the method of Drying Fish at St. Peter and Paul, Kamtschatka. *Hand coloured aquatint, mounted, 295 x 410 mm.* London, Boydell & Co., April 1st, 1809.

85B: WEBBER. *The lying in state of the chief Waheiadooa; the rare sepia issue of the plate.*

84 & 86: WEBBER. *Aquatint from the* Views in the South Seas.

[86C] A VIEW IN THE ISLAND OF PULO CONDORE. *Hand coloured aquatint, mounted, 290 x 415 mm., tear in lower margin extending 50 mm. into the engraved plate.* London, Boydell & Co., April 1st, 1809.

[86D] A VIEW IN OHEITEPEHA BAY, in the Island of Otaheite. *Hand coloured aquatint, mounted, 290 x 410 mm.* London, Boydell & Co., April 1st 1809.

[86E] VIEW OF THE HARBOUR OF TALOO, in the Island of Eimeo. *Hand coloured aquatint, mounted, 280 x 410 mm.* London, Boydell & Co., April 1st 1809.

[86F] THE FAN PALM. *Hand coloured aquatint, mounted, 360 x 270 mm., imprint cropped leaving only the legend "J. Webber fecit, 1788".* [London, Boydell & Co., 1809].

Webber's *Views in the South Seas* were issued both as a full suite of plates and as separate engravings, either sepia or coloured. *Beddie, 1869-1873.*

THE DEATH OF COOK: PROOF ENGRAVING

[87] WEBBER, John. THE DEATH OF CAPTAIN COOK. Engraving by F. Bartolozzi after a drawing by John Webber. *Engraving, 420 x 580 mm., uniformly browned and trimmed to plate mark, mounted.* London, n.d., circa 1784.

A rare proof impression of the separately issued engraving of Cook's death. Webber, the official artist on Cook's third voyage, was at Kealakekua Bay on

February 14th, 1779, and although not an eye witness to Cook's death, he painted a splendid version of it. It was on this painting that the engraving was based. Webber was also publisher of the view, which is the most impressive as well as the most famous of all eighteenth century attempts at portraying the massacre.

The iconography of the various proof plates is extremely complex. Our copy appears to be very early with large sections of the engraved surface uncompleted, and it is entirely without letters. *Not listed in Beddie; see nos. 2608 and 2610 for other proof issues.*

[88] ZIMMERMAN, Heinrich. REISE UM DIE WELT mit Capitain Cook. *Octavo, original cloth; a good modern facsimile.* Mannheim, bei C. F. Schwan, 1781. [Amsterdam, Nico Israel, 1973].

"Zimmerman, a native of Speyer, was coxswain in the Discovery. From the start of the voyage he determined to keep a shorthand journal of the voyage and to retain it, despite the instructions . . . demanding the surrender of all logs and journals. As to be expected in one of his rank and foreign nationality, his account is by no means free from errors, but it has an ingeniousness and charm which differentiate it from the other accounts. His appreciation of Cook's character deserves to rank with that of Samwell" (Holmes). All the early editions of this account are of extreme rarity. *See Holmes, 40.*

V
Cook's Collected
Voyages, and
General Works

By the end of Cook's third voyage and untimely death the face of the Pacific had been changed forever. The memorial to his achievements, the official publication of his journals, had become a lavishly produced and extensive series of volumes.

His achievements included the first crossing of the Antarctic circle, the abandonment of the Southern Continent theory, the abolition of scurvy — the mariners' greatest scourge — and the dismissal of the northwest passage myth. Such was his example that many of the great discoveries to follow were achieved by men who had sailed with him. Men such as Burney, Meares, Vancouver, Bligh, Colnett and Broughton all started their naval careers under Cook's command.

Cook's death was mourned by the whole of Europe. Later navigators spent much of their time almost literally following in his footsteps; even today his charting of some coasts has never been improved.

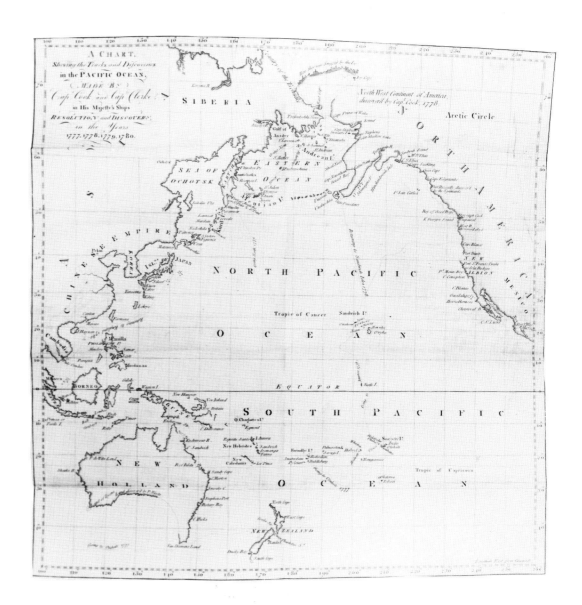

WITH THE RARE SECOND VOYAGE ATLAS

[89] COOK, Captain James. A SET OF THE THREE VOYAGE ACCOUNTS.

FIRST VOYAGE HAWKESWORTH, JOHN. AN ACCOUNT OF THE VOYAGES undertaken by the order of His present Majesty for making Discoveries in the Southern Hemisphere ... *First edition. 3 volumes, quarto*. London, Printed for W. Strahan, and T. Cadell, 1773.

SECOND VOYAGE. COOK, JAMES. A VOYAGE TOWARDS THE SOUTH POLE, and Round the World ... *First edition. 2 volumes, quarto, and a separate folio atlas containing the portrait of Cook and all maps, charts and views*. London, Printed for W. Strahan, and T. Cadell, 1777.

THIRD VOYAGE. COOK, JAMES AND JAMES KING. A VOYAGE TO THE PACIFIC OCEAN ... *First edition. 3 volumes, quarto, and all the separate folio atlas*. London, Printed by W. and A. Strahan, for G. Nicol, bookseller ... and T. Cadell, 1784.

Together 8 volumes, quarto, and 2 folio atlases, the first two voyage texts uniformly bound in contemporary tree calf, extra gilt spines, red and black labels; the third voyage in contemporary calf, extra gilt spines with vine motifs, red and black labels; joints cracked but holding, occasional spotting, generally confined to front and back end leaves; with separate folio atlases to the second and third voyages in original blue paper covered boards as issued, enclosed in modern cloth boxes; paper spines to atlases defective, first few plates of third voyage atlas with marginal dampstaining, not touching images, and plate 52 probably supplied from another copy; but despite defects, both are remarkably fine and fresh copies; most volumes with the armorial bookplate of Edward, Earl of Powis. London, 1773-1784.

A handsome and most desirable set, particularly for the collector of second voyage material. The plates and maps in the second voyage atlas, printed on thicker paper than usual, appear to be proof impressions, and are extraordinarily fresh and bright. Only the largest of the maps and charts are folded, and the views and botanical plates are all the more impressive for their being in uncreased state. Beddie records only one (incomplete) copy of the second voyage plates in this state, and we doubt that it would be possible to find a better set anywhere.

Although the bindings of the third voyage text do not match those of the first two, they are sympathetic, and it is apparent both from the uniform provenance and from the spine labels that the set is as assembled in the eighteenth century. *Beddie, 648, 1216, 1543; Hill, pp. 139-40, 60-62; Holmes, 5, 24, 47.*

A NOTED WOMAN BIBLIOPHILE'S COPY

[90] COOK, Captain James. A SET OF THE THREE VOYAGE ACCOUNTS.

FIRST VOYAGE. HAWKESWORTH, JOHN. AN ACCOUNT OF THE VOYAGES undertaken by the order of His present Majesty for making Discoveries in the Southern Hemisphere ... *First edition: without the directions for placing the cuts as in early issues, but with the "Chart of the Straights of Magellan". 3 volumes, quarto*. London, Printed for W. Strahan, and T. Cadell, 1773.

SECOND VOYAGE. COOK, JAMES A VOYAGE TOWARDS THE SOUTH POLE, and Round the World ... *First edition. 3 volumes, quarto*. London, Printed for W. Strahan, and T. Cadell, 1777.

THIRD VOYAGE, COOK, JAMES KING A VOYAGE TO THE PACIFIC OCEAN ... *First edition. 2 volumes, quarto, and the separate folio atlas*. London, Printed by W. and A. Strahan, for G. Nicol, bookseller ... and T. Cadell, 1784.

Together 8 volumes, quarto; contemporary tree calf,

BARTOLOZZI. *Bartolozzi's engraving of the death of Captain Cook appeared in numerous different forms.*

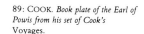

89: COOK. *Book plate of the Earl of Powis from his set of Cook's* Voyages.

90: COOK. *Frances Currer, one of few great women bibliophiles, owned this fine set of Cook's voyages.*

spines extra gilt; neatly rejointed preserving all original spines; with the atlas folio — containing 63 engraved charts, maps and plates — in matching contemporary half calf, marbled boards and endpapers, with the ink inscription "very early impressions, Bohn"; bookplates of Frances Mary Richardson Currer. London, 1773-1784.

A distinguished set, from the celebrated library of Frances Currer (1785-1861), known as the first competitive bibliophile among English women, and one of the great book collectors of all time. Her library at Eshton Hall, Yorkshire, estimated variously between 15 and 20,000 volumes, was rich in works on natural science, topography, antiquities and history, and noted for their choice condition and fine bindings. Dibdin dedicated his *Bibliographical Tour* to her, and referred to her as being "at the head of all female collectors in Europe". *Beddie, 648, 1216, 1543; Hill, pp. 139-40, 60-62; Holmes, 5, 24, 47.*

[91] COOK, Captain James. ANDERSON, George William. A NEW, AUTHENTIC, AND COMPLETE COLLECTION OF VOYAGES ROUND THE WORLD, Undertaken and Performed by Royal Authority. Containing a New, Authentic, Entertaining, Instructive ... Account of Captain Cook's First, Second, Third and Last Voyages ... and now publishing under the immediate direction of George William Anderson, Esq. *Folio, with 80 engraved maps, plans and views; contemporary speckled calf, rebacked, preserving the original red morocco title label; Map of Cooks River (at p. 55) laid down on blank leaf, but a fine copy with the original list of subscribers at end.* London, Printed for Alex. Hogg, at the Original Kings' Arms, 1784-1786.

A popular and important one volume edition of Cook's Voyages. Anderson states that he was "assisted, very materially, by a Principal Officer who sailed in the Resolution ... and by other Gentlemen of the Royal Navy", and the work contains some particulars not found in the official account.

Anderson modestly observes that "some other Editions of these Works (unnecessarily extended to many large volumes, by loose printing, blank paper, and other artifices, practised by many mercinary persons) would cost the purchaser the enormous sum of upwards of Twenty Guineas; so that the thousands of persons who would wish to peruse the valuable discoveries so partially communicated to the world, and view the astonishing fine copper plates, have hitherto been excluded from gratifying their eager curiosity; This Edition, being published in only Eighty Six-penny Numbers (making, when completed, One Large Handsome Volume in Folio) enables every person, whatever may be his circumstances, to become familiarly acquainted with those extraordinary and important voyages and discoveries ... and the obvious intention of the King and Government, that the Improvements and Discoveries ... might be communicated to the whole world, will of course be more fully answered". *Beddie, 19 (but imprint varies).*

[92] COOK, Captain James. ANDERSON, George William. A NEW, AUTHENTIC, AND COMPLETE COLLECTION OF VOYAGES ROUND THE WORLD, Undertaken and Performed by Royal Authority. Containing a New, Authentic, Entertaining, Instructive ... Account of Captain Cook's First, Second, Third and Last Voyages ... and now publishing under the immediate Direction of George William Anderson, Esq. *Folio, with 80 engraved maps, plans and views; nineteenth century dark quarter calf; occasional light spotting to text and a few plates, lacks the list of subscribers at end, but a very good sound copy.* London, Printed for Alex. Hogg, at the King's Arms, circa 1784-1786.

Beddie, 19 (but imprint varies).

[93] COOK, Captain James. HOGG, Capt. John. A NEW, AUTHENTIC, AND COMPLETE COLLECTION OF VOYAGES ROUND THE WORLD: undertaken and performed by Royal Authority. Containing a new, authentic, entertaining, instructive, full, and complete historical account of Captain Cook's first, second, third and last Voyages. *6 volumes, octavo, recently bound in three-quarter calf, red labels, with 131 plates and 28 folding maps and charts; some wear to charts where folded; a good copy.* London, Printed for Alex Hogg [1785].

A popular and now very scarce edition originally published in 80 sixpenny numbers or "handsomely bound and lettered" for two pounds eight shillings. Among the 190 subscribers which the editor assures us represent only a tenth of those on his list, appear George Anderson, editor of the folio edition, and Mrs. Cook at Mile End.

A number of views here not in the folio edition include "A view of the whale fishery" and two of Californian Indians. *Beddie, 21.*

PALMS AND ICEBERGS

[94] COOK, Captain James. NEW DISCOVERIES. NEW DISCOVERIES CONCERNING THE WORLD, AND ITS INHABITANTS. In two parts. Part I. containing a circumstantial account of all the Islands in the South-Sea, that have been lately discovered or explored ... Comprehending all the Discoveries made in the several Voyages of Commodore (now Admiral) Byron, Captains Wallis, Carteret, and Cook, related by Dr. Hawkesworth, Sidney Parkinson, Mr. Forster, and Captain Cook. Together with those of M. de Bougainville ... Part II. Containing a summary account of Captain Cook's Attempts to discover a southern continent in 1773, 1774, 1775. *Octavo, 2 folding maps and 2 folding plates; contemporary half calf, red label, joints cracking but firm, slight wear to extremities, occasional browning of text; a very good copy.* London, Printed for J. Johnson, 1778.

A very early and important compendium of information on the Pacific. Compiled from official and unofficial sources, arranged "in geographical order", each area is described and has an account of its initial discovery and subsequent visits by early explorers. Though most information is from Cook, Hawkesworth, Forster and Parkinson, the compiler states that the relations of Mendana, Quiros, Le Maire and Schouten, Tasman, Dampier, Roggewein and Anson "have been consulted and from them many necessary lights have been derived." Included is the

PERSONS and DRESSES of the INHABITANTS of the SOUTH SEA ISLANDS.

voyage of Constantine John Phipps towards the North Pole in 1773, with a plate showing his ships, the *Racehorse* and *Carcass* in the polar ice.

The second plate depicts Pacific peoples from Easter Island to New Holland, picturesquely arranged in a tropical Eden, with delightful disregard for geography. A Kangaroo sits beside a woman of Otaheite, and a man of the New Hebrides is behind a stately couple from the Marquesas. The harbour, neatly framed by palms, features an iceberg. *Beddie, 9; Hill, p. 210; Kroepelien, 893.*

[95] COOK, Captain James. THE VOYAGES OF CAPTAIN JAMES COOK ROUND THE WORLD. Printed verbatim from the original editions, and embellished with a selection of the engravings. *7 volumes, duodecimo, with a total of 30 engraved portraits, plates and maps; original blue-grey boards, buff paper spines with printed volume numbers and manuscript titles on the spines; top of spine to volume I and bottom of volume 2 chipped, else in very fine condition; untrimmed.* London, Printed for Richard Phillips, 1809.

A most attractive set, rare in this condition. Phillips was a very successful publisher, particularly of children's books, bringing a great number of travel accounts before a wider English reading public than ever before. Vocabularies of Tonga, Nootka and Hawaii are at the end of the last volume, followed by

a general index, probably the first collected edition to have this feature. *Beddie, 73.*

[96] COOK, Captain James. BEAGLEHOLE, J. C. *editor.* THE JOURNALS OF CAPTAIN JAMES COOK on his Voyages of Discovery. *Five volumes, large octavo and a folio atlas of plates; illustrations and maps throughout; a good set in the original blue cloth, dustjackets slightly soiled, small stain to the binding of the atlas volume.* Cambridge, Published for the Hakluyt Society at the University Press, 1967-1974.

Beaglehole's monumental work of scholarship will remain the standard edition of Cook's journals of all three voyages for as long as one can imagine. Complete with the separate pamphlet *Cook and the Russians* (1973).

[97] COOK, Captain James. KIPPIS, Andrew. A NARRATIVE OF THE VOYAGES ROUND THE WORLD performed by Captain James Cook. With an account of his life. *2 volumes, duodecimo; modern half calf; with portrait of Cook, separate engraved title-pages, and 18 wood engravings; light spotting as usual, slight damage to one plate.* Boston, N.H. Whitaker, 1830.

Second American edition, with the engraved title-pages for the first (1828) edition present. A work widely read in America, of which all early editions are very scarce. *Not in Beddie or Hill.*

94: NEW DISCOVERIES. *The topography of the Southern Hemisphere has been rearranged to allow palms and icebergs to appear in the same view.*

95: COOK. *Richard Phillips' edition of Cook's* Voyages *was produced as a popular account.*

THE
VOYAGES
OF
CAPTAIN JAMES COOK
ROUND THE WORLD.

PRINTED VERBATIM FROM THE ORIGINAL EDITIONS, AND EMBELLISHED WITH A SELECTION OF THE ENGRAVINGS.

IN SEVEN VOLUMES.

A

DISCOURSE

UPON

SOME LATE IMPROVEMENTS

Of the MEANS for

Preserving the Health of Mariners.

DELIVERED AT THE

Anniverſary Meeting of the ROYAL SOCIETY,
November 30, 1776.

By Sir JOHN PRINGLE, Baronet,
PRESIDENT.

PUBLISHED BY THEIR ORDER.

LONDON,

PRINTED FOR THE ROYAL SOCIETY.
MDCCLXXVI.

COOK ON SCURVY

[98] COOK, Captain James. A DISCOURSE UPON SOME LATE IMPROVEMENTS OF THE MEANS FOR PRESERVING THE HEALTH OF MARINERS. Delivered at the Anniversary Meeting of the Royal Society, November 30, 1776. By Sir John Pringle, Baronet, President. Published by their Order. *Small quarto, pp. [iv], 44, with the half-title; leaf C4 a cancel as usual; a fine copy with large margins in old calf, neatly rebacked.* London, Printed for the Royal Society, 1776.

Very rare; the first appearance in print of Cook's epoch-making account of the successful measures taken against scurvy on his first two voyages. We know of only five copies sold since 1970, while the National Union Catalog locates only four copies in American libraries — Harvard, John Carter Brown, National Library of Medicine and Naval Observatory Library.

The paper on scurvy was read to the Royal Society by its president, Sir John Pringle — in the absence of Cook himself, then just beginning his final voyage — as the year's Copley medal award, and immediately published in this form. Pringle's long presentation address, quoting directly from Cook and other sources is followed by Cook's paper itself and an extract from a letter by Cook to Pringle written from Plymouth Sound in July 1776.

The paper subsequently appeared in the official account of the second voyage and in the *Philosophical Transactions of the Royal Society*. In 1783, a series of six of Pringle's discourses at the annual presentations of the Copley medal was published in one volume (see below).

The winning of the battle against scurvy was one of the most important achievements in the general field of exploration; it made the major voyages that followed possible. As Robert Hughes has so well put it in *The Fatal Shore*: "malt juice and pickled cabbage put Europeans in Australia as microchip circuitry would put Americans on the moon". *Holmes, 20; Beddie, 1290; Kroepelien, 1065; Garrison & Morton, 2156.*

COOK AWARDED THE COPLEY MEDAL

[99] COOK, Captain James. PRINGLE, Sir John. SIX DISCOURSES, delivered by Sir John Pringle, Bart. when President of the Royal Society; on occasion of six Annual Assignments of Sir Godfrey Copley's Medal. To which is prefixed the Life of the Author. By Andrew Kippis . . . *Octavo, 2 preliminary leaves misbound; a fine copy, with the erratum leaf, entirely uncut in the original blue-grey boards and buff paper spine.* London, W. Strahan and T. Cadell, 1783.

First collected edition of Pringle's presidential addresses to the Royal Society, delivered annually at the presentation of the Society's Copley Medal. The most important address is in honour of Captain Cook, delivered when the Society awarded him the medal for his work on scurvy; the other five recipients honoured here are Priestly (Different kinds of air), Walsh (The torpedo), Maskelyne (Attraction of mountains), Mudge (Reflecting telescopes) and Hutton (Theory of gunnery).

Pringle's long address on Cook, quoting substantially from his paper on the treatment of scurvy and adding recent observations, was delivered at the Society's meeting at the end of 1775. Mrs. Cook accepted the medal in her husband's absence on his second voyage, following Pringle's reading of Cook's *Discourse upon some late improvements of the Means for Preserving the Health of Mariners*, which was separately published in 1775 (see above).

A fine copy, in absolutely original condition. *Holmes, 20 (note); not in Beddie.*

MAPPING OF NEWFOUNDLAND

[100] COOK, Captain James. JAMES COOK SURVEYOR OF NEWFOUNDLAND. Being a collection of charts of the coasts of Newfoundland and Labrador &c. Drawn from original surveys taken by James Cook and Michael Lane . . . with an introductory essay by R. A. Skelton. *Folio, with title and 10 maps (6 folding) and quarto text containing 6 plates, together 2 parts; original blue wrappers with titles on upper covers, enclosed in a fitted linen solander case; box a little soiled, text and plates fine.* San Francisco, David Magee, 1965.

One of 365 copies printed at the Grabhorn Press. In 1763, Cook was sent out on his first command, to make a systematic survey of Newfoundland. The spectacular results, shown here, by which his genius as a navigator and seaman was recognised by the Admiralty, were largely responsible for his securing the command of the *Endeavour*. His meticulously executed charts, published by Thomas Jeffreys in London 1769-1770, reproduced here in the same size as the originals, were not superseded for many years.

The essay by the noted map historian, R. A. Skelton, discusses the maps in particular with remarks on the map publishing businesses of the period. Beautifully printed in black and red by the noted Grabhorn Press in San Francisco, it reproduces material from the Holmes collection, now in the University of California Library, Los Angeles.

OPPOSITE:
98: COOK. *Captain Cook's successful measures against scurvy earned him the Royal Society's Copley Medal (above); the first printing of the full report.*

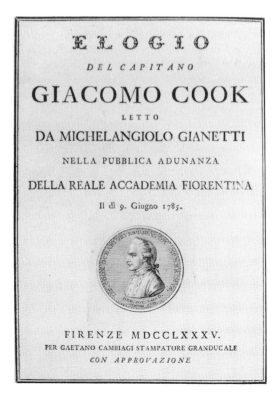

101 & 103: COOK. *Early French and Italian appreciations of Captain Cook.*

SCARCE ELEGY

[101] BLANC GILLI, M[athieu]. ELOGIE DU CAPITAINE COOK. Par M. Blanc Gilli de Marseille. *Octavo; contemporary mottled calf, gilt panelled spine with floral ornaments, red label; slight spotting of text, top corner of front end leaf removed; a very good copy.* Amsterdam, et se trouve a Paris, Chez Morin, 1787.

A very scarce elegy on Cook who, as the author says in his introduction, was as greatly revered in France as in England. It takes the form of a flowery narrative with introduction and notes. *Beddie, 1959; Holmes, 63; O'Reilly-Reitman, 454.*

BOTANY BAY, OR STING-RAY HARBOUR?

[102] BONWICK, James. CAPTAIN COOK IN NEW SOUTH WALES. Or the Mystery of Naming Botany Bay. *Octavo, original wrappers; some browning to text and slight chipping to wrappers, but a good copy of a fragile pamphlet.* London, Sampson Low, 1901.

An attempt to determine at what point "Sting Ray Harbour", so named by Captain Cook, became Botany Bay. The author (1817-1906) noted for his massive transcriptions of early Australian source materials, here examines Cook Logs in the British Museum, documents in the Admiralty, and casts aspersions upon the Cook "Corner" Journal, now in the Mitchell Library, Sydney.

"THIS PRODIGY OF NATURE"

[103] GIANETTI, Michelangiolo. ELOGIO DEL CAPITANO GIACOMO COOK ... Elogy of Captain James Cook composed and publicly recited before the Royal Academy of Florence. *Folio, with titles in Italian and English facing, each with engraved vignette of the Royal Society Medal of Cook; full modern green levant morocco, by Sangorski, gilt panelled spine with anchor ornaments; a very*

fine, tall, clean copy. Florence, Printed for Gaetano Cambiagi, Printer of his Royal Highness, 1785.

Rare. A prose essay honouring Cook in a florid style which would have greatly embarrassed him. Describing his life and achievements in very purple tones, "this prodigy of nature" is lauded for his mapping of the St. Lawrence, to which the author ascribes much of General Wolfe's successes. The voyages are described, and Cook, like many sailors a non-swimmer, is given powers that he never possessed: "From his infancy he was accustomed to the useful practice of swimming, and could cleave the waves of the Ocean with the facility of its inhabitants".

A beautifully printed book in the best Italian eighteenth century traditions, much in the style of Bodoni, using elegant roman and italic types, beautifully composed within ruled borders. Dedicated to Sir Horace Mann, then English ambassador to the Court of Tuscany. *Beddie, 1957; Holmes, 51.*

[104] HOLMES, Sir Maurice. CAPTAIN JAMES COOK, R.N., F.R.S. A Bibliographical Excursion. *Octavo, with 11 plates; tan cloth; one of 500 copies.* London, Francis Edwards Ltd., 1952.

The most important Cook bibliography, describing 157 items together with useful annotations and short biographies of Cook's associates. The plates reproduce many of the most important title-pages.

[105] KING, James. THE DEATH OF CAPTAIN COOK. In "Pacific Adventures" Nos. 1-6. *Six parts complete, octavo; original wrappers as issued, enclosed in a blue cloth case, black label, spine of case faded as often; fine copies.* San Francisco, The Book Club of California, 1940.

A series of "keepsakes" issued by the Book Club for its members, printed by various fine presses in

California, in an edition of 650 copies, with introductory remarks by various authorities. The other numbers include an excerpt from Drake's *Voyage around the World*; a *Description of California* from Shelvocke's *Voyage*; *The Wreck of the Wager* from Byron's *Account*; and *The Manilla Galleons*, from Anson's *Voyage*.

KIPPIS' LIFE OF COOK

[106] KIPPIS, Andrew. THE LIFE OF CAPTAIN JAMES COOK. *Quarto, with engraved frontispiece portrait of Cook; full contemporary tan russia, rebacked, spine with gilt anchor and ship ornaments; tops of several leaves extended at time of original binding, light foxing to title, portrait and a few leaves, but a very good copy.* London, Printed for G. Nicol . . . and G.G.J. and J. Robinson, 1788.

First edition of the first biography of Cook. Using Admiralty sources as well as documents in the possession of Sir Joseph Banks, Kippis attempts a well rounded account of Cook's public life, regrettably omitting anything of a personal nature. Cook's early career on the St. Lawrence River, his surveying, and particularly his three Pacific voyages, are discussed at length. The account of his death is largely drawn from the Samwell account, and Kippis includes part of Miss Seward's *Ode on the Death of Cook*, calling it "the first, both in order of time and of merit". An appendix reprints Miss Williams' ode, *The Morai*. The proposed settlement of Botany Bay is mentioned as a result of the voyages: "If it be wisely and prudently begun and constructed, who can tell what beneficial consequences may spring from it, in future ages?" *Holmes, 69; Hill, p. 163.*

BASLE ISSUE

[107] KIPPIS, Andrew. THE LIFE OF CAPTAIN JAMES COOK. *2 volumes (in 1), octavo, modern half green morocco; slight spotting and fading of spine; a very good copy.* Basle, Printed by J. J. Tournesin, 1788.

First octavo edition, first issue, published in the same year as the London quarto, and the first continental edition, predating both the German and French editions by a year. *Beddie, 33; Holmes, 70; Kroepelien, 649.*

[108] KIPPIS, Andrew. THE LIFE OF CAPTAIN JAMES COOK. *2 volumes, octavo, original pink paper boards as issued, some wear to spines and extremities, very occasional light spotting and browning of text, but a fine copy.* Basle, Printed by J. J. Tournesien, 1788.

First octavo edition, first issue. *Beddie, 33; Holmes, 70; Kroepelien, 649.*

PARIS ISSUE

[109] KIPPIS, Andrew. THE LIFE OF CAPTAIN JAMES COOK. *2 volumes, octavo, contemporary marbled calf, flat spines with gilt urn ornaments, citron and olive labels, marble end papers and blue edges; early and attractive library stamps on titles, occasional light spotting; a very attractive copy.* Basil, Printed by J. J. Tourneisen. Paris, sold by Pissot, Bookseller, 1788.

T H E

L I F E

O F

CAPTAIN JAMES COOK.

Totque Maris vastæque exhausta Pericula Terræ.
VIRG.

B Y

A N D R E W   K I P P I S, D. D. F. R. S. AND S. A.

First octavo edition, second issue, and the rarest of any of the editions of this important life of Cook. Here the title-page has been re-set to include the Paris imprint, and is therefore the first easily available edition for French readers. Much scarcer than the Basle only issue (see above), Holmes knew of it only from a doubtful entry in Jackson's catalogue *Centenaire de la mort de Cook* (Paris, 1879). *Not in Beddie, Holmes (but see no. 70), Hill or Kroepelien.*

106: KIPPIS. *The first biography of the navigator.*

FIRST EDITION IN FRENCH

[110] KIPPIS, Andrew. VIE DU CAPITAINE COOK, traduite de l'Anglois du Docteur Kippis, Membre de la Société Royale de Londres. Par M. Castera. *2 volumes, octavo, with folding plate; modern calf antique, slight insect damage to last few pages of volume 1 not affecting text; a good copy.* Paris, rue de Poitevins, Hotel de Thou, 1789.

First edition in French: the English language version appeared in Basle and Paris editions (see above) before there had been time to arrange translation. The engraved frontispiece here — showing the death of Cook — has been supplied from another source, probably the French edition of Rickman. *Beddie, 36; Kroepelien, 652.*

[111] KIPPIS. BARTOLOZZI, F. after W. Artaud. ANDREW KIPPIS, D.D., F.R.S. and S.A. *Engraved portrait, 327 x 254 mm., in fine condition; mounted.* London, Thomas Macklin, Poets Gallery, Fleet St., October 20, 1792.

A fine portrait of Cook's dour first biographer. *Nan Kivell and Spence, p. 165.*

COOK AND EUROPEAN SETTLEMENT

[112] LEMONTEY, Pierre Edouard. ELOGE DE JACQUES COOK, avec des Notes, discours qui a

111: KIPPIS. *Bartolozzi's portrait of Cook's biographer.*

ÉLOGE

DE JACQUES COOK,

Célèbre Navigateur Anglais, Membre de la Société royale de Londres.

Dans ces jours mémorables où tout Français est appelé par son Roi à la régénération de l'Etat, où l'ame n'a de sentimens, où le génie n'a d'essor que pour les idées patriotiques, irai-je, comme un transfuge, consacrer mes veilles à la mémoire d'un étranger, et troubler la gravité publique par des jeux littéraires? Ah! sans doute si l'éloge de Cook devoit être sans intérêt pour les bons citoyens, son éclat stérile n'auroit ni touché mon cœur ni séduit ma plume. Mais j'ai vu la Seine et la Tamise mêler leurs eaux en murmurant; j'ai vu la paix entre deux peuples généreux ressembler au sommeil de la guerre, et les traités à un joug sous lequel le préjugé agite sa tête impatiente. Qui donc arrachera les dernières racines de cet arbre empoisonné? Quelle main fermera cette plaie profonde creusée par tant d'outrages? Poëtes, Orateurs, Philosophes,

A

112: LEMONTEY *Lemontey's elegy on Cook was read to the Marseilles Academy in 1789.*

remporté le Prix d'eloquence au jugement de l'Academie de Marseille, le 25 Août 1789. *Octavo, tears to first and last leaves repaired without loss, a few stains at beginning and end; half red morocco.* Paris, de l'Imprimerie Nationale, 1792.

First edition, reprinted with other works by Lemontey in 1829. This rare flowery elegy on Cook, read to the Marseilles Academy in 1789 and awarded their prize for eloquence, is of particular interest for the prognostications it makes about Australia in the knowledge that settlement by the first fleet has already taken place: "The position of New Holland will one day make it the world's meeting-place. An English colony will soon attract others to its fertile coasts; China will want to settle her surplus population (the reason for her present weakness) there, lonely Japan will come to mix with the great human family, the European and the Malay, the American and the Asiatic, will meet each other there without surprise . . .".

This is the first appreciation of Cook to acknowledge the European settlement of Australia as a result of his discoveries. *Beddie, 1972 (Mitchell Library's copy); Holmes, 76.*

[113] MERRILL, Elmer Drew. THE BOTANY OF COOK'S VOYAGES, and its Unexpected Significance in Relation to Anthropology, Biogeography and History. *Octavo, with plates and text figures; original cloth; dustjacket worn, but a very good copy.* Waltham, Massachusetts. The Chronica Botanica company, 1954.

The specimens collected by botanists on Cook's first and second voyages form the basis of this study on the distribution of plants in both directions across the Pacific. The author, a botanist of note, draws on his long experience with Pacific basin plant materials, and critically investigates the work of others. A scarce work.

COOK UNVEILED

[114] SYDNEY. UNVEILING OF THE CAPTAIN COOK STATUE, Hyde Park, Sydney, New South Wales, on Tuesday, 25 February, 1879. [*and*] Programme of Proceedings. [*with*] HALLORAN, Henry. The Unveiling the Captain Cook Statue. An exultant ode. *Octavo, caption title, 6 text pp. printed in double columns within red ruled borders, portrait after Dance inside front cover, photograph of statue before first page, and programme inside back cover. The Halloran Ode, 3 (and last blank) pp., duodecimo, laid in; original dark blue morocco, title in gilt on upper cover wihin elaborate fuchsia and fern panel; spine tender, some scuffing to corners; signature of John J. Calvert on first page.* [Sydney, 1879].

A rare group of ephemera reflecting colonial enthusiasm for Cook. "The unveiling of this statue is one of the most pleasing national incidents that has occurred in the history of the Australian colonies". Witnessed by a crowd of 60,000, the procession, estimated at 12,000, included the Woollahra Volunteer Fire Brigade, the Protestant Alliance Friendly Society, and the United Ancient Order of Druids. The enthusiastic speech by the Governor of New South Wales, Sir Hercules Robinson, contains a resume of Cook's life, voyages and achievements, and remarks of the progress of the country in the past 100 years. The purpleness of Halloran's *Ode* is quite startling. *Beddie, 3008, 2355; Ferguson, 8612 (and not noting the Halloran Ode).*

[115] WHITEHEAD, P.J.P. FORTY DRAWINGS OF FISHES made by the artists who accompanied Captain James Cook on his three voyages to the Pacific . . . some being used by authors in the description of new species. *Folio, 36 full page colour illustrations, a fine copy in the original dark blue cloth, dustjacket.* Trustees of the British Museum (Natural History), 1968.

The standard work on the natural history artists who sailed with Cook, concentrating on their watercolours of fish caught during the voyages.

COOK'S BIRTHPLACE

[116] YOUNG, Rev. George. A HISTORY OF WHITBY . . . with a statistical survey of the vicinity to the distance of twenty-five miles. *2 volumes, octavo; 19th century three-quarter brown morocco, marbled boards and endpapers, uncut, top edges gilt; armorial bookplate of the Earl Fitzwilliam; a very good copy.* Whitby, Printed and Sold by Clark and Medd, 1817.

Containing an early and important biography of Cook. It was at Whitby that Cook first apprenticed himself and learnt of ships and the sea. The author, who interviewed friends and members of his family, had access to letters and documents now dispersed, including several which describe his first and second voyages. The work includes a portrait of Cook. *Beddie, 2167, not in Holmes.*

VI
The Settlement of Australia

VIEW of the SETTLEMENT on SYDNEY COVE, PORT JACKSON 20th AUGUST, 1788.

The colonisation of the east coast of Australia and the establishment of a penal colony at Botany Bay were the result of a decision taken by George III in September 1786. The legislative decision had been hotly debated. Rebel American colonists had recently won their independence from Britain and revolutionaries in France were fighting for liberty, while radical intellectuals almost everywhere were urging a wider recognition of human rights. But England needed a "dumping ground" for convicts; the favourable reports of Captain Cook, with the support of Sir Joseph Banks, encouraged the choice of Botany Bay.

The "thief settlement" was quickly moved to Port Jackson, but in the public imagination it was permanently known after the more southern harbour of Botany Bay.

The voyage of the First Fleet was the largest movement of ships into the Pacific until the voyage of the United States Exploring Expedition in the middle of the nineteenth century. It was also the most significant act of long-distance colonisation ever undertaken, and represented the most enduring single change to the history of the Pacific.

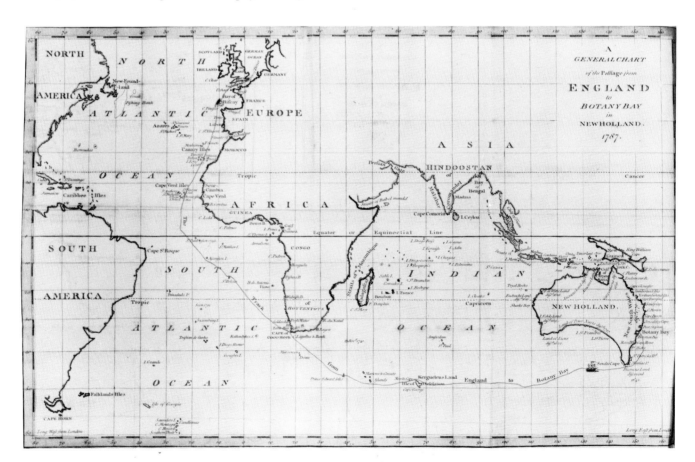

AN EMIGRANT'S GUIDE FOR THE FIRST FLEET

[117] ANONYMOUS. The History of New Holland, from its First Discovery in 1616 to the Present Time. With a Particular Account of its Produce and Inhabitants, and a Description of Botany Bay; also, A list of the Naval, Marine, Military and Civil Establishment. To which is prefixed, An Introductory Discourse on Banishment, by the Right Honourable William Eden. *Octavo, with two folding maps coloured in outline; an excellent uncut copy bound in half polished calf.* London, Printed for John Stockdale, 1787.

First edition; a fine copy of a highly important book, the most widely read and one of the earliest descriptions of Australia, published to coincide with the departure from England of the First Fleet. The anonymous compiler discusses the fleet's imminent departure and lists the numbers and equipment of the fleet as well as the principal officers and the composition of the marine detachment.

The only previous work of this type on Australia was the *Historical Narrative* produced by the London publisher Fielding in the previous year, a much shorter account. The 'Eden' is written, as the author says, "to present at one view a connected description of the whole country of New Holland". The book is clearly aimed at a public eager for information on the new colonial venture, and for details of Botany Bay itself, which is here described at length.

This is the form in which the reading public, and almost certainly many of the participants in the First Fleet themselves, must have absorbed what little information existed about conditions in Australia. The maps show the continent, Botany Bay and most interestingly the 'passage from England to Botany Bay in New Holland 1787', showing clearly the route that the fleet must take. There is also material in both preface and text about transportation, as well as the 'Introductory Discourse' on the subject by William Eden which has often led to the misattribution of the whole book to him. *Ferguson, 24.*

ONE OF THE FIRST ENGRAVINGS TO DEPICT CONVICTS

[118] BARRINGTON, George. A Voyage to Botany Bay with a description of the Country, manners, Customs, religion, &c. of the Natives by the Celebrated George Barrington. To which is added his Life and Trial. *Duodecimo, engraved frontispiece ("An Interesting Discovery in the Woods") and engraved title (convicts disembarking from a long-boat).* London, Printed by C. Lowndes, and Sold by H. D. Symonds [no date; ?1801].

[Bound with:]

A Sequel to Barrington's Voyage to New South Wales comprising an Interesting Narrative of the Transactions and Behaviour of the Convicts; The Progress of the Colony; An Official Register . . . as likewise Authentic Anecdotes Of the most Distinguished Characters, and Notorious Convicts that have been Transported to the Settlement at New South Wales . . . *Duodecimo, small stain to first 5 leaves.* London, Printed and Published by C. Lowndes . . . and sold by H. D. Symonds, 1801.

The 2 pieces bound together in contemporary half calf, a little worn, front joint splitting but the side firmly held.

118: BARRINGTON. *The title-page includes an unusual illustration of convicts disembarking at Botany Bay.*

Scarce semi-chapbook editions of Barrington's popular *Voyage* and its sequel; exactly how much of either, if any, was actually Barrington's work will always be a matter for conjecture, but even if all the published pieces that go under the name of Barrington were concocted from other sources by the London publishers, the 80 entries in Ferguson demonstrate the great popularity that his accounts had with the contemporary reader. These early editions represent the form in which information about New South Wales reached those of the public who could not afford the expensive quartos published by members of the First Fleet.

The first piece here is conjecturally dated circa 1795 by Ferguson, but it is on paper watermarked 1800; it was put out by the same partnership (Lowndes and Symonds) as the second piece, which is dated 1801. The 2 pieces are also bound together in the Oxley Library and the Allport copies.

The vignette on the title-page is one of very few illustrations of convicts in the early days of the colony, a subject that was curiously avoided by illustrators of the period. *Ferguson, 206 & 328.*

[119] BRADLEY, Lieutenant William. A Voyage to New South Wales. The Journal of Lieutenant William Bradley, R.N. of H.M.S. Sirius 1786-1792. *2 volumes, quarto, the second volume a portfolio of charts; the first volume a facsimile of the original manuscript with colour illustrations; a fine copy in the original cloth, dustjacket.* Sydney, The Trustees of the Public Library of New South Wales, 1969.

BAKER'S FARM,
High land on the banks of the River.

The first publication of William Bradley's beautiful manuscript journal of the First Fleet.

[120] CLARK, Lieutenant Ralph. THE JOURNAL AND LETTERS OF LT. RALPH CLARK 1787-1792. *Quarto, photographic illustrations; a fine copy in the original cloth, dustjacket.* Sydney, Australian Documents Library, 1981.

The first publication of this First Fleet journal, held in the Mitchell Library and probably the most intimate of all First Fleet journals, as Clark freely records all his most personal feelings including lascivious dreams.

"THE MOST VALUABLE PRINTED RECORD"

[121] COLLINS, David. AN ACCOUNT OF THE ENGLISH COLONY IN NEW SOUTH WALES: with Remarks on the Dispositions, Customs, Manners &c. of the Native Inhabitants of that Country. To which are added, Some Particulars of New Zealand; compiled, by permission, from the Mss. of Lieutenant-governor King. *Quarto, with a frontispiece chart and folding map and altogether 22 engravings, 18 as plates and 4 as vignettes in the text; a little light staining, but an excellent copy in contemporary calf, rebacked.* London, Printed for T. Cadell, 1798.

First edition of the earliest history of Australia as an English settlement. "The work, apart from its singular, almost painful interest as a narrative, is of especial value as the first official account of the infant colony . . ." (DNB). Collins travelled as Deputy-Judge-Advocate on the first fleet, and later became Secretary to the Governor and the second most powerful man in the colony. He served under Phillip, Grose, Paterson and Hunter during the first ten years of the colony, returning to England in 1796. His book, as a factual account of the formative period of the country, has been described as "beyond doubt, the most valuable printed record of the period".

The last of the First Fleet journals to be published, Collins' book is the earliest history of Australia as an English colony, and contains the most detailed and painstaking of all descriptions of the voyage and first settlement found in any of the early narratives. It also contains the account of the voyage by Bass and Flinders in which they discovered Bass Strait and circumnavigated Tasmania, taken from Bass' Journal, which has since disappeared, making this the only contemporary printed record.

The engraved views are among the best published illustrations of early Sydney. They were engraved in London by the well known artist Edward Dayes from sketches made by the convict artist Thomas Watling. The natural history plates, including those of a lyrebird, wombat and wedge-tailed eagle, are all very early representations of these species. Another of the plates illustrates the "Plan and Elevation of a Church Built at Parramatta, New South Wales, during the Government of John Hunter". This is almost certainly the first published plan of a public building in New South Wales; the church, St. John's, was later added to by Governor Macquarie.

A second, supplementary volume, was issued in 1802, and an abridged edition was published in 1804. *Ferguson, 263; Wantrup, 19.*

ORIGINAL BOARDS

[122] COLLINS, David. AN ACCOUNT OF THE ENGLISH COLONY IN NEW SOUTH WALES, from its first Settlement in January 1788, to August 1801; with Remarks on the Dispositions, Customs, Manners, &c. of the Native Inhabitants of that Country. *Quarto, with*

NON COMMISSION Officers EMBARKING for BOTANY BAY

a portrait, two maps, 23 engraved plates and 8 half-page engravings; original boards uncut, spine repaired, a small portion of board replaced on upper spine not affecting original label, a repaired tear in the Chart of New Zealand, with no paper loss. London, Printed by A. Strahan . . . for T. Cadell and W. Davies, 1804.

The second edition, abridged from the first edition of 1798 and its 1802 supplement, with considerable changes and additions; edited by Collins' wife, Maria, who continued her husband's revision and completed the book with new information available to the end of 1803.

This is the rare issue with the 3 natural history plates uncoloured and all the illustrations, except the Chart of New Zealand, grouped together at the front rather than placed throughout the text as the binders instructions indicate. It appears from our records that this grouping is found only in copies in original boards. *Ferguson, 390; Wantrup, 21.*

DIE NEUESTEN REISEN

[123] FORSTER, Johann Reinhold. DIE NEUESTEN REISEN NACH DER BOTANY-BAY UND PORT-JACKSON. Nebst Nachrichten von den Fortschritten und Entdeckungen in New-Sudwallis und der Sudsee . . . Aus dem Englischen ubersetzt . . . *Two volumes, octavo, containing altogether four engraved plates (two folding) and two engraved folding maps; in fine condition in the original plain brown boards.* Berlin, In der vossischen Buchhandlung, 1794.

Two volumes of early Australian material in digested form, compiled by Forster. According to Ferguson three volumes altogether appeared, but "each of the volumes seems to be independent (the National Library has vols. II and III as separate items, without

any indication that they form part of another work) . . .".

The first of the two volumes contains versions of the voyages of Bligh and of de Surville; at the end of the second volume is a separate printing (104 pages) of Hamilton's account of the Pandora voyage, separately described by Ferguson (no. 182).

The second volume contains Forster's versions of Hunter and Phillip and closes with King's account of Norfolk Island. *Ferguson, 178 (but see also 182 and 184).*

THE FIRST TRANSPORTATION

[124] GILLRAY, James. NON COMMISSION OFFICERS EMBARKING FOR BOTANY BAY. *Engraving, 366 x 525 mm., with partial handcolouring, as issued; a skilfully repaired tear extends 55 mm. into image on upper right corner without loss; framed.* London, November 1st, 1786.

The first print to show transportation to Botany Bay and also the first satirical reference to the colony.

The imaginary First Fleet sets sail in this rare caricature with the Prince of Wales sitting astride a barrel of wine drinking. On his right is the unpopular whig and radical, Burke, and on his left is another whig, Charles Fox, with his cronies. The Prince is depicted leaving his lover and weeping money-lenders on the shore. This thinly disguised attack on the Prince of Wales illustrates strong public opinion that he had abused his position and should be the first to suffer under the harsh government legislative decision of 14th September 1786 on transportation to Botany Bay.

A rare and important image of the new colony. Reproduced by Jonathan King, *The Other Side of the Coin: A Cartoon History of Australia,* p. 19.

124: GILLRAY. *Gillray's caricature, although entirely imaginary, is the first depiction of transportation to Botany Bay.*

123: FORSTER. *A German compilation of early Australian material.*

Die neuesten Reisen
nach der
Botany-Bay und Port-Jackson.
Nebst Nachrichten
von den Fortschritten und Entdeckungen
in
Neu-Südwallis und der Südsee.
Aus dem Englischen übersetzt.
Mit Anmerkungen
von
J. Reinhold Forster,
Professor in Halle, und Mitglied der Königl. Akademie der
Wissenschaften in Berlin.
Dritter Theil.
John Hunter's Reise nach Neu-Südwallis;
Arthur Phillip's Tagebuch während eines Aufenthaltes eben daselbst;
und
Lieutenant Kings Nachrichten von der Norfolk-Insel.
Mit Kupfern und Karten.
Berlin, 1794.
In der Vossischen Buchhandlung.

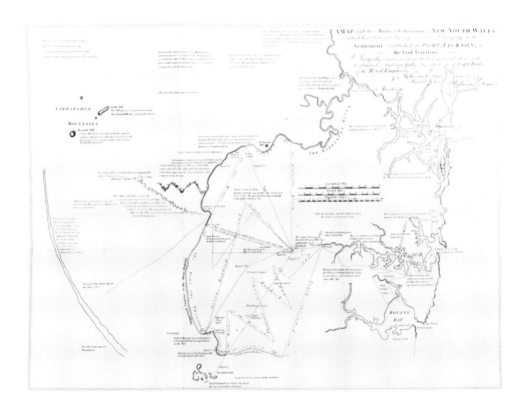

125: HUNTER. *Dawes' map of New South Wales which appears in Hunter's* Historical Journal *is one of the first published maps of the colony.*

127 & 128: PHILLIP. *The two issues of the title-page of Phillip's* Voyage to Botany Bay *may be clearly distinguished by the names around the Wedgwood medallion.*

HUNTER: A LARGE COPY

[125] HUNTER, John. AN HISTORICAL JOURNAL OF THE TRANSACTIONS AT PORT JACKSON AND NORFOLK ISLAND, with the Discoveries which have been made in New South Wales and in the Southern Ocean . . . including the Journals of Governors Phillip and King, and of Lieut. Ball. *Quarto, with 17 engraved plates and charts; an excellent and large copy (with at least a quarter of an inch below the date, which is often cropped) in contemporary half calf, joints repaired.* London, Printed for John Stockdale, January 1, 1793.

Hunter's *Journal* is equal in importance to Phillip's and White's as an account of the first years of settlement at Sydney. Captain John Hunter was appointed second captain of HMS *Sirius* under Phillip for the voyage to Botany Bay. Once in New South Wales he was actively engaged in surveying and exploration, and only left for England in late 1791 after the loss of the *Sirius* at Norfolk Island while under his command. He spent the next few years in England, where he wrote the *Journal*.

Hunter gives an excellent account of many activities, particularly exploration and the settlement at Norfolk Island, which are treated more cursorily by the other First Fleet chroniclers. The engraved plates and maps, many of the latter from original cartography by Hunter, Dawes and Bradley, are very fine. The plates include the well known 'View of the Settlement at Sydney Cove, Port Jackson, 20th August 1788' (the first published engraving of Sydney) and P. G. King's 'A Family of New South Wales'. *Ferguson, 152; Wantrup, 13.*

[126] KING, Philip Gidley. THE JOURNAL OF PHILIP GIDLEY KING: Lieutenant, R.N. 1787-1790. *Quarto, photographic illustrations; a fine copy in the original cloth,* dustjacket. Sydney, Australian Documents Library, 1980.

First publication of a First Fleet journal of particular interest for the material recorded by King during his two year stay on Norfolk Island.

THE OFFICIAL ACCOUNT

[127] PHILLIP, Arthur. THE VOYAGE OF GOVERNOR PHILLIP TO BOTANY BAY, with an Account of the Establishment of the Colonies of Port Jackson & Norfolk Island . . . to which are added the Journals of Lieuts. Shortland, Watts, Ball & Capt. Marshall . . . embellished with fifty-five copper plates. *Quarto, with an engraved portrait of Phillip and an engraved title, 7 folding engraved charts and 46 engraved plates; the vulpine opossum plate in the first ("wulpine") issue; an excellent copy in contemporary polished calf, flat spine gilt in compartments with anchors, very skilful repair to joints.* London, John Stockdale, 1789.

The official account of the first settlement of Australia: a very good copy of the first edition.

The *Voyage of Governor Phillip*, based on Phillip's journals and despatches and assembled into book form by the London publisher Stockdale, is without a doubt — as the official record — the single most important book to describe the journey to Botany Bay and the foundations of settlement. It describes the events from March 1787, just before the First Fleet sailed from the Isle of Wight, up to September 1788. There is a chapter dealing with the fauna of New South Wales, appendices detailing the routes of various ships to Botany Bay, from Botany Bay to Norfolk Island and from Port Jackson to various other ports, and finally a list of convicts sent to New South Wales. The Voyage also contains some excellent maps by John Hunter and

William Dawes, including the first of the Sydney Cove settlement, which shows in detail the buildings and 'progress' which had been made by July 1788.

Davidson in *A Book Collector's Notes* (p. 71) summarises the importance of this volume: "Being the authentic record of first settlement the work's importance cannot be over-emphasised, and no collection (of Australiana) can be complete without a copy", and Wantrup in *Australian Rare Books* notes that "as a detailed and officially sanctioned account of the new colony, the first edition of Stockdale's Phillip is a key work and essential to any serious collection of Australian books".

This copy is an example of the "wulpine" issue, so named because the plate illustrating the vulpine opossum facing page 150 has the word *wulpine* instead of *vulpine*. This error indicates an early state of this particular plate, although not necessarily an early issue of the entire book. *Ferguson, 47; Wantrup, 5.*

FIRST ISSUE, IN CONTEMPORARY COLOURING

[128] PHILLIP, Arthur. THE VOYAGE OF GOVERNOR PHILLIP TO BOTANY BAY, with an Account of the Establishment of the Colonies of Port Jackson and Norfolk Island . . . to which are added the Journals of Lieuts. Shortland, Watts, Ball & Captain Marshall . . . embellished with fifty-five copper plates. *Quarto, with an engraved portrait of Phillip and an engraved title, 7 folding engraved charts and 46 engraved plates; the natural history plates in fine contemporary hand colouring; contemporary tree calf, skilfully rebacked preserving the original label; some foxing to title-page and frontispiece; preliminary pages with some marginal repairs, otherwise an excellent copy.* London, John Stockdale, 1789.

The title-page of this copy is in the rare first state, with the name of the artist Henry Webber under the engraving of the Wedgwood medallion. At the request of Josiah Wedgwood, Webber's name was subsequently removed.

Copies of Phillip's *Voyage* with the plates in contemporary colouring are scarce and an issue combining the rare title-page with this beautiful form of the plates must be considered extremely desirable. *Ferguson, 47; Wantrup, 5.*

FIRST FRENCH PHILLIP

[129] PHILLIP, Arthur. VOYAGE DU GOVERNEUR PHILLIP A BOTANY-BAY, Avec une déscription de l'établissement des Colonies du port Jackson et de l'ile Norfolk; Faite sur des Papiers authentiques, obtenus des divers Departemens, auxquels on a ajouté les Journaux des Lieutenans Shortland, Watts, Ball, et du Capitaine Marshall, avec un récit de leurs nouvelles Découvertes . . . *Octavo; contemporary sheep, rather worn, but a sound and clean copy.* Paris, chez Buisson, 1791.

The first French edition of Phillip's *Voyage to Botany Bay*, describing the voyage of the First Fleet and the earliest days of the colony. The original English publication in 1789 led to world-wide interest in British achievements in Australia, which the French observed with considerable acquisitive interest. *Ferguson, 112.*

[130] RUMSEY, Herbert. THE PIONEERS OF SYDNEY COVE. *Quarto, illustrations by James Emery; a fine copy in the original cloth, dustjacket.* Sydney, The Sunnybrook Press, 1937.

One of 150 numbered copies: a full listing of the First Fleet members with biographies where available.

[131] SMYTH, Arthur Bowes. THE JOURNAL OF ARTHUR BOWES SMYTH: Surgeon, Lady Penrhyn 1787-1789. *Quarto, numerous illustrations, a fine copy in the original cloth, dustjacket.* Sydney, Australian Documents Library, 1979.

The first publication of this First Fleet journal; the *Lady Penrhyn* carried more than 100 female convicts to Sydney in the First Fleet.

VISCOUNT SYDNEY

[132] [SYDNEY] YOUNG, Jno. LORD VISCOUNT SYDNEY. *Mezzotint engraving, 440 x 310 mm., after the original painting by Gilbert Stuart, framed.* London, n.d. (circa 1790).

Viscount Sydney, a strong supporter of Young and Matra in their plans for the colonisation of the east coast of Australia, was Secretary for the Home Department when the decision was finally made to colonise New South Wales, and he was the first to announce (in August 1786) George III's decision to send out the First Fleet. When Phillip finally decided to establish the settlement at Port Jackson, rather than Botany Bay, he paid the Home Secretary the compliment of naming Sydney after him.

A fine and fresh impression. *Nan Kivell and Spence, p. 300 (and reproduced p. 317).*

129: PHILLIP. *The first illustration of the Australian cassowary, from the coloured issue of Phillip's* Voyage to Botany Bay.

132: SYDNEY. *Lord Sydney, the Home Secretary in 1786, for whom the capital was named.*

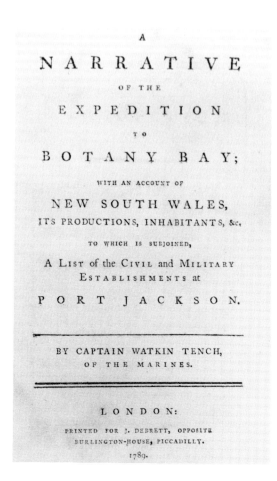

A

NARRATIVE

OF THE

EXPEDITION

TO

BOTANY BAY;

WITH AN ACCOUNT OF

NEW SOUTH WALES,

ITS PRODUCTIONS, INHABITANTS, &c,

TO WHICH IS SUBJOINED,

A LIST of the CIVIL and MILITARY
ESTABLISHMENTS at

PORT JACKSON.

BY CAPTAIN WATKIN TENCH,
OF THE MARINES.

LONDON:

PRINTED FOR J. DEBRETT, OPPOSITE
BURLINGTON-HOUSE, PICCADILLY.
1789.

133: TENCH. Watkin Tench's Narrative was the first authentic account of settled Australia to be published.

THE EARLIEST ACCOUNT

[133] TENCH, Watkin. A NARRATIVE OF THE EXPEDITION TO BOTANY BAY; with an Account of New South Wales, its Productions, Inhabitants, &c., to which is subjoined a list of the Civil and Military Establishments at Port Jackson. By Captain Watkin Tench of the Marines. *Octavo, without the half title and the (often missing) leaf of advertisements; a good copy in modern calf.* London, Printed for J. Debrett, 1789.

First edition of this important first settlement book, now conclusively proved to have been the first authentic account of settled Australia to be published. Tench's book not only predates the other First Fleet accounts, but it is also arguably the most readable and the most sympathetic. The others are often more or less official in tone, and none has the directness of Tench's descriptions of life in the first days of the colony.

Tench must have made arrangements before he left England with the London publisher Debrett; certainly his book appeared quickly, first being put on sale on the 24th April 1789. It proved extremely popular, not surprisingly in view of the large public that would have been curious for news of the colony, and three editions in English, a Dublin piracy and French, German and Dutch translations all appeared quickly.

Tench spent altogether four years in the colony (in 1793 producing a second book on the settlement — see below) carrying out his military duties as a marine, but giving as much time as he could to the business of exploration. He discovered the Nepean River and

traced it to the Hawkesbury, and began the many attempts to conquer the Blue Mountains. He was a lively and cultured member of the new society, and these qualities come through in his book which gives a vivid picture of the voyage out, and the establishment of the town at Sydney Cove. Apart from its importance as the first genuine description, Tench's *Narrative* provides us with the clearest of the surviving images of the first crucial months of settlement.

"It is a rare book in first edition and much sought after, even more so as collectors gradually realise its significance as the earliest printed record of the first settlement . . ." (Wantrup, pp. 56-57). *Davidson, pp. 75-6 ("increasingly rare"); Ferguson, 48; Wantrup, 2.*

THE FIRST YEARS OF THE COLONY

[134] TENCH, Captain Watkin. A COMPLETE ACCOUNT OF THE SETTLEMENT AT PORT JACKSON, in New South Wales, including an Accurate Description of the Situation of the Colony; of the Natives; and of its Natural Productions: taken on the spot, by Captain Watkin Tench, of the Marines. *Quarto, with a folding map; repair to head of title-page, a substantially good copy in recent full hard-grain morocco.* London, Sold by G. Nicol . . . and J. Sewell, 1793.

First edition. One of the scarcest of the First Fleet accounts, the second of the two books by Tench on the first settlement. Tench had arrived in Botany Bay on 20th January 1788; a Captain-Lieutenant, he explored the country around Sydney as well as carrying out his military duties, and was the discoverer of the Nepean River. His *Complete Account* was published on his return to England.

"As an accurate, well-written and acutely observed account of the earliest years of Australia's colonisation it is a most important addition to any collection of Australian books. It is rare despite the hundreds of copies that were originally printed and is much in demand . . ." (Wantrup, p. 72). *Ferguson, 171; not in Hill (although the octavo "Narrative of the Expedition to Botany Bay" by Tench is held by the collection, catalogue p. 290); Wantrup, 16.*

[135] TENCH, Captain Watkin. A NARRATIVE OF THE EXPEDITION TO BOTANY BAY. *Octavo, with coloured woodcuts and drawings by Adrian Feint; a fine copy, uncut, as issued in the original quarter cloth and canvas, dustjacket.* Sydney, Australian Limited Editions Society, 1938.

One of 500 numbered copies, reprinting the text of the third edition (1789) of the classic account of the First Fleet, and a particularly handsome publication.

SURGEON WHITE

[136] WHITE, John. JOURNAL OF A VOYAGE TO NEW SOUTH WALES, with sixty-five plates of nondescript animals, birds, lizards, serpents . . . by John White Esqre. Surgeon General to the Settlement. *Quarto, 65 engraved plates, in fine contemporary colouring; contemporary diced russia, spine neatly repaired; some browning to preliminaries and a marginal repair, but a very good copy.* London, J. Debrett, 1790.

An excellent copy of the rare coloured issue. Like

Phillip's *Voyage to Botany Bay*, White's *Journal* is normally seen with the plates uncoloured, although there was a special issue in which the plates were coloured by hand. In this form, White's *Journal* is one of the most beautiful of Australian colour-plate books, and one of the most attractive as well as one of the earliest of Australian bird books.

White was chief surgeon of the First Fleet, and was particularly successful in that he overcame serious medical problems in appalling conditions both on the voyage out and when the settlement was founded. He was also a keen amateur naturalist, and after arriving at Port Jackson found time to accompany Phillip on two journeys of exploration. On joining the First Fleet he had begun to keep a journal in which he made notes about birds in the new colony. It was this manuscript which formed the nucleus of his *Journal*.

It is the natural history content of the published account which makes White particularly noteworthy amongst the First Fleet journals. Many of the plates were drawn in England by leading natural history artists of the day, such as Sarah Stone, from original sketches done in the colony. The plates of birds are particularly magnificent, especially when they are seen in their coloured versions, as in this copy.

White's *Journal* also contains an interesting and valuable account of the voyage from London, with long detailed accounts of the stops at Rio de Janeiro, Cape Town and of the colonial voyages to Norfolk Island. The *Journal* was an immediate success, with subscribers alone accounting for 700 copies. This indicates the great interest in the exploration and settlement in the South Pacific which had swept England and Europe since Cook's discoveries.

White's interest in natural history continued during his whole stay in New South Wales until December 1794. When the convict artist Thomas Watling arrived in the colony in October 1792 he was assigned to White, and in the next two years made many drawings of birds for him. It is possible that White himself had some skill as an artist, and that he himself was responsible for the original sketches of some of the engravings here. *Ferguson, 97; Wantrup, 17.*

A REVOLUTIONARY WHITE

[137] WHITE, John. VOYAGE A LA NOUVELLE GALLES DU SUD, à Botany-Bay, au Port Jackson, en 1787, 1788, 1789; par John White, Chirugien en chef de l'établissement des Anglais, dans cette partie du globe; Ouvrage où l'on trouve de nouveaux détails sur le caractère et les usages des habitans du cap de Bonne-Espérance, de l'île Ténériffe, de Rio-Janeiro et de la Nouvelle Hollande ... *Octavo; contemporary quarter calf, flat spine gilt in compartments, mottled boards.* Paris, Chez Pougin, An 3 de la Republiquen (1795, vieux style).

First French edition of the surgeon White's journal, describing the First Fleet and the earliest days of the settlement; the original English edition had been published in London in 1790. It contains considerable additional material by the translator, Pougens, including an introduction in which he discusses the economic hazards facing the English in their colonial undertakings but applauds the humane principles of the transportation system. The revolutionary government he says, should recognise that "Nul n'a droit d'ordonner la mort de son semblable ... Il n'est point d'homicide legal ..." and agree that "tuons les crimes, mais non les coupables ...". *Ferguson, 231 (calling, in error, for two plates).*

[138] WHITE, John. TAGEBUCH EINER REISE NACH NEW-SUD-WALLIS. *Octavo, 136 pages; wrappers.* Berlin, n.d. [1791]

Extracted from *Magazin von Merkwurdigen neuen Reisebeschreibungen*; a German translation of John White's *Voyage to Botany Bay*, plainly presented. Issued originally as volume 5 of the *Magazin*, it also contains a version of Bligh's account of the mutiny on the *Bounty*. *Ferguson Addenda, 88b.*

[139] WORGAN, George B. JOURNAL OF A FIRST FLEET SURGEON. ... *Octavo, photographic frontispiece; a fine copy in the original cloth.* Sydney, Library Council of New South Wales, 1978.

First publication of the journal of the surgeon on H.M.S. *Sirius*.

"A NEW COLONY OF THIEVES AND RUFFIANS"

[140] [WRAXALL, Sir Nathaniel William]. A SHORT REVIEW OF THE POLITICAL STATE OF GREAT BRITAIN at the Commencement of the Year One Thousand Seven Hundred and Eighty Seven. *Octavo, wrappers.* London, 1787.

One of the earliest references to the transportation of convicts to Botany Bay. The *Short Review* was published anonymously, but its author was Sir Nathaniel Wraxall; he criticises the Government transportation act — "The measure, adopted by Government, for the exile and removal, rather than the punishment of malefactors, known by the name of 'The Expedition to Botany Bay', and now on the point of its execution ..." — and goes on to ask "If ... we are reduced to the melancholy and lamentable necessity of annually transporting a considerable portion of [England's] inhabitants to some foreign colony, or distant quarter of the world; is there no part of the planet, except New-Holland, to which we can have recourse? — Geography itself had not extended its discoveries so far, when Swift, in the beginning of the present century, ventur'd to place his 'Lilliput and Blefuscu' as he imagin'd, on the extreme verge of Nature. Unconscious as he was, and ignorant of futurity, which in the reign of George the Third, and under the auspices of a Sydney, spurns the narrow bound; and through stormy seas, and inclement latitudes, forms a new colony of thieves and ruffians, in another hemisphere, under the Southern Pole!"

This edition, the sixth, "with additions", the first version of the text to contain the criticism (pages 77-83), is one of the earliest printed references to transportation to Botany Bay. *Ferguson, 27.*

140: WRAXALL. *Wraxall's pamphlet contains one of the first references to Australian transportation.*

A
SHORT REVIEW
OF THE
POLITICAL STATE
OF
GREAT-BRITAIN
AT THE
Commencement of the Year One Thousand
Seven Hundred and Eighty-Seven.

—" *Nec demere quisquam, et sine
Odio dicendus est.*"

THE SIXTH EDITION,
WITH ADDITIONS.

LONDON:
PRINTED FOR J. DEBRETT, OPPOSITE
BURLINGTON-HOUSE, PICCADILLY.
M,DCC,LXXXVII.

OVERLEAF:
136: WHITE. *One of the natural history plates in the fine coloured issue.*

The Small Paroquet.

London Published as the Act directs Dec.20 1789 by I.Debrett.

VII
Bligh and the
Breadfruit Voyages

William Bligh was sailing master of the Resolution *on Cook's third voyage, which touched Australia at Adventure Bay in Tasmania in 1777. As commander of the* Bounty *bound for Tahiti he again visited Australia 11 years later. In August 1806 he was installed as Governor of New South Wales, only to be deposed in the "Rum Rebellion" of January 1808; but it was as commander of the* Bounty *that Bligh's name has become immortalized.*

The Bounty *voyage was unambiguously a botanical "collect and carry" mission. In 1787 Lord Sydney officially informed the Admiralty of King George III's intentions for a South Sea voyage for breadfruit — "the Merchants and Planters interested in His Majesty's West India Possessions have represented that the Introduction of the Bread Fruit Trees into the Islands in those Seas to constitute an Article of Food would be a very essential Benefit to the Inhabitants . . .".*

The mutiny that took place on this voyage on 28th April 1789, resulting in Bligh and 18 others being cast adrift in an open boat, is the most infamous in history.

As Governor of New South Wales from 1806 to 1810, Bligh suffered a further uprising, in the form of the "Rum Rebellion", but it was the Bounty *mutiny and its ramifications that would haunt Bligh for ever, although his reputation was also for ever redeemed by the epic open boat voyage of 6,000 kilometres across the Pacific and by the part he played in the battle of Copenhagen alongside Nelson.*

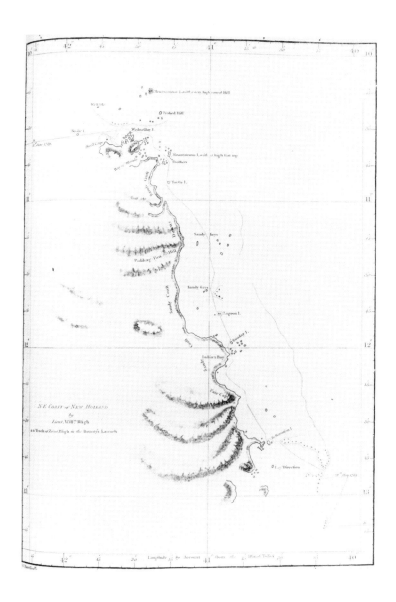

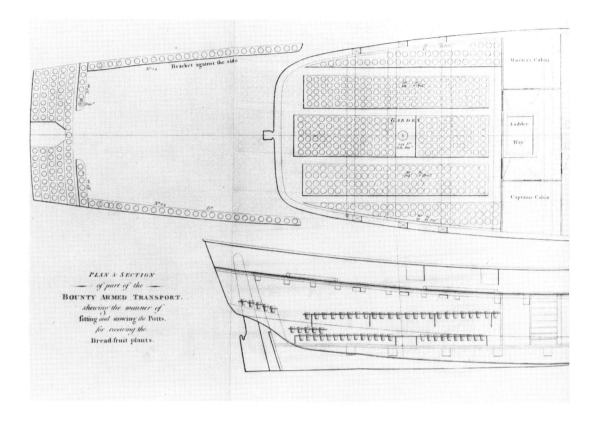

PLAN & SECTION
— of part of the —
BOUNTY ARMED TRANSPORT.
shewing the manner of
fitting and stowing the Pots.
for receiving the
Bread-fruit plants.

THE MUTINY ON THE BOUNTY

[141] BLIGH, William. A Narrative of the mutiny, on board His Majesty's Ship Bounty; and the Subsequent Voyage of Part of the Crew, in the Ship's Boat, from Tofoa, one of the Friendly Islands, to Timor, a Dutch Settlement in the East Indies. *Quarto, with a plate and 3 charts (one folding); a good copy in early calf.* London, Printed for George Nicol, 1790.

First edition. This is Bligh's own account of the most notorious incident in maritime history, and predates his full account of the voyage by two years. Bligh was anxious to have an account of the mutiny itself available to safeguard his own reputation and so that he could present copies to the Lords of the Admiralty before the court-martial of the mutineers, to absolve himself from any blame. *Ferguson, 71; Hill, p. 26; Wantrup, 61.*

THE FULL ACCOUNT OF THE VOYAGE

[142] BLIGH, William. A Voyage to the South Sea, undertaken by Command of His Majesty, for the purpose of conveying the Bread-fruit Tree to the West Indies, in His Majesty's Ship the Bounty . . . including an account of the mutiny on board the said ship, and the subsequent voyage of part of the Crew, in the Ship's Boat, from Tofoa, one of the Friendly Islands, to Timor, a Dutch settlement in the East Indies. *Quarto, with frontispiece portrait, and 6 plans and charts; contemporary calf, rebacked, retaining original red label; portrait, title-page and folding chart (Map of the Track of the Launch) foxed, text generally good; with the armorial bookplate of G.H.D. Tennant.* London, Printed for George Nicol, 1792.

First edition of the official narrative of Bligh's voyage in the *Bounty* and the mutiny. Bligh was at the

time of this publication on his second breadfruit voyage, and the work was edited by James Burney, with the assistance of Sir Joseph Banks.

This, the full account of the voyage, contains a slightly altered version of Bligh's own account of the mutiny, which had been published two years earlier (see above). *Ferguson, 125; Hill, p. 27; Wantrup, 62a.*

[143] BLIGH, William. A Voyage to the South Sea, undertaken by Command of His Majesty, for the purpose of conveying the Bread-fruit Tree to the West Indies, in His Majesty's Ship the Bounty . . . *Quarto, frontispiece portrait, 4 charts and maps, 3 plates; modern tan calf, red label; light browning of title, occasional spotting to text, early and skilful repair to margin of portrait; the plate with a plan of the Bounty's Launch torn and neatly laid down with slight surface loss.* London, Printed for George Nicol, 1792.

First edition. *Ferguson, 125; Hill, p. 27; Wantrup, 62a.*

THE VERY RARE ADVANCE ISSUE OF THE VOYAGE

[144] BLIGH, William. A Voyage to the South Sea, undertaken by Command of His Majesty, for the purpose of conveying the Bread-fruit Tree to the West Indies, in His Majesty's Ship the Bounty . . . *Quarto, frontispiece portrait, 4 charts and maps, 3 plates; old calf, that spine gilt with red and green labels; joints repaired, sides somewhat scarred, but an excellent copy with wide margins.* London, Printed for George Nicol, 1792.

Of the greatest rarity: one of only very few known copies of a special advance issue of Bligh's description of his voyage in the *Bounty*. This issue contains the original 1790 printing of Bligh's *Narrative of the*

141: BLIGH. *HMS* Bounty *was extensively re-built to transport breadfruit seedlings to the West Indies.*

MINUTES

OF THE

PROCEEDINGS

OF THE

COURT-MARTIAL held at PORTSMOUTH,
AUGUST 12, 1792.

ON

TEN PERSONS charged with MUTINY on Board
His Majesty's Ship the BOUNTY.

WITH AN

APPENDIX,

CONTAINING

A full Account of the real Causes and Circumstances of that unhappy
Transaction, the most material of which have hitherto been
withheld from the Public.

LONDON:

Printed for J. DEIGHTON, opposite Gray's-Inn, Holborn.

MDCCXCIV.

Mutiny on board His Majesty's Ship Bounty (see 141 above), bound up with a special advance printing of the additional narrative prepared by Bligh detailing the remainder of the voyage, later published in full as the *Voyage to the South Sea* of 1792.

In this version, the account of the voyage goes to p. 153; p. 154 is left deliberately blank, and p. 246 (with p. 245 also a blank) takes up the story again; it was intended that the mutiny account should have been bound to fill the hiatus between pp. 154 and 245.

We can find no published record of any copy of this issue having been offered for sale since the F.G. Coles copy was auctioned in 1965 for the then remarkable sum of five hundred pounds; later in the same year the Cook copy was sold privately in Melbourne for eight hundred pounds. *Ferguson, 126 (listing only the Mitchell Library copy); Wantrup, 62b.*

FIRST FRENCH EDITION

[145] BLIGH, William. RELATION DE L'ENLEVEMENT DU NAVIRE LE BOUNTY, appertenant au Roi d'Angleterre, & commandé par le Lieutenant Guillaume Bligh; avec le voyage subsequent de cet officier & d'une partie de son equipage dans sa caloupe. *Duodecimo, with 3 folding maps; old half calf, an attractive copy.* Paris, Chez Firmin Didot, 1790.

First French edition of the official account of the voyage.

ONE OF THE GREATEST PACIFIC RARITIES

[146] BOUNTY MUTINY. MINUTES OF THE PROCEEDINGS OF THE COURT-MARTIAL HELD AT PORTSMOUTH August 12, 1792. On Ten Persons charged with Mutiny on Board His Majesty's Ship the Bounty. With an Appendix [by Edward Christian] containing A Full Account of the real Causes and Circumstances of that unhappy Transaction, the most material of which have hitherto been withheld from the Public. *Quarto, original full calf, gilt, spine neatly renewed; with a contemporary owner's inscription on upper right edge of title-page; an extremely good copy, fine and clean, with very large margins.* London, J. Deighton, 1794.

Exceedingly rare. The trial of the *Bounty* mutineers: an exceptionally fine copy of one of the most important Pacific rarities. This account of the proceedings was published in only a very small number of copies for distribution among the interested parties and the ministers of state at the time. We can find no record of a copy catalogued for sale by a bookseller since a copy was (at forty pounds) one of the most expensive items in Messrs. Francis Edwards' 1934 catalogue of the remarkable Edge-Partington collection, where they noted that "not more than three or four copies appear to be known, none of which is in the British Museum".

The *Appendix* contains a defence of the conduct of Fletcher Christian by his brother Edward Christian, Professor of Laws. It contains a considerable amount of information not found elsewhere, relating both to events preceding and subsequent to the mutiny, none of which was mentioned at the Court Martial. It evoked a reply from Bligh in which he said "this

---

RELATION
DE L'ENLEVEMENT
DU NAVIRE
LE BOUNTY,

Appartenant au Roi d'Angleterre, & commandé par le Lieutenant GUILLAUME BLIGH; avec le Voyage subséquent de cet Officier & d'une partie de son équipage dans sa Chaloupe, depuis les ÎLES DES AMIS dans la mer du Sud, jusqu'à TIMOR, établissement Hollandais aux îles Moluques.

Écrit en Anglais par M. WILLIAM BLIGH, Lieutenant de la Marine d'Angleterre ; & traduit par DANIEL LESCALLIER, Commissaire général des Colonies, ci-devant Ordonnateur dans la Guiane Hollandaise, & en-suite dans la Guiane Française, Correspondant de la Société Royale d'Agriculture de Paris.

OUVRAGE ORNÉ DE TROIS CARTES.

A PARIS,
Chez FIRMIN DIDOT, Libraire, rue Dauphine, N° 116.
Et se trouve
À AMSTERDAM, chez GABRIEL DUFOUR, Libraire.

─────────

1790.

Appendix is the Work of Mr. Edward Christian ... written apparently for the purpose of vindicating his brother at my expense ...". *Ferguson, 175; Hill, pp. 200-201.*

THE OPEN BOAT LOG

[147] BLIGH, William. THE BLIGH NOTEBOOK. 'Rough account — Lieutenant Wm. Bligh's voyage in the Bounty's Launch from the Ship to Tofua and from thence to Timor' 28 April to 14 June 1789. With a draft list of the Bounty mutineers. *2 volumes, quarto and octavo, encased in a silk lined green buckram box.* Canberra, National Library of Australia, 1986.

A facsimile of Bligh's notebook, kept at sea during the open boat voyage; edited by John Bach, and limited to 500 copies. The notebook, published for the first time in both facsimile and transcription, provides an opportunity to reassess William Bligh and the *Bounty* mutiny of April 1789 from direct evidence of Bligh's own notes.

On 28 April 1789 Bligh and eighteen others were set adrift from the *Bounty*. A landing on nearby Tofua to take on food and water almost ended in disaster when the natives attacked and killed one man. The survivors then sailed in a 23 foot open boat almost 6,000 kilometers across the Pacific Ocean and the Timor Sea. On this perilous voyage Bligh continued his former *Bounty* task of keeping the ship's log, but now the record was made in a small notebook and the entries show the stress of events as well as the author's powers of observation and attention to detail.

The editor, John Bach, supplies an informed commentary on the transcription and the book is well illustrated from originals produced close to the date of the voyage. Included, as in the original, is the first

145: BLIGH. The first French edition of Bligh's account of the mutiny.

OPPOSITE:
146: BOUNTY MUTINY. The court-martial of the Bounty mutineers: one of the rarest of all Pacific books.

Dangerous Situation of Captain BLIGH and his Crew.

THE
DANGEROUS VOYAGE
PERFORMED BY
Captain Bligh,
WITH A PART OF THE CREW OF
HIS MAJESTY'S SHIP BOUNTY,
IN AN OPEN BOAT,
Over Twelve Hundred Leagues of the Ocean;
IN THE YEAR
1789.

TO WHICH IS ADDED,
An Account of the Sufferings and Fate of the
Remainder of the Crew of said Ship.

DUBLIN:
PRINTED BY R. NAPPER, 140, CAPEL-ST.
1824.

rough list of the *Bounty* mutineers.

This is the first published account of Bligh's original record of events as they occurred on his incredible open boat voyage across the Pacific from Tofua to Timor after the mutiny on the Bounty — one of the great epics of the sea.

THE RESOURCE AND VLYDT LOGS

[148] BLIGH, William. BLIGH'S VOYAGE IN THE RESOURCE. From Coupang to Batavia, together with the Log of his subsequent Passage to England in the Dutch Packet Vlydt, and his remarks on Morrison's Journal . . . with an introduction and notes by Owen Rutter, & engravings on wood by Peter Barker-Mill. *Small folio, with chart and page of log in facsimile; original blue and fawn cloth; an excellent copy.* London, Golden Cockerel Press, 1937.

The full text of Bligh's log kept on the *Resource* (including little-known details of another near mutiny) during his voyage from Timor to Batavia after the mutiny on the *Bounty*, and his subsequent journey back to England in the *Vlydt*. Both logs are printed here for the first time from the originals in the Mitchell Library. A beautifully printed and illustrated book: one of 350 numbered copies. *Hill, p. 27.*

THE PROVIDENCE LOG

[149] BLIGH, William. THE LOG OF H.M.S. PROVIDENCE, 1791-1793 [with an introduction by Lord Mountbatten of Burma]. *Folio, with colour frontispiece (Parkinson's watercolour of the breadfruit), maps (5 folding), folding plate of the Providence and numerous other illustrations; original half calf.* Guildford, Genesis Publications Limited, 1976.

A splendid facsimile of Bligh's log, reproduced in full for the first time, together with all correspondence leading up to the first breadfruit voyage, and articles on Bligh by D.G.C. Allen and Stephen Walters, with

notes on the breadfruit tree by David Bellamy. Included is a facsimile of John Ellis' monograph *A description of the Mangosteen and the Breadfruit* (London, 1775), which first suggested the possibilities of transplanting the tree to the West Indies. One of 500 numbered copies. *Hill, p. 357.*

[150] [BARROW, Sir John] THE EVENTFUL HISTORY OF THE MUTINY AND PIRATICAL SEIZURE OF H.M.S. BOUNTY: its cause and consequences. *Small octavo, with a frontispiece and 5 etched plates, contemporary half calf, joints splitting and spine worn.* London, John Murray and Sold by Thomas Tegg, 1835.

Second edition of a popular account of the *Bounty* story. The plates, after drawings by Batty, include the familiar image "Residence of John Adams, Pitcairns Island". *Hill, pp. 346-7 (other editions).*

THE DANGEROUS VOYAGE

[151] CHAPBOOK. THE DANGEROUS VOYAGE PERFORMED BY CAPTAIN BLIGH, with a part of the crew of His Majesty's Ship Bounty, in an open boat, Over Twelve Hundred Leagues of the Ocean; in the year 1789. To which is added, An Account of the Sufferings and Fate of the Remainder of the Crew of said Ship. *Duodecimo, with a frontispiece; a little stained but a sound copy in the original blind-stamped cloth, spine lettered in gilt, somewhat worn, small hole at base of spine.* Dublin, Printed by R. Napper, 1824.

An early edition of the anonymous *Dangerous Voyage* chapbook, the very popular cheap account of Bligh's adventures still selling well thirty-five years after the events it chronicles.

THE DISCOVERY OF THE MUTINEERS

[152] DELANO, Amasa. A NARRATIVE OF VOYAGES AND TRAVELS, IN THE NORTHERN AND SOUTHERN HEMISPHERES; comprising three voyages round the

world; together with a voyage of survey and discovery in the Pacific Ocean and Oriental Islands. *Octavo, with portrait frontispiece, portrait of Abba Thule, folding map of Pitcairn Island; quarter tan calf antique, preserving the original spine, marble paper covered boards; moderate foxing and staining to text as in all copies; a very good copy.* Boston, Printed by E. G. House, for the Author, 1817.

First edition. Delano was a 12 year veteran of the sea, when attracted, as much of New England was, by the lucrative China trade. He made three important Pacific voyages: the first, 1790-1792, to Canton on the ship *Massachusetts,* visiting New Guinea, Timor, Borneo, the Celebes, Macao, Bombay and Calcutta; the second, 1799-1802, on the *Perseverance* via Cape Horn, Chile, Hawaii and China; the third, 1803-1807, on the *Perseverance* and the *Pilgrim,* via the Cape of Good Hope, Australia, Hawaii and China.

Delano has much to say of great relevance to the earliest permanent settlement of Tasmania. He met Governor Collins and Lt. Bowen in 1803 shortly after their arrival at the Derwent. Sealing in Bass' Straits was the main reason for his visit, and he found himself an early subject of protectionism by a Port Jackson gang who considered he had no right to that privilege near the colony. The Australian section contains extensive natural history notes, one of the earliest sources of such knowledge for American readers.

But of the greatest interest is the long section on Bligh, the *Bounty* and Pitcairn. While at Timor, Delano found and copied a manuscript account by Captain Edwards of the cruise of the *Pandora,* part of which he reproduces; he also gives Bligh's account with remarks based on his own experience, reprints the *Quarterly Review* article in which Folger's and Staines' letters announced the discovery of the mutineers, and reproduces the Carteret map with an account of that voyage. Delano, who knew Folger, reproduces an unpublished letter, along with notes of

conversations with him. *Ferguson, 673; Hill, p. 83; Judd, 51.*

"MA NOW, WA, EHO, MAA!"

[153] [HEYWOOD] TAGART, Edward. A MEMOIR OF THE LATE CAPTAIN PETER HEYWOOD, R.N. with extracts from his diaries and correspondence. *Octavo, contemporary presentation inscription; a little light spotting, but a good copy in the original cloth, rubbed, spine faded and printed paper label somewhat worn, joints strengthened.* London, Effingham Wilson, 1832.

Scarce: the principal source for the biography of Heywood, probably the best known of the captured mutineers of H.M.S. *Bounty.* Tagart deals with the mutiny itself, Heywood's trial, his condemnation to death and his ultimate pardon — as well as the remainder of an interesting naval career including spells at Buenos Aires and Montevideo where he was stationed to safeguard British interests during the revolutions. At the end of Heywood's naval career in 1816 he was nearly at the head of the list of captains of the Royal Navy having survived the disgrace of the mutiny so early in his career.

Heywood's early experiences proved useful in one minor episode in 1816: his biographer records a touching episode at Gibraltar when he finds that there are two Tahitians aboard the *Calypso.* "Never, as long as I live, shall I forget the emotions of these poor creatures, when, on entering the door of my cabin I welcomed them in their own way by exclaiming: 'Ma now, wa, Eho, maa! Yowra t'Eatooa, te harre a mye!' . . .". *Hill, p. 287.*

[154] [MORRISON] MONTGOMERIE, H. S. THE MORRISON MYTH. A pendant to William Bligh of the Bounty in Fact and in Fable. *Octavo, original tan paper covered boards as issued; a fine copy.* London, Privately Printed, 1938.

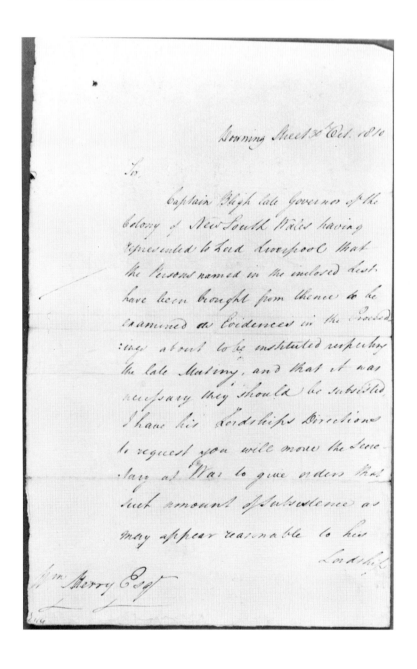

155: PEEL. *Sir Robert Peel and William Bligh are linked in this original letter from Downing Street.*

An examination of the authenticity of one of the key documents in the history of the *Bounty* mutiny. James Morrison's *Journal*, which Montgomerie shows was written after the fact, forms the basis for the attack on Bligh.

LETTER FROM DOWNING STREET

[155] PEEL, Sir Robert. AUTOGRAPH LETTER SIGNED to William Merry (?). *Small folio, 2 pp., legibly written in brown ink. Originally folded. Reinforced on central fold.* Downing Street, 30th October, 1810.

An important letter linking two major figures, Sir Robert Peel and William Bligh. Robert Peel was in 1810 the undersecretary for war and the colonies. The secretary of state was at this time Lord Liverpool. Peel writes to William Merry that:

"Captain Bligh late Governor of the Colony of New South Wales having represented to Lord Liverpool that the persons named in the inclosed List have been brought from thence to be examined as Evidences in the Proceedings about to be instituted respecting the late Mutiny, and that it was necessary they should be subsisted, I have his Lordship's Directions to request you will move the Secretary at War to give orders that such amount of Subsistence as may appear reasonable to his Lordship may be issued to them respectively . . .".

The list of defence witnesses referred to in this letter for the George Johnston/William Bligh "Rum Rebellion" trial of 1811 has not survived.

The witnesses in Bligh's defence were 19 in all and included leading New South Wales men such as Robert Campbell, Palmer, Fulton, Gore and George Suttor. This letter, written only five days after Bligh arrived in London from Sydney, is testimony to his troubled life and continued public humiliation.

PITCAIRN'S ISLAND. See also nos. 50-53 (Hawkesworth) and 225 (Tagus).

VIII
La Pérouse, and the
search for him

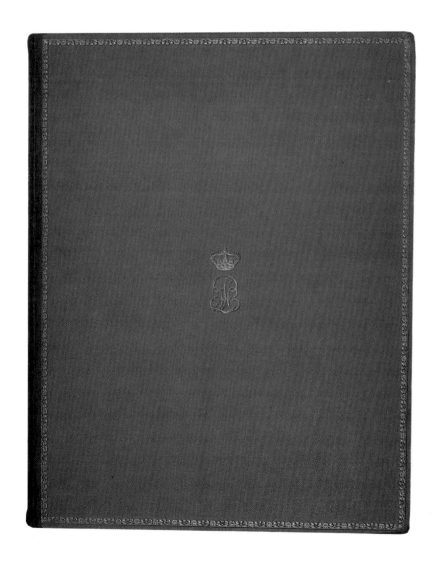

La Pérouse's was one of the greatest exploring voyages of the eighteenth century. After extensive exploration in the Pacific, he arrived in Botany Bay on the 24th January 1788, six days after the arrival of the First Fleet. The French spent almost seven weeks in the new colony. When the Boussole *and the* Astrolabe *sailed out of Botany Bay on 10th March 1788 they were never seen again, and this disappearance became the greatest maritime mystery of the eighteenth century. Not until 40 years later was it established by the sea-captain Dillon that the expedition had ended its days on the island of Vanikoro.*

The French authorities responded to La Pérouse's disappearance by commissioning a major expedition in search of the voyagers. The Recherche *and the* Esperance *were put into commission and set sail in September 1791 under the command of Antoine-Raymond-Joseph de Bruni d'Entrecasteaux, one of the most experienced French captains.*

D'Entrecasteaux had also been entrusted with scientific and exploratory goals, and his work on the Australian coasts is of the greatest significance. The exploration of Tasmania — and particularly the south-east coast — was of major importance, and it was their examination of the Derwent River in 1792-3 that focused attention on its suitability for settlement. The fine maps by Beautemps-Beaupré, the expedition's cartographer, contained in the official account here are the first detailed maps of the site of Hobart, and were almost certainly themselves partly responsible for prompting hasty British settlement of the area to pre-empt French ambitions.

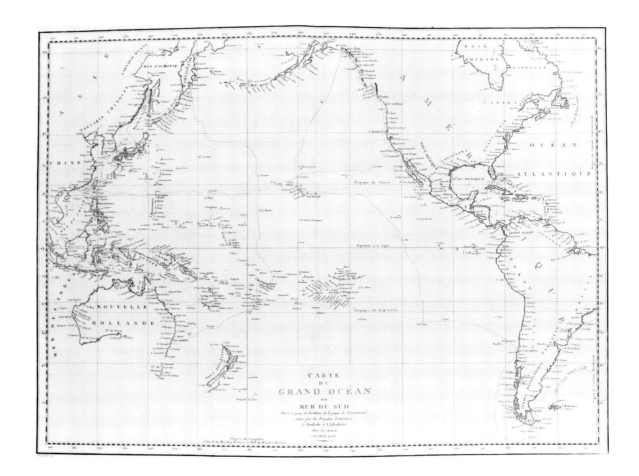

THE OFFICIAL ACCOUNT OF LA PEROUSE'S VOYAGE

[156] LA PEROUSE, Jean Francois Galaup de. VOYAGE DE LA PEROUSE AUTOUR DU MONDE, publié conformément au décret du 22 Avril 1791, et redigé par M.L.A. Milet-Mureau. *4 volumes, quarto, with engraved frontispiece portrait, modern pink mottled paper covered boards, paper title labels; [with] Atlas folio, containing engraved title, 69 maps, charts, and plates (21 folding), modern pink mottled paper covered boards; text printed on pale blue paper, spines faded, and slight dampstaining to tops of portion of text; both text and atlas entirely uncut, the atlas with all plates extraordinarily fresh.* Paris, de l'Imprimerie de la République, An V. (1797).

First edition. The tragedy of the disappearance of the entire La Pérouse expedition, overshadows what was in reality a great Pacific voyage. While primarily a voyage of exploration and discovery, the possibilities of the fur trade and of French expansion into the Pacific and Asia were evidently investigated in depth.

The most significant results of the voyage are the charts of the imperfectly known asiatic side of the Pacific. Enroute to Kamschatka, La Pérouse was the first to safely navigate and chart the Japan Sea and the strait between the Island of Sakahlin and the northernmost island of Japan, which bears his name. At Kamschatka he received instructions to proceed to Australia to assess the extent of British plans in New South Wales. Travelling via Samoa where he discovered Savaii, Manono and Apolima Islands in

December 1787, and through the Tongan group, he arrived at Botany Bay in January 1788, just hours after Governor Phillip had arrived with the First Fleet.

La Pérouse's habit of forwarding records whenever opportunity offered ensured their survival. The first portion was forwarded by sea from Macao; the second (Macao to Kamschatka) went overland with de Lesseps (see 159 below), and the final despatches from Botany Bay. The folio atlas contains magnificent maps of Russian Asia, Japan, the Pacific Northwest Coast, San Francisco and Monterey. This is a particularly good copy of the atlas, with larger margins than the Yale University Library copy described by Lada-Mocarski and the John Howell-Books copy, (their fiftieth anniversary catalogue 1982) described as "the finest we have ever seen". *Ferguson, 268; Hill p.173; Lada-Mocarski, 52.*

FROM THE BELGIAN ROYAL LIBRARY: A FINE COPY

[157] LA PEROUSE, Jean Francois Galaup de. ATLAS TO THE VOYAGE. *Folio, containing engraved title and 69 maps, charts and plates, of which 21 are folding; an extremely good copy with especially good impressions of the plates, in contemporary quarter red morocco and glazed boards, royal cypher in gilt on covers and spines.* Paris, de l'Imprimerie de la République, An V. (1797).

A particularly fine copy of the splendid La Pérouse atlas by itself, from the Belgian Royal Library, with the royal cypher in gilt on the binding and a library stamp on the front endpaper.

160: LABILLARDIERE. *The great flower painter Redouté was responsible for most of the botanical plates in Labillardière's account of the d'Entrecasteaux expedition, including this elegant engraving of a eucalypt.*

THE BEST ENGLISH EDITION

[158] LA PEROUSE, Jean Francois Galaup de. A VOYAGE ROUND THE WORLD, performed in the Years 1785, 1786, 1787 and 1788, by the Boussole and Astrolabe, under the command of J.F.G. de la Perouse. *2 volumes, quarto, with engraved frontispiece portrait, half tan speckled calf, rebacked, but preserving original gilt spines, red and green labels; [with] Atlas folio, with engraved title, and 69 maps and plates, the large folding map of the voyage coloured in part; old half calf, red and green labels; titles and portrait slightly browned, text generally very clean, some spotting to plates; bookplate of Hugh A. Wyndham.* London, Printed by A. Hamilton, for G. G. and J. Robinson, J. Edwards, and T. Payne, 1799.

Best English edition, and the first to contain a full translation of the text of the French edition. Most of the engraved plates are by Heath, engraver of some plates for Cook's third voyage. The translator modestly announces "The book now laid before the world is one of the most magnificent in its conception, and recent in its execution". Hill calls this edition "an extremely rare work". *Ferguson, 288 "the best English edition"; Hill, p.174.*

DE LESSEPS' OVERLAND JOURNEY WITH DESPATCHES

[159] [LA PEROUSE] LESSEPS, Jean Baptiste Barthélemy, *Baron de.* JOURNAL HISTORIQUE DU VOYAGE DE M. DE LESSEPS. . . employée dans l'expédition de M. le comte de La Pérouse. . . depuis l'instant ou il a quitté les frégates Francaises au port Saint-Paul de Kamschatka jusqu'à son arrivée en France, le 17 Octobre 1788. *2 volumes, octavo, with 2 maps and 1 plate; contemporary mottled calf, gilt panelled spines with floral designs, red and black labels; joints a little tender and slight wear to tops of spines; a fine copy.* Paris, de l'Imprimerie Royale. . . 1790.

First edition. An epic journey across Russia by which a substantial portion of the records of the La Pérouse voyage were preserved. De Lesseps, the young son of the French Consul-General at St. Petersburg, and himself Russian interpreter on the voyage, left the expedition at Kamschatka in September 1787, with charts, views and La Pérouse's journal from Macao to Kamschatka, to travel overland to France. He thus became the only survivor of the ill fated expedition. This graphic account of his travels over enormous distances and under hostile conditions with his eventual arrival at Versailles in October 1788, is an important adjunct to the voyage. In 1829, De Lesseps had the melancholy duty of positively identifying the relics brought back to France by Peter Dillon. *Hill, p.178.*

FIRST ACCOUNT OF THE D'ENTRECASTEAUX EXPEDITION

[160] LABILLARDIERE, Jacques Julien Houton de. RELATION DU VOYAGE A LA RECHERCHE DE LA PEROUSE, fait par ordre de l'Assemblée Constituante, pendant les annees 1791, 1792, et pendant la 1ère et la 2de année de la République Francaise. *2 volumes, quarto, original tan calf spines, vellum corners and blue-green mottled paper boards, as issued; [with] Atlas folio, with engraved title, folding chart of the voyage and 43 engraved maps, charts, elevations and plates; modern green morocco spine and corners, preserving the original green glazed paper boards; spines of text volumes a little scuffed, two corners bumped, but text generally clean and free from spotting; some dampstaining to lower portion of plates; a very good untrimmed copy.* Paris, Chez H. J. Jansen, Imprimeur-libraire, An VIII de la République Francoise (1800).

First edition, and the first published results of this voyage: a narrative by the naturalist on the d'Entrecasteaux expedition, in which Australia was circumnavigated twice, and the islands surrounding investigated for traces of La Pérouse. The work is particularly interesting for its descriptions (and illustrations) of Tasmania, Tonga, New Caledonia, and New Guinea, and the Atlas contains outstanding and important views of these areas by the official artist Piron. Included is the first large depiction of the Black Swan. The 14 botanical plates, all by or produced under the direction of Redouté, the most famous of all botanical artists, include 2 of Eucalypts and 2 of Banksias.

It was a notable voyage in itself, although also beset by tragedy: the commander, D'Entrecasteaux, died of a "dreadful cholic" shortly before the expedition collapsed in Batavia. There they learned of the French Revolution, and d'Auribeau, then commander, and the principal officers being monarchists, put themselves under Dutch protection, arrested the remainder of the officers, including Labillardière the naturalist, and Piron the artist, and disposed of the ships. D'Auribeau in turn died, and was succeeded by Rossel, who managed to return to Europe and later edited the manuscripts for the official account (see below). The papers and natural history specimens were seized enroute and carried to England, but in 1796, with the urging of Sir Joseph Banks, were returned to France under a flag of truce.

Because Labillardière was a "Republican", his account appeared first, while that of d'Entrecasteaux had to wait until the restoration of the monarchy. The atlas appeared a year earlier than the text. *Ferguson, 307; this edition not in the catalogue of the Hill collection.*

[161] LABILLARDIERE, Jacques Julien Houton de. RELATION DU VOYAGE A LA RECHERCHE DE LA PEROUSE, fait pendant les années 1791, 1792, et pendant la 1ère et la 2de année de la République Francaise. *2 volumes, quarto; full contemporary mottled gilt embossed calf, gilt panelled spines, red morocco title labels, marble endpapers. [with] Atlas folio, with engraved title, folding map of the voyage and 43 engraved maps, charts, elevations and plates, in contemporary half green morocco, green cloth boards, gilt panelled spine, pink embossed floral design end papers; joints of text just cracking but firm; text very clean; a fine set.* Paris, Chez H. J. Jansen, Imprimeur-libraire . . . An VIII (1800).

First edition. *Ferguson, 307; this edition not in the catalogue of the Hill collection.*

"THE RUDIMENTS OF SOME GREAT EMPIRE"

[162] LABILLARDIERE, Jacques Julien Houton de. VOYAGE IN SEARCH OF LA PEROUSE. Performed by order of the Constituent Assembly, during the years 1791, 1792, 1793, and 1794, and drawn up by M. Labillardière. *2 volumes, octavo, with folding chart and 45 engraved plates; contemporary black half straight-grained morocco; occasional foxing, titles and frontispiece plates browned, but a fine set.* London, Printed for John Stockdale, Piccadilly, 1800.

First octavo English edition, published simultaneously with the quarto issue; with a new introduction discussing voyages of discovery and the possibilities of transferring the "advantages of civilization. . . to those remote countries":
"If so, the period may arrive, when New Zealand may produce her Lockes, and Newtons, her Montesquieus; and when great nations in the immense region of New Holland, may send their navigators, philosophers, and antiquaries, to contemplate the ruins of ancient London, and Paris, and to trace the languid remains of the arts and sciences in this quarter of the globe. Who can tell, whether the rudiments of some great empire may not already exist at Botany Bay?" *Ferguson, 310; Hill, P. 168.*

[163] LABILLARDIERE, Jacques Julien Houton de. VOYAGE IN SEARCH OF LA PEROUSE. Performed by order of the Constituent Assembly, during the years 1791, 1792, 1793 and 1794, and drawn up by M.

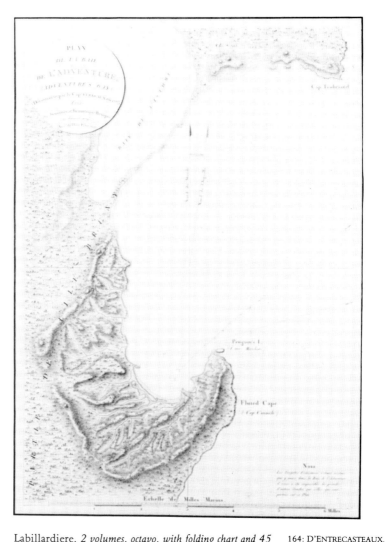

Labillardiere. *2 volumes, octavo, with folding chart and 45 engraved plates; contemporary speckled calf, rebacked, black labels; occasional foxing to titles, frontispiece plates browned, but a good clean set.* London, John Stockdale, 1800.

First octavo English edition. *Ferguson, 310; Hill, p.168.*

THE OFFICIAL ACCOUNT, FROM D'ENTRECASTEAUX'S PAPERS

[164] D'ENTRECASTEAUX, Antoine Raymond Joseph de Bruni. VOYAGE DE DENTRECASTEAUX, ENVOYE A LA RECHERCHE DE LA PEROUSE. Publié par ordre de sa Majesté l'Empereur et Roi. . . Redigé par M. de Rossel, ancienne capitaine de vaisseau. *2 volumes, quarto, with 32 folding engraved plates in volume I, original blue-green marbled paper covered boards, printed spine labels, [with] Atlas, imperial folio, containing separate title leaf and explication leaf, and 39 charts and maps (29 double folding); modern dark green morocco spine and corners, original blue-green marbled paper covered boards; joints of text a little worn, slight scuffing to spine and dust stains to edges, but a very fine crisp copy in the original boards, as issued; endpapers of atlas spotted, but all maps very fresh and bright; a fine set in original and desirable condition.* Paris, de l'Imprimerie Impériale, [1807]-1808.

The official commander's account of the search for La Pérouse, published posthumously. The Republican Labillardière's account had already appeared some

164: D'ENTRECASTEAUX.
Adventure Bay, Tasmania: one of the magnificent Australian maps contained in the official account of the D'Entrecasteaux voyage.

7 years before the monarchist D'Entrecasteaux's narratives, edited from his manuscripts by Rossel, the last commander of the expedition.

The series of 12 magnificent maps of Western Australia and Tasmania contained in the fine atlas here record much of these coasts accurately for the first time and are among the most important ever made. Of prime importance to Tasmania, it was d'Entrecasteaux's explorations of 1792 and 1793 which focussed attention on the Derwent River area (now Hobart) as a suitable place of settlement.

A particularly attractive copy of a very scarce voyage account, of great importance to Australia and the Pacific. *Dunmore, French Explorers in the Pacific, Vol. I (1969), pp. 283-341; Ferguson, 443, 461; Hill, p.97; Wantrup, 64a-64b.*

[165] [D'ENTRECASTEAUX]. HULOT, Le Baron. D'ENTRECASTEAUX 1737-1793. *Octavo, with 4 portraits, and folding map; modern blue cloth; light foxing to end papers, with presentation inscription from the author on half title.* Paris, Société de Géographie, 1894.

An important biography. Very scarce. *Not in Ferguson; not in Hill.*

A PRESENTATION COPY

[166] DILLON, Peter. NARRATIVE AND SUCCESSFUL RESULT OF A VOYAGE IN THE SOUTH SEAS, performed by order of the Government of British India, to ascertain the actual fate of La Perouse's Expedition, interspersed with accounts of the religion, manners, customs and cannibal practices of the South Sea Islanders. *2 volumes, octavo, 2 folding lithographs (1 coloured), plate of a canoe, folding map; contemporary green panelled morocco, rebacked; armorial bookplates of the 13th Earl of Derby (1775-1851), with presentation inscription to the 13th Earl and date 1841 on front blank leaf of Vol. I and further marked "garden library" which may account for the light foxing.* London, Hurst, Chance, 1829.

First edition: a presentation copy. Forty years after the disappearance of La Perouse, Peter Dillon, a

sandalwood trader, called at the Solomons, and when a silver sword guard was brought out, suspected he had stumbled on the solution. He returned to India, persuaded the government of Bengal to sponsor an expedition and sailed to the Solomons via Tasmania, New Zealand and Tonga. At Vanikoro, he conducted a careful investigation among the natives regarding the shipwrecks, and was able to obtain many relics including a portion of the stern of the *Boussole*, ships' bells stamped "Bazin m'a fait", monogrammed silver, metal fragments and mill stones known to have been aboard. One native (depicted on a folding plate) had a glass piece from a thermometer in his nose. On the successful receipt of his report and this material in France, Dillon was made a Chevalier of the Legion of Honour, his expenses defrayed and granted a pension.

Dillon, described as "eccentric, quick of temper and with a vivid vocabulary" (Dunmore), includes a scathing examination of the legal system of Tasmania and New South Wales. Aboard ship had been a Dr. Robert Tytler with whom relations were so strained that Dillon was accused of insanity, the doctor in turn arrested for attempts to incite mutiny, and upon arrival at Hobartown, assault charges were placed against Dillon and the ship sequestered. Over 40 pages relate to the questionable legal proceedings between judge and governor, and the appendix reprints articles from Australian and Indian sources on Dillon's treatment in what he called a "land of corruption and injustice". *Ferguson, 1255; Hill, pp. 83-84.*

[167] DILLON, Peter. VOYAGE AUX ILES DE LA MER DU SUD, en 1827 et 1828, et Rélation de la Découverte du Sort de La Pérouse. *2 volumes, octavo, modern half calf antique with 3 lithograph plates (2 folding) and chart of the island of Mannicolo, title-pages repaired where library stamps have been removed, text fine and free from spotting.* Paris, Chez Pillet Ainé . . . 1830.

First French edition. This edition contains a dedication to Charles X, King of France, and the attractive plates are by Engelmann, the inventor of lithography. *Ferguson, 1336; Hill, p. 84.*

IX
The Northwest Coast

As a result of Cook's discoveries on the Northwest coast of America, the King George's Sound Company was formed in London on 1st May 1785 by Richard Cadman Eitches and other traders, for the purpose of fur trading between the Northwest coast of America and China.

They obtained a licence from the South Sea Company and another from the East India Company, and fitted out two ships, the King George and the Queen Charlotte. Although both began and ended together, and overlapped in parts, their voyages are essentially different as, although their motive was commercial, important geographical discoveries were made by each. Both captains had previously sailed with Cook on his third voyage: Portlock as master's mate on the Discovery, and Dixon as petty officer on the Resolution. Portlock was to make a further Pacific voyage in command of the Assistant brig, tender to the Providence on her voyage to the Pacific to bring breadfruit plants to the West Indies.

John Meares was sent out from India by a group of merchants under a foreign fiat to avoid paying a duty to the English monopoly. He established a settlement at Nootka and engaged Colnett to join him in the enterprise. When the Spanish, attempting to enforce their rights in the area, seized Meares' ships, the resulting clash led to the "Nootka Controversy", settled in 1790 by a convention between England and Spain, which virtually guaranteed Britain's supremacy in the area. French interests in the Northwest are also reflected in La Pérouse's voyage, which explored the coast in 1788, as well as in the explorations of Marchand, on the first French commercial voyage to the Northwest coast in 1791.

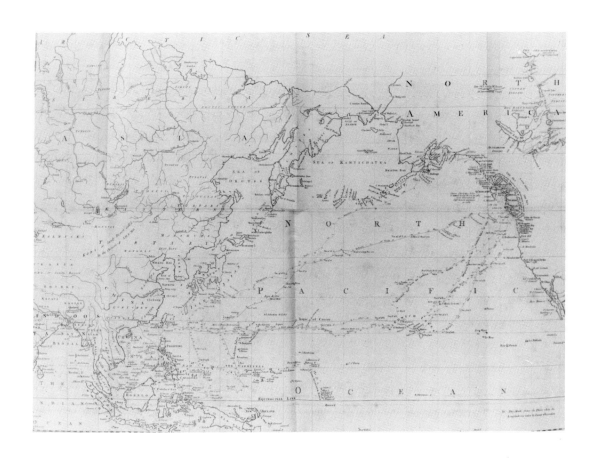

WITH CONTEMPORARY ANNOTATIONS THROUGHOUT

[168] BROUGHTON, William Robert. A VOYAGE OF DISCOVERY TO THE NORTH PACIFIC OCEAN... Performed in His Majesty's Sloop Providence and her tender, in the years 1795, 1796, 1797, 1798. *Quarto, half calf antique, contemporary stamps of the "Royal Astronomical Society" and "Smithfields Mathematical Society" on title-page, and with contemporary manuscript annotations throughout.* London, Printed for T. Cadell and W. Davies, 1804.

First edition of the work upon which Great Britain based her claim to the Oregon Territory in 1846. Broughton, commander of Bligh's old ship the *Providence*, was ordered to the Northwest Coast of America to join Captain Vancouver. He sailed to Nootka Sound via Rio de Janeiro, Australia, Tahiti and the Hawaiian Islands. His stop in Australia in August 1795 included a week at Port Stephens where he found four white men whom he described as "miserable half starved objects, depending on the hospitality of the natives...". A short visit was also made to Port Jackson. When he did not find Vancouver at Nootka, he headed down the coast to Monterey and across the Pacific, visiting Hawaii again enroute. For four years he surveyed the coasts of Asia and the islands of Japan and produced important maps of Japan, Korea and Formosa, off which coast the *Providence* was wrecked. Hill calls it a "scarce and exceedingly important work".

This is an interesting copy. Though the extensive annotations are nowhere identified, it is obvious they were made by someone intimately connected with the voyage, perhaps even John Crossley the astronomer aboard ship. The text has been altered and corrected throughout, particularly the nautical readings which have been also compared with those of other voyages, and their discrepancies explained. An entry on p. 94 is a fair example: where the printed text reads "Our watches this day differed so considerably that we could place no dependence upon them...", the owner of this copy has noted in manuscript "The altitudes of the Sun observed this day by Mr. Haywood are very erroneous, which is the cause of the watches giving the Longitude so differently this day from the preceding ones". *Ferguson, 389; Hill, pp. 35-36; Lada-Mocarski, 59 "extremely rare... of prime importance".*

FIRST FRENCH EDITION

[169] BROUGHTON, William Robert. VOYAGE DE DECOUVERTES DANS LA PARTIE SEPTENTRIONALE DE L'OCEAN PACIFIQUE... pendant les années 1795, 1796, 1797 et 1798. *2 volumes, octavo, with 6 folding maps, charts and profile views and 1 plate; contemporary black half morocco, gilt spines.* Paris, Dentu, 1807.

First French edition of this important Pacific voyage: a very fine copy.

[170] COLNETT, James. A VOYAGE TO THE SOUTH ATLANTIC AND ROUND CAPE HORN INTO THE PACIFIC OCEAN, for the purpose of extending the Spermacetti Whale Fisheries, and other objects of commerce, by ascertaining the Ports, Bays, Harbours, and Anchoring

Births in certain islands and coasts in those seas at which the ships of the British merchants might be refitted. *Quarto, with 9 folding maps, charts and plates; original cloth; a good modern facsimile.* London, Printed for the author, by W. Bennett, 1798. [Amsterdam, Nico Israel, 1968].

The main portion of this narrative by Colnett, one of the principal players in the Northwest coast drama concerns his voyage in the *Rattler* around South America, and includes accounts of the islands off that coast. The lengthy preface contains Colnett's account of his previous activities in the Pacific, during which he made two voyages to China laden with furs from the Northwest coast, and figured largely in the dispute between England and Spain. *Hill, p. 58.*

WITH PORTLOCK AND MEARES AT NOOTKA SOUND

[171] DIXON, Captain George. A VOYAGE ROUND THE WORLD; but more particularly to the North-West Coast of America: performed in 1785, 1786, 1787, and 1788, in the King George and Queen Charlotte by Captains Portlock and Dixon. *Quarto, with 21 maps and plates (of which 7 folding), including the indian song plate facing p. 243; contemporary tree calf, raised spines, red label; top of spine sympathetically repaired; a fine clean copy, complete with the often missing half title, in an attractive contemporary binding.* London, Published by Geo. Goulding, 1789.

Dixon's account of his voyage in the *Queen Charlotte*, dedicated to Sir Joseph Banks, forms a companion to Portlock's account (see no. 180). The ships sailed together as far as Prince William Sound. There they parted on May 15, 1787. Dixon followed the coast making a series of landfalls, discovered and closely observed Queen Charlotte's Island, and entered Dixon's Straits, before ultimately arriving at Nootka where he joined both Portlock and Meares.

168: BROUGHTON. *The knowledgeable annotations in this copy of Broughton's* Voyage *may be by the expedition's astronomer.*

169: BROUGHTON. *The first French edition of Broughton's* Voyage.

171: DIXON. *View of the Volcano, Cook's River; engraving from Dixon's* Voyage.

The *Queen Charlotte* made two visits to Hawaii, in November-December 1786 and September 1787, trading at Oahu and Kauai. The book includes a long account of commercial transactions at Canton. Though often catalogued as the work of William Beresford whose letters to a friend signed W.B. form the basis of this work, Dixon added substantially to the text and edited the whole. *Hill, p. 23; Judd, 53; Lada-Mocarski, no. 43.*

FIRST FRENCH EDITION

[172] DIXON, Capt. George. VOYAGE AUTOUR DU MONDE, et Principalement à la cote Nord-Ouest de l'Amerique, fait en 1785, 1786, 1787 et 1788, à bord du King-George et de la Queen-Charlotte, par les Capitaines Portlock et Dixon. *Quarto, with folding chart of the voyage and 20 plates, maps and charts (including the indian song plate); half calf antique, light rubbing to boards, internally a clean bright copy.* Paris, chez Maradan, 1789.

First French edition. *Judd, 53.*

PRESENTATION COPY

[173] FRANCHERE, Gabriel. NARRATIVE OF A VOYAGE TO THE NORTHWEST COAST OF AMERICA in the years 1811, 1812, 1813 and 1814. Or the first American settlement on the Pacific. *Octavo, with 3 woodcuts; original dark green cloth, rebacked, preserving all original spine, with presentation inscription from the author to Joseph Houquet on title page; enclosed in a dark green morocco backed box; a fine copy.* New York, Redfield, 1854.

First edition in English: a key Northwest coast narrative. Franchere was a member of the party sent out by John Jacob Astor on the *Tonquin* to found a fur trading post at Astoria, at the mouth of the Columbia River. Hill calls it "the most important source for the adventures of Astor's Pacific Fur Company". The account of his three year stay, his inland travels, the transfer of Astor's company to the North West Fur Company of Canada in 1813 and subsequent actions of the British, is lengthy and important.

On the way out, the *Tonquin* stopped in Hawaii, in February 1811, and Franchere gives a good account of the customs and political situation in the islands as well as a biography of Kamehameha I.

This work became a key in the boundary disputes, and was referred to by Senator Benton in his famous Oregon Question speech in the United States Senate, May 1846. *Hill, p. 110-111; Judd, 69.*

[174] HOWAY, Frederick W. THE DIXON-MEARES CONTROVERSY. Containing, Remarks on the Voyages of John Meares by George Dixon, An Answer to Mr. George Dixon, by John Meares, and Further Remarks on the Voyages of John Meares, by George Dixon. *Octavo, with 2 maps, illustration and facsimiles of title-pages; original cloth; a good modern facsimile.* Toronto, The Ryerson Press, n.d., circa 1929. [Amsterdam, Nico Israel, 1969].

The great pamphlet war of the Northwest Coast. Soon after the publication of Meares' *Voyage*, Dixon issued a pamphlet charging him with false statements; Meares answered in an attempt to free himself from the allegations and charged that Dixon failed to respond to his requests for aid on the seizure of his ships by the Spanish. Dixon countered with *Further Remarks*. The original pamphlets are of the greatest rarity.

[175] HOWAY, Frederick W. VOYAGES OF THE "COLUMBIA" to the Northwest Coast 1787-1790 and 1790-1793. *Octavo, with a map and 11 illustrations; original cloth; a good modern facsimile.* Boston, The Massachusetts Historical Society, 1941. [Amsterdam, Nico Israel, 1969].

As a result of the publication of Cook's third voyage, a group of Boston merchants, led by Joseph Barrell, realised the immense profits to be made in Northwest Coast furs as a means of developing trade with China. In 1787, six partners purchased and outfitted the *Columbia Rediviva* and the *Lady Washington* and both set sail from Boston for the Northwest coast on September 30, 1787. The *Washington*, commanded by John Kendrick, never saw Boston again, but the *Columbia* became the first ship to carry the American flag around the world. The *Columbia* sailed again in 1790-1793.

This work includes Logs, Narratives and miscellaneous papers relating to the voyage of the two ships, and the second voyage of the *Columbia*.

FROM THE LIBRARY OF JEROME BONAPARTE

[176] [MARCHAND] FLEURIEU, Charles Pierre Claret de. VOYAGE AUTOUR DU MONDE, pendant les années 1790, 1791, et 1792, par Etienne Marchand, précédé d'une introduction historique; auquel on a joint des recherches sur les terres australes de Drake, et un examen critique du voyage de Roggeween. *4 volumes, quarto, with folding table in volume I, and 15 folding engraved maps, and 1 plate in volume IV; original half red morocco, pink glazed boards, slight wear to boards, a few corners bumped, slight insect holes to gutters of several volumes, occasional light spotting to text, but a fine crisp, large paper copy, with the gilt cypher of Jerome Bonaparte on spines.* Paris, de l'Imprimerie de la République, An VI-VIII [1798-1800].

The first French commercial voyage to the Northwest coast, and only the second French circumnavigation in the course of a single voyage. Marchand, on his return from Bengal in 1788, met Portlock at St. Helena, and learned of the lucrative fur trade between the Northwest coast and China. The trading firm of Baux in Marseilles underwrote the expedition, and purchased and fitted out the copper sheathed ship, the *Solide*. After a delay due to the Nootka dispute between England and Spain, the ship sailed in December 1790 via Cape Horn. At the Marquesas, Marchand took possession of two islands, Uapou and Nukuhiva (which he named "Ile Baux") not knowing of Ingraham's visit on the *Hope* two months earlier (and which the world at large was not to know until details of Ingraham's voyage became known — see item 274). At the Northwest coast he obtained a large cargo of furs, sailed south to Hawaii, through the Marianas and reached Macao November 27, 1791.

Marchand was unable to sell the furs in China, and upon his return to France, they were impounded during the counter-revolutionary movement in southern France, and eventually perished, the firm of Baux thereby losing two-thirds of their capital in the venture. Nevertheless, Marchand proved that in times of peace, the French could compete successfully in the Pacific trade. As Marchand died in 1793, the work was actually written by Count Charles Pierre Fleurieu, himself an explorer. It includes a good account of discoveries along the American coast, from Cortes in 1537 to Malaspina in 1790, including records of Drake, Juan de Fuca, Cook, La Perouse, Meares, Colnett, Portlock and Dixon. Considerable text is devoted to descriptions of natural history specimens collected enroute. The final volume contains a critical analysis of Roggeween's voyage, and the engraved plates include 5 of Alaska and the Northwest coast, 4 of Marquesan interest and 1 of Hawaii, while the China Sea chart contains important corrections. Lada-Mocarski calls it "a very important and authoritative work for the history of the Northwest coast".

A remarkable copy, from the library of Jerome Bonaparte, on very large paper: measuring 320 x 240 mm., it is larger than the fine Lada-Mocarski copy by nearly 15 mm. *Hill, pp. 105-6; Lada-Mocarski, 54; see also Dunmore, French Explorers in the Pacific, pp. 342-353, for a discussion of the voyage and its importance.*

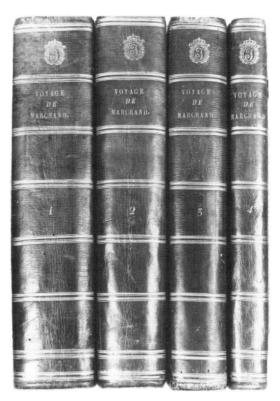

FROM THE LIBRARY OF THE RUSSIAN IMPERIAL GENERAL STAFF

[177] [MARCHAND] FLEURIEU, Charles Pierre Claret de. VOYAGE AUTOUR DU MONDE, pendant les années 1790, 1791, et 1792, par Etienne Marchand, précédé d'une introduction historique; auquel on a joint des recherches sur les terres australes de Drake, et un examen critique du voyage de Roggeween. *4 volumes, quarto, with folding table in volume I, and 15 folding engraved maps and 1 plate in volume IV; original half calf, red labels, marbled boards, extremities of spines expertly repaired, library stamp and cancel on title-pages.* Paris, de l'Imprimerie de la République, An VI-VIII [1798-1800].

A fine copy, from the library of the Russian Imperial General Staff, with their bookplate — a particularly apt provenance as so much of the history of the Northwest coast concerns the struggle between the French and the Russians, and so much of the Russians' exploring soon to come was prompted by their commercial interest in the west coast of America.

THE NOOTKA CONTROVERSY

[178] MEARES, John. VOYAGES MADE IN THE YEARS 1788 AND 1789, FROM CHINA TO THE NORTH WEST COAST OF AMERICA. To which are prefixed, An Introductory Narrative of a Voyage performed in 1786, from Bengal, in the ship Nootka; observations on the probable existence of a North West Passage; and some account of the trade between the North West Coast of America and China; and the latter country and Great Britain. *Quarto, with frontispiece portrait, 7 maps and charts and 21 plates; contemporary tree calf, rebacked, maroon label, light occasional spotting as usual; contemporary signature on title page; a very good copy.* London, Printed at the Logographic Press, 1790.

"One of the early and fundamental books on the

176: MARCHAND. *Jerome Bonaparte's splendid copy of the Marchand voyage.*

177: MARCHAND. *The bookplate in the Russian Imperial General Staff copy of the Marchand voyage.*

178: MEARES. Engraved portrait of the voyager John Meares from his account of his travels.

Northwest coast of America in general and on Alaska in particular" (Lada-Mocarski). Meares made two fur trading voyages. The first, sponsored by Bengal merchants, included the ships *Nootka* and the *Sea Otter* and sailed from Calcutta on March 2, 1786. Meares reached Alaska and visited Kodiak, but was constantly frustrated by the presence of the Russians. On the Northwest coast he met Portlock and Dixon. In June 1787 he sailed to Hawaii and continued on to Canton.

His second voyage to the American coast was to alter the course of history. In 1788 he determined to establish a permanent fur trading settlement at Nootka, and engaged Colnett of the *Argonaut* and Hudson of the *Princess Royal* to accompany him. Shortly after arrival, the ships *Iphigenia*, *Argonaut* and *Princess Royal* were seized by a Spanish frigate, and the resulting action, known as the "Nootka Controversy" nearly precipitated a war between England and Spain. The appendices contain letters and instructions, Duffin's journal while exploring the Straits of Juan de Fuca, July 1788, and Meares' *Memorial to the House of Commons* of May 13, 1790, claiming exclusive rights to Nootka and the prior raising of the British flag.

Meares' account was central to British claims to the Northwest territory and led to the convention by which Spain's claim was finally disallowed. *Hill, p. 195; Judd, 123; Lada-Mocarski, 46.*

CARRIED ON BAUDIN'S VOYAGE

[179] [MEARES] VOYAGES A LA CHINE A LA COTE NORT-OUEST D'AMERIQUE, fait dans les années 1788 et 1789. . . Traduite de l'Anglois par J.B.L. Billecocq, citoyen Francais. *3 volumes, octavo; full contemporary tree calf, gilt spines, blue endpapers; volume III spine neatly repaired, library stamps removed from title pages at an early date, with "La Corvette Le Naturaliste" in ink on each title of text; light spotting of text. [with] Quarto atlas, with separate title leaf and 28 plates, maps and charts (part folding); contemporary mottled calf, gilt spine, red morocco title label, marble endpapers.* Paris, chez F. Buisson, An 3e de la Republique [1794].

First French edition, and of extraordinary association interest, being the copy carried on the Baudin expedition to Australia and the Pacific; it travelled in the ship's library on the corvette *Naturaliste* commanded by Jacques-Felix-Emmanuel Hamelin, the second ship under Baudin's command.

All expeditions were routinely fitted out with scientific libraries which included the most important and relevant voyages and travels. In the detailed list of supplies furnished by "citizen Fonchevreuil" to the *Naturaliste*, Case 48 contained Cook's *Voyages*, Dalrymple, Bougainville, Macartney, Phillip's *Voyage*, Bligh's *Voyage of the Bounty* and this copy of Meares. (See *The Journal of Post Captain Nicolas Baudin. . . Translated by Christine Cornell*, Adelaide, 1974, Appendix VII, p. 592).

Copies of voyages actually carried aboard ship are of the utmost rarity, as most would have remained official libaries; we do not know of any other such examples. A fine copy of an important Pacific voyage, carried and used on one of the most important voyages to Australia.

THE COMMANDER'S ACCOUNT OF THE EXPEDITION

[180] PORTLOCK, Captain Nathaniel. A VOYAGE ROUND THE WORLD; but more particularly to the North-West Coast of America: performed in 1785, 1786, 1787, and 1788, in the King George and Queen Charlotte. . . by Captain Nathaniel Portlock. *Quarto; contemporary russia, rebacked, with frontispiece portrait, and 19 maps, plans and plates; title page and plates foxed with some offsetting to text, but with the natural history plates in colour; armorial bookplates.* London, Printed for John Stockdale, 1789.

Portlock, in command of the expedition, sailed on the *King George* in 1785, to the Northwest coast. There, he and Dixon went up the Cooks River, past Kodiak Island and cruised around Montague Island and Prince William Sound, looking for furs. There they parted, Portlock sailing directly to Nootka. His stay at Nootka was longer than that of Dixon and the narrative is "of great value" (Hill) and contains vivid encounters with the American Indians and the Russians. Portlock's chart, published almost five months after that of Dixon does not show the Queen Charlotte Islands, thus giving Dixon full credit for their discovery.

The *King George* made two stops in Hawaii in 1786, and another in 1787, trading there at Hawaii, Oahau, Kauai and Niihau. Portlock made extensive notes on trading, the chiefs, the death of Cook and the development of the Islands since his visit with Cook on the *Discovery*.

Portlock's notes on a mutiny aboard the *Belvedere* while at Whampoa and the subsequent Court of Inquiry are curious when it is recalled that he was later to sail with Bligh. *Hill, p. 239; Judd, 147; Lada-Mocarski, 42.*

X
The Missionaries

PREVIOUS PAGE:
182: DUFF VOYAGE: *The cession of Matavai; engraving by Bartolozzi after Smirke.*

At the end of the eighteenth century, the Pacific was effectively waiting to be taken. Colonisation had begun — in Australia and elsewhere — but the next thrust was to come from a surprising direction. If the greatest cliché of the early discovery of the Pacific Islands is the 'noble savage', its equivalent in the post-Cook period is the mission house; the activities of the missionaries were far wider than this, however, in their effect: to a large extent they were to determine the political boundaries of the Pacific.

"In 1795 a group of evangelists formed the London Missionary Society . . . Thomas Haweis, one of the founders, preached the opening sermon on 'the innumerable islands which spot the bosom of the Pacific Ocean'; where 'savage nature still feasts on the flesh of its prisoners —appeases its gods with human sacrifices — whole societies of men and women live promiscuously and murder every infant born among them' . . ."

The voyage of the Duff *effectively ended the age of innocence for the Pacific islanders. As Alan Moorehead notes, the missionaries "were not collectors like Banks, nor were they concerned with scientific discoveries of any kind, nor had they any of Cook's tolerance and gift for compromise. They were practical workers in the cause of the Lord, and they were determined to recreate the island in the image of lower-middle-class Protestant England.*

"It was a strange boatload that drew up to the black sand beaches of Matavai Bay in March 1797 after sailing nearly 14,000 miles without sighting land, perhaps the longest ocean journey ever known. The company of thirty-nine included only four ordained clergymen, the rest being made up of butchers, carpenters, weavers, tailors, harness-makers, bricklayers, shopkeepers and domestic servants. There were also six wives and three children . . ."

BELOW:
181: DUFF VOYAGE. *Map of the Fiji Islands from the official account of the voyage of the* Duff.

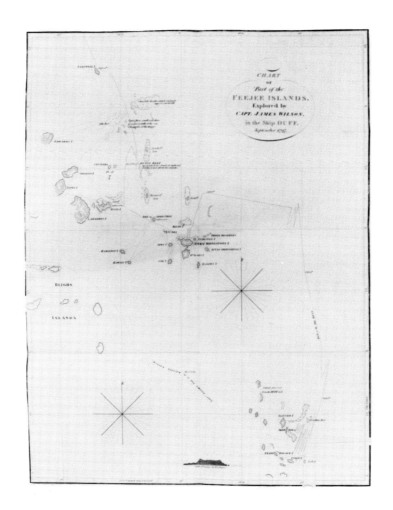

THE FIRST MISSIONARY VOYAGE TO THE PACIFIC

[181] [DUFF VOYAGE] HAWEIS, Thomas, *editor*. A MISSIONARY VOYAGE TO THE SOUTHERN PACIFIC OCEAN, performed in the years 1796, 1797, 1798, in the Ship Duff, commanded by Captain James Wilson. Compiled from Journals of the Officers and the Missionaries. . . With a Preliminary Discourse on the Geography and History of the South Sea Islands and an Appendix, including details never before published, of the Natural and Civil State of Otaheite. . . *Quarto, with 6 plates and 7 maps, of which 5 are folding; some sporadic foxing, mainly affecting the maps; a large copy, on fine paper, in contemporary russia, corners worn, old rebacking, all edges gilt; from the library of the Earl of Derby, with his bookplate.* London, Printed by S. Gosnell, for T. Chapman, 1799.

First edition of the full official account of the first missionary voyage to the South Pacific.

The *Duff* set out for Tahiti in 1796, but visited many island groups, including particularly Tonga and the Marquesas. A new group of islands, the "Duff Group", was discovered among the Santa Cruz islands. The maps here include a large chart of the Fiji islands as well as charts of Tongataboo, the Gambier Islands, the Marquesas, Tahiti and the Duff Group; the plates include an engraved view of Rio de Janeiro.

There is much of Australian interest in the account of the voyage including a mention of escaped Botany Bay convicts, and the flight of several missionaries from Tonga, where three were killed, to Sydney. Some of the missionaries made their homes in Australia and founded families later to become important in Australian history. *Ferguson, 301; Hill, p. 184; Kroepelien, 528.*

ENGRAVED BY BARTOLOZZI

[182] [DUFF VOYAGE] SMIRKE, R. (*after*). THE CESSION OF THE DISTRICT OF MATAVAI IN THE ISLAND OF OTAHEITE to Captain James Wilson for the use of the Missionaries sent thither by that Society in the Ship Duff. Is most respectfully Dedicated by their most obedient Servants, Will, Jeffreys & Co. To the Treasurer and Directors of the London Missionary Society. *Hand coloured engraving, framed.* Painted by R. Smirke, R.A., London, Jan. 1st, 1803.

A fine, separately issued print, engraved by Bartolozzi after Smirke's original oil painting, a sketch for which is held in the National Library, Canberra. Captain Wilson (1760-1814) was master of the missionary ship *Duff*, despatched by the newly formed London Missionary Society in 1796. Trouble arose with natives in Tonga and three of the missionaries were killed, while others were compelled to seek refuge in Sydney.

PRESENTATION COPY: HAWAIIAN (AND SURFING) CLASSIC

[183] ELLIS, Rev. William. NARRATIVE OF A TOUR THROUGH HAWAII, OR OWHYHEE; with remarks on the History, traditions, manners, customs and language of the inhabitants of the Sandwich Islands. *Octavo, frontispiece portrait, folding map of Hawaii and 7 engraved plates; contemporary calf, rebacked, preserving all original spine, occasional spotting; with contemporary ms. inscription "from the Author. London, May 1826" to the missionary Charles Stewart.* London, Published for the Author, by H. Fisher, Son and P. Jackson, 1826.

First edition in this form: one of the most important books on Hawaii. Ellis, who had recently arrived after a long residence in the Society Islands, joined a deputation of missionaries making a tour of the island from June to September 1823. The purpose was to select eligible sites for mission stations, also to observe "the structure of the island, its geographical character, natural scenery, productions, and objects of curiosity. . . traditions, manners and customs of the inhabitants". All of this Ellis was to accomplish due to his familiarity with a similar language. One of his informants was Governor Kuakini of Kailua with whom he frequently conversed "on the history and traditions of the island".

Ellis' narrative contains one of the earliest detailed descriptions of surfing in chapter 13 where he describes the sport itself, its popularity amongst the islanders, the use of a *papa he nalu* or "wave sliding board" five or six feet long which is greased with coconut oil. "Those who are expert frequently change their position on the board, sometimes sitting and sometimes standing erect in the midst of the foam. . . we have seen Karaimoku and Kaikiowe, some of the highest chiefs in the island, both between 50 and 60 years of age, and large corpulent men, bouncing themselves on their narrow board, or splashing about in the foam, with as much satisfaction as youths of sixteen."

An earlier version appeared in Boston in 1825, but this is so extensively revised and enlarged as to make it virtually a new work. The engraved plates include views of the City of Refuge, a Hula performance and the Volcano. *Hill, II, p. 413.*

[184] ELLIS, Rev. William. NARRATIVE OF A TOUR THROUGH HAWAII, OR OWHYHEE; with observations on the natural history of the Sandwich Islands, and remarks on the manners, customs, traditions, history and language of their inhabitants. *Octavo, frontispiece portrait and one of the plates somewhat foxed; a good uncut copy in the original boards, spine and paper label replaced.* London, H. Fisher [and 8 others], 1827.

Second edition, enlarged and with some revisions. This popular account of Hawaii also appeared in a third edition in the same year. *This edition not in the catalogue of the Hill collection.*

[185] [ELLIS] [SANDERS, Mrs. Elizabeth Elkins]. REMARKS ON THE "TOUR AROUND HAWAII", by the missionaries Messrs. Ellis, Thurston, Bishop and Goodrich, in 1823. *Octavo, 42 pp.; original printed wrappers; apart from slight soiling to covers and browning to top edge, a fine copy.* Salem [Massachusetts], Printed by the Author, 1848.

A very rare and curious review of William Ellis' classic *Tour of the Hawaiian Islands* (see no. 183). The authoress, Mrs. Sanders (1762-1851) was a noted

185: SANDERS. *An unusual attack on the role of the missionaries in Hawaii.*

REMARKS

ON THE

"TOUR AROUND HAWAII,"

BY THE MISSIONARIES,

MESSRS. ELLIS, THURSTON, BISHOP, AND GOODRICH,

IN

1823.

SALEM:
PRINTED FOR THE AUTHOR.
1848.

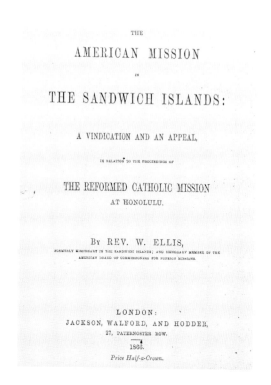

THE

AMERICAN MISSION

IN

THE SANDWICH ISLANDS:

A VINDICATION AND AN APPEAL,

IN RELATION TO THE PROCEEDINGS OF

THE REFORMED CATHOLIC MISSION

AT HONOLULU.

BY REV. W. ELLIS,

FORMERLY MISSIONARY IN THE SANDWICH ISLANDS; AND HONORARY MEMBER OF THE
AMERICAN BOARD OF COMMISSIONERS FOR FOREIGN MISSIONS.

LONDON:
JACKSON, WALFORD, AND HODDER,
27, PATERNOSTER ROW.
1866.
Price Half-a-Crown.

190: ELLIS. *The English edition of Ellis' work on the Hawaiian mission.*

philanthropist, social reformer and proponent of the rights of native American indians.

Mrs. Sanders was pleased to learn from Ellis' *Narrative* that "although these natives had suffered much from their intercourse with civilized man", they still retained "a portion of those primitive virtues, which had engaged the respect and sympathy of the wise and good". She was dismayed to read the appendix which enumerated all "their odious vices" which she reported "can be found to exist in every country, although practised in secret". She makes frequent reference to the Wilkes narrative, not only in reference to Hawaii, but also in discussing Tonga and Burma.

"Nothing is more calculated to excite in the natives, bad passions, than to be debarred from all their innocent and useful recreations. . . and to insist on their passing the Sabbath and some other days in perfect inactivity, thus leading them to the practice of secret vices which they would have once shuddered to commit".

History is silent as to the reasons for this review and its tardy appearance.

TAHITI BY ONE OF THE MOST PERCEPTIVE OF THE MISSIONARIES

[186] ELLIS, William. POLYNESIAN RESEARCHES, during a residence of nearly six years in the South Sea Islands; including descriptions of the natural history and scenery of the islands — with remarks on the history, mythology, traditions, government, arts, manners, and customs of the inhabitants. *2 volumes, octavo, with portrait of Pomare, 2 folding maps, 7 engraved plates and 16 wood engravings; modern half blue calf, red labels; light foxing of text, and slight darkening of endpapers.* London, Fisher, Son & Jackson, 1829.

First edition: one of the most important works on the history and ethnology of the Society Islands, by

one of the most perceptive of the missionary travellers in the Pacific. The work begins with the author's voyage in which he visited and described Rio de Janeiro, Sydney, and New Zealand. He was in Tahiti from 1816 to 1822, during which time very little seems to have escaped his notice. A very popular and influential work, its publication "went far to redeem the character of missionaries in the eyes of those who had thought of them as ignorant and narrow minded men" (Hill). *Not in Ferguson; Hill, p. 96; Judd, 61 (listing the 1831 edition).*

AN UNCUT COPY

[187] ELLIS, William. POLYNESIAN RESEARCHES, during a Residence of nearly six years in the South Sea Islands. . . *2 volumes, octavo, with portrait, 2 folding maps, 7 plates and 16 wood engravings; modern half calf, uncut.* London, Fisher, Son & Jackson, 1829.

First edition; a fine uncut copy.

[188] [ELLIS, William] ELLIS, John Eimeo. LIFE OF WILLIAM ELLIS, missionary to the South Seas and to Madagascar. By his son John Eimeo Ellis. With a supplementary chapter. . . by Henry Allom. *Octavo, frontispiece portrait; original decorated plum cloth, black endpapers, slight fading of spine, uncut and partially unopened; a fine copy.* London, John Murray, 1873.

The only biography to date of this famous and important missionary, with much information not otherwise available.

AMERICAN MISSIONARIES IN HAWAII

[189] ELLIS, Rev. William. THE AMERICAN MISSION IN THE SANDWICH ISLANDS; a vindication and an appeal, in relation to the proceedings of the Reformed Catholic Mission at Honolulu. *Octavo, original half black calf, green printed boards; some browning to covers and blank leaves, but a very good copy; scarce.* Honolulu, H. M. Whitney, 1866.

A plea against the intrusion by the Church of England into a missionary sphere for forty years occupied by another body of Christians. Ellis, a distinguished member of the London Missionary Society, and a former missionary to Hawaii (1823-1824) here draws on his great knowledge of the subject to demolish the 14 reasons set forth by the English church for the formation of a mission, and includes the original letters from Hawaii requesting English clergymen. His text includes much information on local customs and history of the islands.

AN IMPORTANT ASSOCIATION COPY

[190] ELLIS, William. THE AMERICAN MISSION IN THE SANDWICH ISLANDS. A vindication and an appeal. *Octavo, stitched as issued, lacking back wrapper, slight soiling of upper wrapper and last page of text, else very good.* London, Jackson, Walford and Hodder, 1866.

Presentation copy from the author to James Hunnewell of Boston, one of the most influential supporters of the American Mission in Hawaii, and founder in 1826 of the oldest business house in

Hawaii, C. Brewer & Co. The English edition of this work is much scarcer than the Honolulu edition.

"SLANDERS TRIUMPHANTLY REFUTED"

[191] [EVARTS, Jeremiah]. An Examination of Charges against the American Missionaries at the Sandwich Islands, as alleged in the Voyage of the Ship Blonde, and in the London Quarterly Review. *Octavo, 67 [+ last blank] pp.; original buff wrappers, wrappers chipped, occasional marginal tears to text, but withal a fine copy of a very rare pamphlet.* Cambridge [Mass.], Hilliard, Metcalf and Company, 1827.

An important review of the published accounts of the voyage of HMS *Blonde*, and in itself a significant account of mission activities in the central Pacific.

Evarts (1781-1831) was one of the principal founders and corresponding Secretary (1821-1831) of the American Board of Commissioners for Foreign Missions, the governing body of American protestant missions worldwide, and had an intimate knowledge of mission affairs. Remarks in Byron's voyage are contrasted with statements made by William Ellis, and the Rev. C. S. Stewart; the article was written in answer to an article published in the *London Quarterly*, which was also answered by Orme — see 194.

Evarts had ample materials to use to form his answer and his biographer crows that "never were slanders more triumphantly refuted, or the shallow arts of accusing ignorance and malice more thoroughly exposed". The account of the *Blonde*, he asserts, was "a booksellers' speculation prepared by another and unfriendly hand, from certain papers obtained from the chaplain of the Blonde"; the missionaries were treated with "contempt and calumny"; Bingham was not credited as the source of a native song in the appendix; another prayer had been copied directly from Mr. Stewart's journal but given as "from the missionaries". "Mrs. Graham calls herself the editor . . .", Evarts says, but "we should call her the fabricator . . .". The review first appeared in the *North American Review*, but is here re-printed with additional material. *Not in the catalogue of the Hill collection; see E.C. Tracy, "Memoir of the Life of Jeremiah Evarts", Boston, 1845.*

FRENCH SOVEREIGNTY AND THE MISSIONS

[192] LONDON MISSIONARY SOCIETY. Expose des Faits qui ont accompagné l'aggression des Francais contre l'Ile de Tahiti, par les Directeurs de la Société des Missions de Londres. Traduit de l'Anglais. *Octavo, viii, 80 pp., worm hole at base of extreme inner margin, well clear of all text, otherwise a fine uncut copy in the original wrappers.* Paris, L.-R. Delay, 1843.

Very scarce. This discussion of the issue of French sovereignty in Tahiti is collected and translated from publications of the London Missionary Society, and publishes material from various sources including Captain Fitzroy's address to the Missionary Society, details of the visit of the *Artemise* to Tahiti and the various manoeuvrings of its Captain, La Place; details on the Moerenhout incident, and other articles on the Catholic missions in Tahiti. *O'Reilly-Reitman, 7696; not in the catalogue of the Hill collection.*

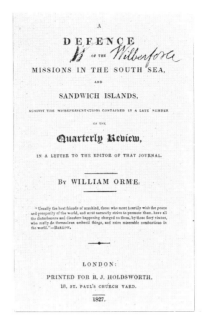

194: ORME. *The abolitionist William Wilberforce's copy of a defence of the Hawaiian missionaries.*

THE MISSIONARIES IN TAHITI

[193] LONDON MISSIONARY SOCIETY. REED, Andrew. The Case of Tahiti etc. An Appeal to the Constituents of the London Missionary Society, in reply to the "Statement of the Directors". *Octavo, (iv), 28 pp.; quarter calf.* London, Ward & Co., 1847.

Very scarce: continuing disputes on the role of the missionaries in Tahiti. *Not in O'Reilly; not in the catalogue of the Hill collection.*

DEFENDING THE HAWAIIAN MISSIONARIES

[194] ORME, William. A Defence of the Missions in the South Sea, and Sandwich Islands, against the misrepresentations contained in a late number of the Quarterly Review, in a letter to the editor of that journal. *Octavo, 142 [+ 2] + Advt. leaf; original boards, uncut, title label on upper cover, contemporary signature "W. Wilberforce" on cover and title-page; spine worn and joints cracked, but firm; a fine copy.* London, Printed for B. J. Holdsworth, 18 St. Paul's Churchyard, 1827.

A contemporary criticism of the published account of the voyage of HMS *Blonde*, and of the greatest importance regarding the first decade of American missionary activities in Hawaii. It was written in reply to the "Sandwich Islander", an article which appeared in the *Quarterly Review* for March 1827, which professed to be drawn up from *The Voyage of HMS Blonde*, from the *Narrative of a Tour Through Hawaii or Owhyhee*, by Ellis, and from unpublished letters of Captain Beechey. Orme calls the *Blonde* narrative "a piece of patch work", calls Beechey a "meddler" and exposes the famous letter from Chief Boki dated Woahoo January 24, 1826 in which he criticises the missionaries as a complete fabrication. The postscript (pp. 81-82) is made up of letters and press notices (including those from America) which "completely corroborate and authenticate the statements and reasonings of Mr. Orme's letter".

An interesting copy, owned by William Wilberforce (1759-1833) philanthropist, noted parliamentarian reformer, abolitionist and Evangelical

197: WILLIAMS. *This memorable portrait of the missionary John Williams was published shortly after his death at the hands of natives of the New Hebrides.*

Zealand and a long stay in New South Wales. The narrative contains a good description of Sydney, their travels to Parramatta, the Rev. Samuel Marsden, a female factory, Allan Cunningham the botanist, and their discussions on settling Mr. Threlkeld as a missionary to the aborigines near Bathurst. The last volume describes their travels to China, India and Madagascar.

Their visit to Hawaii on the *Mermaid* in 1822, was with fellow passenger Rev. William Ellis. Accompanying them was the schooner *Prince Regent* built at Port Jackson and presented to Kamehameha II as a gift from the King of England to fulfil a promise made by Vancouver to Kamehameha I. *Ferguson supplement, 1598a; Judd, 177 note; O'Reilly-Reitman, 802 (listing the English edition).*

QUAKER MISSIONARY VOYAGE

[196] WHEELER, Daniel. EXTRACTS FROM THE LETTERS AND JOURNAL OF DANIEL WHEELER, while engaged in a religious visit to the inhabitants of some of the Islands of the Pacific Ocean, Van Dieman's Land, New South Wales, and New Zealand. *Octavo, original brown blind stamped cloth, slight fading of spine, slight wear to top and bottom of spine, occasional light foxing as usual; with contemporary signature of Josiah B. Sharpless; a very good copy.* Philadelphia, Printed by Joseph Rakestraw, 1840.

First American edition. An account of a celebrated Quaker missionary voyage to the Pacific. The author, accompanied by his son Charles, sailed in the *Henry Freeling*, a Post Office packet, purchased and fitted out by the Society of Friends in London. They sailed from London in November 1833, went via the Cape of Good Hope, and made Hobart Town on September 10, 1834. Wheeler visited Sydney and Parramatta, and with James Backhouse, the celebrated reformer and naturalist, held meetings in Sydney and visited Norfolk Island. The most extensive portions of the text are devoted to travels through the Society, Tonga and Hawaiian Islands. This edition, corrected from the London edition, contains documents not previously published. *Ferguson, 3125; this edition not in the catalogue of the Hill collection; Judd, 187 (the London edition.)*

THE MISSIONARY COLLECTOR

[197] [WILLIAMS] ANELAY, Henry. REV. JOHN WILLIAMS. Missionary to the South Sea Islands. *Coloured lithograph, 49 x 35 cms., framed.* London, G. John Snow, n.d., circa 1840.

One of the most striking and memorable images of the missionaries in the Pacific: Williams is portrayed standing on board ship pointing to a collection of native artefacts from the South Seas.

Williams, regarded as the most enterprising missionary in the islands, paid a three month visit to Sydney in 1821 where he preached and addressed public meetings. In 1838 he returned and was influential in establishing the local Aborigines Protection Society. The following year he was violently killed by natives at Eromanga in the New Hebrides. *Nan Kivell, Portraits of the Famous and Infamous, p. 321.*

Christian, and one of the founders of the Church Missionary Society in 1798 (see DNB). *Not in the catalogue of the Hill collection.*

WITH KOTZEBUE IN TAHITI FOR THE CORONATION

[195] TYERMAN, Rev. Daniel and George BENNET. JOURNAL OF VOYAGES AND TRAVELS by the Rev. Daniel Tyerman and George Bennet, Esq. Deputed from the London Missionary Society, to visit their various stations in the South Sea Islands, China, India, &c. between the years 1821 and 1829. Compiled from original documents by James Montgomery. *3 volumes, octavo, with frontispiece portrait of Tyerman and 4 engraved plates of Tahiti and Hawaii; original tan glazed cloth, rebacked, preserving all original spines, paper title labels reading "Library of Religious Knowledge", occasional foxing as usual, but a fine untrimmed copy.* Boston, Crocker and Brewster, 1832.

First American edition, containing three letters and notes not in the first edition. The work was edited by Rev. Rufus Anderson, Secretary of the ABCFM in Boston, and contains his notes and additions bringing the Hawaii section up to 1830. The authors, travelling on the *Tuscan*, first made a thorough tour of the Society Islands (with a side trip to Hawaii) met Kotzebue at Huaheine and witnessed the coronation of Pomare III in 1824; made a short stay in New

XI
English Voyages
after Cook

PREVIOUS PAGE:
198: ARROWSMITH. *The fine engraved cartouche from Arrowsmith's immense nine-sheet map of the Pacific.*

The various nations which remained attentive to developing colonies and trade in the newly opened Pacific were rewarded by wealth and territory; the English quickly met the challenge set by the earlier navigators and excelled in exploration and colonial expansion. They were prominent in the South Sea sperm whale fishery business and traded in furs and other commodities. The official voyages increasingly followed the fashion for the intense study of ethnography and natural history, and they vied with the French for scientific recognition.

BELOW:
202: BEECHEY. *Map of the Pacific from the account of the* Blossom *voyage.*

Private commercial voyages became both more important and more frequent; as trading routes were established, more and better information was sent back to map publishers like Arrowsmith. The frontiers of geographical knowledge were pushed back further every year.

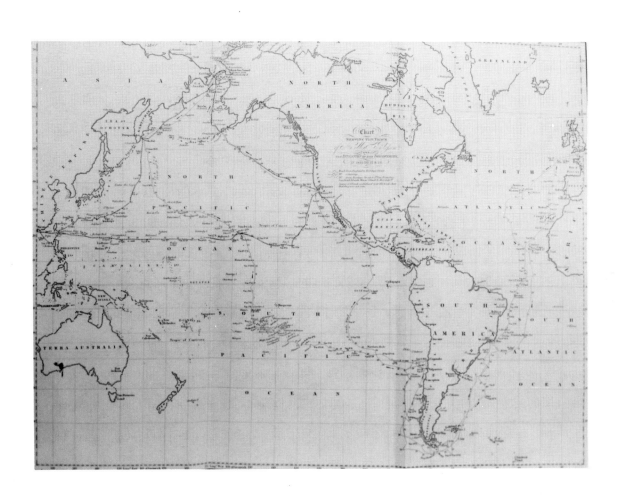

ARROWSMITH'S NINE-SHEET PACIFIC MAP

[198] ARROWSMITH, Aaron. CHART OF THE PACIFIC OCEAN. Drawn from a great number of Printed and MS. Journals by A. Arrowsmith. Engraved by George Allen. *9 sheets each 63 x 79 cms., with elaborately engraved cartouche of tropical scene surrounding title of map; the 9 sheets assembled to form the full map, measuring approximately 189 x 236 cms., and mounted on canvas; framed and glazed; in particularly good condition.* London, Published Oct. 1st 1798; additions to 1810 and 1814.

A fine copy: perhaps the greatest of all Pacific maps. First published in 1798, the Arrowsmith *Chart of the Pacific Ocean* was in continual revision. This version shows all knowledge of the Pacific Ocean as available — that is, reported by explorers — up to 1814.

The map is dedicated to Joseph de Mendoza Rios, the Spanish astronomer and Fellow of the Royal Society, who worked for many years in England on navigation and nautical astronomy. The Arrowsmith family were the leading British map publishers in the first half of the 19th century. They were particularly renowned for their nautical charts, and established the standard format later adopted by the Royal Navy's Hydrographic Office. Aaron Arrowsmith, the founder of the firm, was a scrupulous worker, who constantly revised his maps to show the latest geographical discoveries, and took great pride in producing publications combining accuracy and a functional beauty. The publication of a detailed chart such as this one of the Pacific Ocean only decades after Cook's discoveries in the region shows the intense interest in new frontiers and the knowledge that sea-power was the key to empire. *Tooley, Printed Maps of Australia (Map Collector's Circle, 1970, no. 60)* — "a landmark in the early cartography of Australasia. . . all editions are rare and valuable".

COLONEL HARBOTTLE

[199] AYLING, Thomas. COLONEL JOHN HARBOTTLE, A NATIVE CHIEF OF THE SANDWICH ISLANDS, taken by my Friend Thos. Ayling Esq. of H.M. Sloop Champion. *Watercolour portrait, partially silhouette, on sheet measuring 230 x 175 mm., caption in ink at base; partly defective at lower margin and repaired.* Hawaii, December 1843.

Thomas Ayling was assistant surgeon on H.M.S. *Champion*, one of the ships under the command of Admiral Thomas, which arrived in Honolulu in October 1843 and stayed until December.

A friendship developed between the surgeon and John Harbottle, the subject of this silhouette portrait, and the son of one of Hawaii's earliest foreign settlers. John Harbottle senior had arrived in Honolulu as mate aboard the English trader the *Jackall* (whose captain, William Brown, was probably the first foreigner to examine Honolulu harbour) in 1792-1793. He subsequently captained the *Lelia Byrd* for Kamehameha I, and was one of the principal foreigners who assured the King's rise to power, particularly in the crucial battle on Oahu in 1795. Harbottle was rewarded with land for his service, became a permanent resident of Hawaii, married a Hawaiian woman of high rank, and was appointed by

199: AYLING. *John Harbottle, the son of one of Hawaii's earliest foreign settlers.*

the King as harbourmaster — in which capacity he is mentioned by both Broughton (see items 168-9) and von Chamisso (item 265). Several sons followed his seafaring activities, acting as navigators and mates on various ships owned by the King. There is no record that we can find of how John Harbottle Junior earned his title of "Colonel" but it may well have come from his work on one of the King's boats. He was probably born in about 1810, and died at the end of 1862, leaving two small children.

FAMILY PRESENTATION

[200] AYLMER, Capt. Fenton (*editor*). A CRUISE IN THE PACIFIC. From the log of a naval officer. *2 volumes, octavo, original violet cloth, spines faded; a fine partially unopened copy with contemporary inscription "Michael Aylmer from his affect. mother 1860".* London, Hurst and Blackett, 1860.

A rarely seen narrative. Aylmer (1835-1862), a Captain of the 97th Regiment, who later served in the Crimea, visited the Pacific in 1858 on a vessel identified only as a "steamer man of war". Ports of call included Tahiti, the Marquesas, with an extensive account of his stop in Honolulu and visit to the Volcano on the island of Hawaii, before cruising to Kamschatka. Aylmer describes whaling enroute and tries dog sledding upon arrival at Petropauvloski. Most of the second volume records his stay in Vancouver and the Pacific Northwest, his hunting exploits with the Indians, whom he describes in some detail, his

NARRATIVE

OF A

Geo. Wyndham
R.N.

VOYAGE TO THE PACIFIC

AND

BEERING'S STRAIT,

TO CO-OPERATE WITH

THE POLAR EXPEDITIONS:

202: BEECHEY. The Blossom voyage was one of the most important early nineteenth century English expeditions. This copy, in an unusual English binding of the period (below) is from the library of Lord Egremont. See also the illustration on p.75.

trips to the Dalles, Kettle Falls on the Columbia River and Grand Coulee. He includes interesting observations on the Frazer River Gold Rush. *Not in Hill or Judd; O'Reilly-Reitman, 1214.*

SUFFERINGS AND ADVENTURES

[201] BARNARD, Charles H. A NARRATIVE OF THE SUFFERINGS AND ADVENTURES OF CAPT. CHARLES H. BARNARD, in a Voyage Round the World, during the years 1812, 1813, 1814, 1815 and 1816; embracing an account of the seizure of his vessel at the Falkland Islands, by an English crew whom he had rescued from the horrors of a shipwreck. *Octavo, with folding frontispiece map and 6 engraved plates; modern cloth spine, preserving the original title label; contemporary marble paper covererd boards, occasional spotting to text as in all copies, upper corners of 3 leaves repaired; a good copy.* New York, Printed for the Author by J. Lindon, 1829.

While on a sealing expedition to the Falklands during the war of 1812, Barnard rescued the crew and passengers of the *Isabella* enroute to England from Port Jackson, only to have them seize his ship and abandon him. The leader of this action was the "convict adventurer" and builder of Vaucluse House, Sydney, Sir Henry Brown Hayes (1762-1832), returning from a fourteen year stay in New South Wales. Barnard includes choice remarks on Hayes and his association in Sydney with Governor Bligh, whom he says obtained his pardon. Barnard spent nearly two years in the Falklands, before being rescued, and finally made his way to Hawaii, arriving there on December 7, 1815 on the *Millwood* from New York.

During his stay at Kailua, the *Pedlar* arrived carrying Dr. Schaefer (here spelled Shafford), a key figure in the expansion of Russian activities on the island of Kauai. Barnard describes the method of collecting taxes, an eclipse of the moon, native customs, has a long and important interview with

John Young regarding Capt. Metcalf and the "Olawalu massacre" and includes a short but perceptive comment on Kamehameha. *Ferguson, 1241 (listing only 2 copies); not in Hill.*

VOYAGE OF THE BLOSSOM

[202] BEECHEY, Frederick W[illiam]. NARRATIVE OF A VOYAGE TO THE PACIFIC AND BEERING'S STRAIT, to co-operate with the Polar Expeditions: performed in His Majesty's Ship Blossom. . . in the years 1825, 26, 27, 28. *2 volumes, quarto, with 2 large folding engraved maps, a double page map, 23 plates (including 4 double page); contemporary half crimson morocco, marbled sides, spines extra gilt, occasional light spotting, but a fine copy; with bookplate of the Earl of Egremont.* London, Henry Colburn and Richard Bentley, 1831.

"One of the most valuable of modern voyages" (Sabin). H.M.S. *Blossom* was ordered by the Admiralty as a relief expedition to Bering Straits to await the expeditions of Captains Parry and Franklin on their search for a Northwest passage. Beechey was also instructed to explore those areas of the Pacific in his route and to reach Bering Strait no later than July 10, 1826.

The ship visited Easter Island, Pitcairn and the Mangareva Islands (on which Beechey was the first European to land), sailed through the Tuamotus, reached Tahiti and made a short stop in Hawaii. At Kamchatka he learned of Parry's return, and spent July to October in Kotzebue Sound, tragically missing Franklin near Point Barrow, Alaska by fifty leagues. The next year he continued in his explorations of the Arctic, entering Kotzebue Sound from the west. The narrative contains extensive accounts of his stops at San Francisco, Monterey, Honolulu and Okinawa.

The most celebrated portion of the narrative describes the stop at Pitcairn Island where an account of the mutiny of the *Bounty* was related to Beechey by

John Adams, the last of the survivors.

The fine engravings made after drawings by William Smyth, Captain Beechey and his nephew, include two of Pitcairn (see illustration on p. 75), one of California and five of Okinawa. *Hill, p. 19; Lada-Mocarski, 95.*

THE "ADMIRALTY" EDITION

[203] BEECHEY, Frederick William. NARRATIVE OF A VOYAGE TO THE PACIFIC AND BEERING'S STRAIT, to co-operate with the Polar Expeditions; performed in His Majesty's Ship Blossom. . . a new edition. *2 volumes, octavo, with 25 maps and plates, including several folding or double page; contemporary tree calf, neatly rebacked, red labels.* London, Henry Colburn and Richard Bentley, 1831.

First octavo edition, published the same year as the quarto. A fine copy. *Ferguson, 1419; Hill, p. 19.*

HOOKER'S BOTANY

[204] [BEECHEY] HOOKER, Sir William Jackson and ARNOTT, G. A. Walker. THE BOTANY OF CAPTAIN BEECHEY'S VOYAGE; containing an account of the plants collected by Messrs. Lay and Collie and other officers of the expedition, during the voyage to the Pacific and Bering's Strait. . . in the years 1825, 26, 27 and 28. *Quarto, with 79 engraved and 20 lithographed plates; modern half green morocco, light spotting and browning, embossed stamp and release of Chicago Natural History Library on recto and verso of title.* London, Henry G. Bohn, 1841.

The botanical collections of the *Blossom's* voyage, arranged in order of places visited, with extensive sections relating to Chile, the Society Islands, Hawaii, Mexico, California and China. The California supplement illustrates and describes plants collected for the Royal Horticultural Society by David Douglas, and the Mexico supplement specimens collected by Dr. Sinclair, surgeon of H.M.S. *Sulphur*, 1837-1838. *O'Reilly-Reitman, 2513.*

WHALING

[205] BENNETT, Frederick Debell. NARRATIVE OF A WHALING VOYAGE ROUND THE GLOBE, from the year 1833 to 1836. Comprising sketches of Polynesia, California, the Indian Archipelago. . . with an account of Southern whales, the sperm whale fishery, and the natural history of the climates visited. *2 volumes, octavo; white and blue cloth, as issued; a good modern facsimile.* London, Richard Bentley, 1840. [Amsterdam, Nico Israel, 1970].

"According to Herman Melville, this is one of the best works on the whale fishery" (Hill). Bennett sailed on the *Tuscan* from London in 1833, with several LMS missionaries bound for the Society and Marquesas Islands as fellow passengers. The ship made stops at Pitcairn, Tahiti and the Marquesas, and Hawaii was visited three times (1834-35) in the course of the voyage. The author was specifically assigned to observe southern whales in order to determine improvements in the sperm whale fishery business, and collected important information, as well as natural

THE

BOTANY

OF

CAPTAIN BEECHEY'S VOYAGE;

COMPRISING

AN ACCOUNT OF THE PLANTS

COLLECTED BY

MESSRS LAY AND COLLIE,

AND OTHER OFFICERS OF THE EXPEDITION,

DURING THE VOYAGE TO THE PACIFIC AND BERING'S STRAIT, PERFORMED IN HIS MAJESTY'S SHIP BLOSSOM,

UNDER THE COMMAND OF

CAPTAIN F. W. BEECHEY, R.N., F.R. & A.S.,

IN THE YEARS 1825, 26, 27, AND 28.

BY

SIR WILLIAM JACKSON HOOKER, K.H., LL.D., F.R., A., & L.S.,

MEMBER OF THE IMPERIAL ACADEMY NATURÆ CURIOSORUM, HONORARY MEMBER OF THE ROYAL IRISH ACADEMY, ETC., ETC., AND REGIUS PROFESSOR OF BOTANY IN THE UNIVERSITY OF GLASGOW.

AND

G. A. WALKER ARNOTT, Esq., LL.D., F.R.S.E., F.L.S.,

MEMBER OF THE IMPERIAL ACADEMY NATURÆ CURIOSORUM, ETC., ETC.

ILLUSTRATED BY NUMEROUS PLATES.

PUBLISHED UNDER THE AUTHORITY OF THE RIGHT HONOURABLE THE SECRETARY OF STATE FOR COLONIAL AFFAIRS.

LONDON:
HENRY G. BOHN, No. 4, YORK STREET, COVENT GARDEN.

MDCCCXLI.

history specimens. Most of the second volume contains notes on his scientific research. *Hill, p. 22; Judd, 19.*

204: BEECHEY. The official botanical results of the Blossom voyage.

VOYAGE OF THE BLONDE

[206] BYRON, George Anson. VOYAGE OF H.M.S. BLONDE TO THE SANDWICH ISLANDS, in the years 1824-1825. Captain the Right Hon. Lord Byron, Commander. *Quarto, with folding aquatint frontispiece, chart of the voyage, 8 other aquatint plates, 3 engraved portraits, plan of Kilauea volcano and a woodcut; half calf antique, moderate foxing to text.* London, John Murray, 1826.

This voyage has been termed "one of the most gracious acts that one country has ever extended to another" (Buck). Kamehameha II of Hawaii and his Queen Kamamalu, were on a visit to London in 1824, when they both died of measles, for which they had no immunity. This voyage, with the cousin of the poet in command, was undertaken by the British government, specifically to return their bodies to the Hawaiian Islands. The work contains a history of their visit to London, a resume of the discovery and visits to Hawaii by British explorers, as well as the main narrative, compiled by Maria Graham from journals kept by the naturalist Bloxam as well as from official papers.

The stay in Hawaii contains an interesting account of travels to Hilo, and the Volcano, Kealakekua, Lahaina and Honolulu. The aquatint views by Robert

Dampier include a large view of Kilauea crater, 2 of Honolulu, 4 of Hilo, and one each of the City of Refuge near Kealakekua and Lahaina on Maui. *Hill, p. 309; Judd, 76.*

FROSTBITE ON KODIAK ISLAND

[207] CAMPBELL, Archibald. A VOYAGE ROUND THE WORLD, FROM 1806 TO 1812; in which Japan, Kamschatka, the Aleutian Islands, and the Sandwich Islands, were visited. . . With an account of the present state of the Sandwich Islands, and a vocabulary of their language. *Octavo, with folding map coloured in part; contemporary diced calf, gilt spine, black label, joints weak, slight staining to upper cover, text good; with signature of the early Hawaiian collector, Fred. Wundenberg (1850-1908).* Edinburgh, Printed for Archibald Constable, 1816.

A Pacific narrative, published in aid of a crippled seaman, remarkable for its descriptive accounts of the Northwest coast, Alaska and Hawaii. Archibald Campbell, a Scot of humble origin, was already an experienced seaman when in 1806 he signed on the *Thames* Indiaman. In China in 1807 (using an assumed name), he signed on the *Eclipse* from Boston, and made stops at Nagasaki, Kamschatka and Alaska. The ship was wrecked at Sannack, and Campbell continued in the long boat to Kodiak. He describes his sufferings (ultimately losing both feet from frostbite), spent almost a year on Kodiak, met Baranov, and includes a good description of that island.

His lengthy account of Hawaii in 1809-1810 is of the greatest importance, being the first narrative from the viewpoint of a resident rather than a visitor. He lived with the King and royal family for some time, then with Isaac Davis, of all of whom he gives a good account. The social structure and agricultural pursuits of the islanders are discussed, and the author identifies some of the early foreign residents, a number of whom were Botany Bay men. The 29 pp. vocabulary includes 3 pp. of dialogues useful for the sailor and trader, and the Hawaiian names of several resident foreigners. *Not in Ferguson; Hill, p. 45; Judd 30, Lada-Mocarski, 71.*

FIRST AMERICAN EDITION

[208] CAMPBELL, Archibald. A VOYAGE ROUND THE WORLD, FROM 1806 TO 1812; in which Japan, Kamschatka, the Aleutian Islands, and the Sandwich Islands were visited; including a narrative of the author's shipwreck on the Island of Sannack, and his subsequent wreck in the ship's long-boat; with an account of the present state of the Sandwich Islands, and a vocabulary of their language. *Duodecimo, folding frontispiece map; original tree calf, rebacked; contemporary owner's inscription on front blank, text lightly spotted, but a very good copy.* New York, Printed by Broderick and Ritter, 1819.

Very scarce: the first American edition to be published, and containing the earliest printing of a Hawaiian vocabulary in America. The various American editions contain considerable information not in the English edition. Tipped in is a printed commendation to readers from Governor De Witt Clinton of New York. *Hill, p. 45* — "American imprints of this date, relating to Pacific voyages, are rare. . .".

THE NORTHERN PACIFIC

[209] CORNEY, Peter. VOYAGES IN THE NORTHERN PACIFIC. Narrative of several Trading Voyages from 1813 to 1818, between the Northwest Coast of America, the Hawaiian Islands and China, with a Description of the Russian Establishments on the North-West Coast. Interesting Early Account of Kamehameha's Realm; Manners and Customs of the People, etc. And Sketch of a Cruise in the Service of the Independents of South America in 1819. *Duodecimo, old half grey morocco, slight fading to spine.* Honolulu, Thos. G. Thrum, 1896.

First edition in book form: the author spent four years voyaging on the *Columbia*, a British schooner trading in furs between the North West Coast and China. The introductory chapters contain a general account of the development of the Northwest trade. The *Columbia* was bought by King Kamehameha of Hawaii, and Corney's four chapters on Hawaii include much on the King as well as a description of the Islands and an account of Russian activities on Kauai between 1815 and 1817.

The narrative which originally appeared in a London literary magazine, was here edited with the addition of much material by W. D. Alexander, a prominent Honolulu historian. *Hill, p. 65.*

ADVENTURES IN THE PACIFIC

[210] COULTER, John. ADVENTURES IN THE PACIFIC; with observations on the natural productions, manners and customs of the Natives of the various islands; together with remarks on missionaries, British and other Residents. *Octavo; contemporary blue cloth, yellow endpapers, slight fading to spine, joints a little tender, occasional spotting to text.* Dublin, William Curry; London, Longmans, Brown; Edinburgh, Fraser and Co., 1845.

First edition: with a detailed account (on more than 100 pages) of the Marquesas in the 1830s. There, the author assumed native dress, was tattooed (described at length) and became involved in a tribal war.

Coulter, a surgeon on the *Stratford* during her voyage in 1832-1836, visited various South American ports, and the Galapagos Islands, gives an account of whaling and curiously calls the sperm whale "a very large fish".

A long stay was made at the Chatham Islands where he toured the island and found a skeleton in an abandoned hut. He made three stops at Tahiti and gives a general account and discusses the English missionaries there in some detail. *Hill, p. 70; O'Reilly-Reitman, 903.*

THE WRECK OF THE GUARDIAN

[211] DODD, R. PART OF THE CREW OF HIS MAJESTY'S SHIP GUARDIAN endeavouring to escape in the boats. *Handcoloured aquatint, 410 x 600 mm.; print surface worn with minor loss, generally aged, framed.* London, July 1st, 1790 by J. & J. Boydell.

When the colony of New South Wales was established in 1788, it was expected that supplies from England would arrive at regular intervals. However, one of the first two supply ships never arrived, when disaster overtook H.M.S. *Guardian*, commanded by Lieut. Edward Riou. The *Guardian*, laden with two years' provisions for the new colony, left London in July 1789, but was wrecked on an iceberg twelve days out of Cape Town. Three accounts of the disaster were published immediately in 1790, as well as this magnificent aquatint by Robert Dodd (1748-1816), a well known marine painter of the period.

All contemporary material relating to the *Guardian* disaster is scarce and highly sought after. The double-column caption gives a description of the disaster in the form of the text of a letter from Riou to the Admiralty. *Nan Kivell & Spence, p. 265 (illustrated p. 293).*

CONRAD MARTENS' COPY OF EARLE

[212] EARLE, Augustus. A NARRATIVE OF A NINE MONTHS RESIDENCE IN NEW ZEALAND IN 1827. Together with a Journal of a Residence in Tristan d'Acunha, an Island situated between South America and the Cape of Good Hope. *Octavo; illustrated with seven plates by Augustus Earle; slight repair to top right hand corner of title-page; bound in half tan polished calf, gilt panelled spine with dark green labels, maroon cloth boards, marbled endpapers, speckled edges, by the colonial binder, Conyber, with his ticket (13, Park St., Sydney).* London, 1832.

This copy of Earle's description of his voyage to New Zealand belonged to the artist Conrad Martens — Earle's successor as official artist on HMS *Beagle* — and bears manuscript annotations in Martens' hand.

On p. x is a marginal note in black ink and on p. 371 is added a postscript of six lines describing Augustus Earle's death.

With the opening up of vast new territories in the nineteenth century, and before the beginnings of photography, the travelling artist, like both Earle and Martens, held a unique position in the documentation of the Pacific. Free of the burdens of Admiralty regulations and the constraints of the patron, Earle's work offered a refreshing spontaneity and he was soon recognised as the recorder of places "hitherto unvisited by any artist". He indulged his love of travelling and explored the world at will. In 1828-29 he visited New Zealand and on his return to England wrote and illustrated this book. Even before its publication he had left England again aboard the *Beagle*, as official artist accompanying his friend Charles Darwin. His deteriorating health forced him to leave the expedition at Montevideo where his place was taken by Conrad Martens.

A fine association copy of an important travel account, one of few first-hand narratives of exploration by a professional artist in the Pacific. *Hocken, p.51; not in Abbey.*

THE INVESTIGATOR VOYAGE

[213] FLINDERS, Matthew. A VOYAGE TO TERRA AUSTRALIS; undertaken for the purpose of completing the Discovery of that vast Country, and prosecuted in the years 1801, 1802, and 1803 in His Majesty's Ship the Investigator, and subsequently in the Armed Vessel Porpoise and Cumberland Schooner. With an Account of the Shipwreck of the Porpoise. *2 volumes, large quarto, with 9 engraved plates of views, and a folio atlas containing the 16 large folded charts, 2 plates of coastal*

211: DODD. *Dodd's magnificent aquatint shows the wreck of HMS Guardian, the supply ship desperately awaited by the Australian colonists.*

212: EARLE. *This copy of Earle's Narrative has the ticket of an early Sydney binder.*

CONYBER, BOOK.BINDER, 13, PARK ST., Sydney.

Ueber Neuholland und Australien, bei Gelegenheit von Flinders's Entdeckungsreise in der Südsee. *)

Aus dem Englischen.

Flinders hatte als Lieutenant auf einem königlichen Schiffe, auf der Station von Neusüdwales, im Jahr 1798 manche Gelegenheit, seinen heißen Wunsch zu erfüllen, seine große Erfahrung in Erforschung unbekannter Küsten und Häfen zu bewäh-

---

*) A Voyage to Terra Australis, undertaken for the Purpose of completing the Discovery of that vast Country, and prosecuted in the Years 1801, 1802, and 1803 in his Majesty's Ship Investigator, and subsequently in the Armed Vessel Porpoise and Cumberland Schooner. With an Account of the Shipwreck of the Porpoise, Arrival of the Cumberland at Mauritius, and Imprisonment of the Commander during six Years and a half in that Island. By Mathew Flinders, Commander of the Investigator. In Two Volumes, with an Atlas. London 1814.

215: FLINDERS. *The first appearance of Flinders in German.*

views and 10 botanical plates; the plates in the text volumes a little foxed and offsetting slightly as usual, some light spotting in the atlas volume; overall an excellent copy in a sympathetic modern binding of full calf, spines gilt, atlas in matching half calf and marbled boards. London, Printed by W. Bulmer and Co., 1814.

The first circumnavigation of Australia. A good copy of the first edition of this classic voyage account. The important charts in the folio atlas are all present in their earliest issue — a significant point since they remained standard charts for many parts of the Australian coast for a long time, and were continually revised and updated as new information came to hand.

The engraved views in the text volumes are by the landscape painter William Westall, who travelled as official artist on the voyage, while the botanical plates in the atlas are by the renowned flower painter Ferdinand Bauer. *Ferguson, 576; Wantrup, 67a.*

THE VOYAGE IN THE FRANCIS

[214] FLINDERS, Matthew. MATTHEW FLINDERS' NARRATIVE OF HIS VOYAGE IN THE SCHOONER FRANCIS: 1798; preceded and followed by notes on Flinders, Bass, the wreck of the Sidney Cove, &c. by Geoffrey Rawson, with engravings by John Buckland Wright. *Quarto, with a map and wood engravings by John Buckland Wright; original green cloth, gilt spine title and ship ornament on upper cover, deckle edges; ink presentation inscription on front flyleaf; an excellent copy.* Golden Cockerel Press, 1946.

One of 750 numbered copies: the first publication from the manuscript in the State Library of Victoria of Flinders' account of his voyage in the schooner *Francis* in 1788, partly to locate the wreck of the *Sydney Cove*, which had sailed from Bengal, in one of the first attempts to open up a regular trade between Bengal and Australia. Her loss led to the further exploration

of Bass Strait by Flinders and also led to the discovery of the Illawarra coal seams by Bass and the first export of coal from Australia.

FIRST ACCOUNT IN GERMAN

[215] FLINDERS, Matthew. UEBER NEUHOLLAND UND AUSTRALIEN, bei Gelegenheit von Flinders's Entdeckungsreise in der Sudsee [on pages 51-89 of] Miscellen aus der neuesten auslandischen Literatur. . . Zehntes oder Vierten Bandes erstes heft. *Small octavo, original wrappers preserved bound in quarter buckram.* Leipzig, in der Expedition der Minerva, 1815.

A rare abridgment of Flinders' voyage, apparently the first appearance of any account of the voyage in German. *Not in Ferguson.*

THE FIRST AUSTRALIAN TRADING VOYAGE

[216] GILBERT, Thomas. VOYAGE FROM NEW SOUTH WALES TO CANTON, in the year 1788, with Views of the Islands discovered. *Quarto, with an engraved vignette on the title and four large folding plates; without the half-title or final advertisement leaf; occasional spotting; fine period-style half calf.* London, Printed by George Stafford, for J. Debrett, 1789.

First edition. The first trading voyage out of Australia: Gilbert commanded the *Charlotte*, one of the First Fleet transports carrying convicts to Botany Bay. With one of the other ships, the *Scarborough* under Captain Marshall, he was contracted by the East India Company to take a cargo of tea from China back to England. After a brief description of the colony, in which he expresses disappointment with the country around Botany Bay, but is optimistic for the prospects northward, Gilbert describes their voyage to Canton, including the discovery of the islands that bear his and Marshall's names. Although "the actual Australian interest of this volume is limited. . . it is an important and scarce work, particularly from the point of view of general Pacific discovery" (Rodney Davidson, *A Book Collector's Notes*, p. 79). *Crittenden, 106; Ferguson, 38; Hill, p. 124.*

THE WRECK OF THE ANTELOPE

[217] KEATE, George. AN ACCOUNT OF THE PELEW ISLANDS, situated in the western part of the Pacific Ocean. Composed from the Journals and communications of Captain Henry Wilson, and some of his officers, who, in August 1783, were shipwrecked, in the Antelope. *Octavo, with frontispiece portrait of Wilson, and 3 portraits; calf antique, red label; light browning to part of text.* London, Printed for W. Nicoll, 1788.

First octavo edition of one of the most popular eighteenth century books on the Pacific. In 1783, the *Antelope* was wrecked on an uncharted reef near Palau; the crew reached shore and were well treated by the natives. From the wreck they built a small boat which they managed to get to Macao, taking with them Prince Lee Boo, the son of King Abba Thule. Lee Boo travelled with them to England, but tragically died soon after of smallpox. This account did much to reinforce the idea of the noble savage, but was also the main source of early knowledge of the Palau Islands in Micronesia. *This edition not in Hill.*

SCARCE AMERICAN EDITION

[218] [KEATE, George] AN ACCOUNT OF THE PELEW ISLANDS, situated in the Great South Sea. Composed from the Journals of Capt. Henry Wilson, and his Officers; who, in August, 1783, were there shipwrecked in the Antelope Packet. *Duodecimo, iv + 96 pp., quarter calf.* Wilmington [Delaware], Printed for the Rev. M.L. Weems, by Samuel and John Adams, 1794.

Scarce American printing of the highly popular account of the wreck of the Antelope. This edition does not appear in the Hill catalogue, although the catalogue notes the existence of this printing and of others in Philadelphia (1789, 1791, 1792, and 1796), New York (1796), Rutland (1797), Katskill (1797) and Brookfield (1800). *Hill, p. 464.*

THE RARE SUPPLEMENT

[219] [KEATE] HOCKIN, John Pearce. A SUPPLEMENT TO THE ACCOUNT OF THE PELEW ISLANDS; compiled from the journals of the Panther and the Endeavour, two vessels sent by the Honourable East India Company to those islands in the year 1790; and from the oral communications of Captain H. Wilson. *Quarto, with 5 engraved plates; slight worming in outer margin, well clear of text; a good, large copy in contemporary calf, rubbed, spine renewed.* London, Printed for Captain Henry Wilson, by W. Bulmer and Co., 1803.

Very scarce: a companion piece to Keate's *Account of the Pelew Islands*, it was originally printed as a supplement to the fifth edition of Keate's book, which appeared in 1803, but copies are known to have been available separately for owners of the earlier editions to bind or shelve together. The Hill catalogue notes that "separately issued copies of Hockin in contemporary bindings are extraordinarily rare".

The *Supplement* contains narratives of the activities of the *Panther* and the *Endeavour*, East India Company ships which spent over a year in the Palau Islands, leaving at various points to survey the coast of New Guinea and to visit the coast of China. *Hill, p.449.*

LEFT FOR DEAD ON TONGA

[220] MARINER. MARTIN, John. AN ACCOUNT OF THE NATIVES OF THE TONGA ISLANDS, in the South Pacific Ocean. With an original grammar and vocabulary of their language. *2 volumes, duodecimo, with 4 engraved plates (including 2 of Tongan music) and folding map; original rose glazed boards, paper spine labels, some fading to boards, joints cracking, light foxing to text; uncut and partially unopened.* Edinburgh, Printed for Constable and Co., 1827.

Third and "considerably improved" edition of this Pacific classic. Mariner was a young British sailor on the *Port au Prince*, a whaler which sailed in 1805, but spent much of her time attacking Spanish shipping. In the spring of 1806 she captured two ships, the brig *Santa Isidora* and the corbeta *Santa Maria*, both of which were then sent to Port Jackson to be sold. The

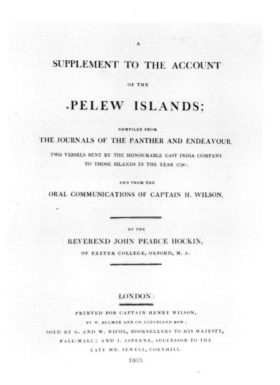

Port au Prince visited Hawaii in September-October 1806, then sailed with a number of Hawaiian crew. At Tonga the crew mutinied, and most were massacred by the natives, but Mariner came under the protection of the King and lived there as his adopted son for four years.

Mariner's story was cited by Byron as one of the two sources for his poem *The Island, or Christian and his Comrades*, a romantic narrative of the *Bounty* mutiny. The work includes a grammar and a Tongan-English dictionary, with a further important appendix "on the surgical skills of the Tonga people", with references to similar practices in Hawaii. *Hill, p. 192.*

THE "OFFICIAL" ACCOUNT

[221] MORTIMER, George. OBSERVATIONS AND REMARKS MADE DURING A VOYAGE to the islands of Teneriffe, Amsterdam, Maria's Islands near Van Diemen's Land; Otaheite, Sandwich Islands; Owhyhee, the Fox Islands on the North West Coast of America, Tinian, and from thence to Canton, in the brig Mercury, commanded by John Henry Cox, Esq. *Quarto, with two folding charts; original cloth, a good modern facsimile.* London, Printed for the Author, and sold by T. Cadell, in the Strand, 1791. [Amsterdam, Nico Israel, 1975].

The "official" account of a puzzling voyage. The voyage of Cox in the *Mercury* has always puzzled historians of the South Seas, but it has now been demonstrated that the *Mercury* was in fact the *Gustaf III*, a privateer sailing under the Swedish flag sent by the King of Sweden to attack Russian fur trade settlements in the North Pacific, during the war between Sweden and Russia in 1788-90; (see the article by R. Du Rietz, "The Voyage of H.M.S. Pandora", in *Ethnos*, 28 (1963), pp. 210-18, where the principal literature on the subject is listed).

219: KEATE. Hockin's supplement to Keate's Pelew Islands.

218: KEATE. An unusual early American printing of Keate.

Engelsmannen
JOH. HINDRIC COX
RESA
Genom Söderhafvet
Till
On Amsterdam, Marien-Oarna,
O-Taheiti, Sandvichs- och
Raf-Oarna, Tinian, Unalaska
och Canton i China.

Utgifven
af
GEORG MORTIMER.

NYKÖPING,
Tryckt hos Peter Winge 1798.

No. 141 Mortimer

THE

LIFE AND ADVENTURES

OF JOHN NICOL,

MARINER.

WILLIAM BLACKWOOD, EDINBURGH:
AND T. CADELL, LONDON.
MDCCCXXII

222: MORTIMER. *The Swedish account of the voyage of the* Mercury *(in fact the Gustaf III), an espionage voyage to the South Seas.*

223: NICOL. *John Nicol's account of his experiences includes one of very few printed accounts of the voyage of the second fleet to Australia.*

SWEDISH SPY VOYAGE

[222] MORTIMER, George. ENGELSMANNEN JOH. HINDRIC COX Resa Genom Soderhafvet Till On Amsterdam, Marien-Oarna, O-Taheiti, Sandvichs-och Raf-Oarna, Tinian, Unalaska och Canton i China. Utgifven af Georg Mortimer. *Octavo, 77 pp. and a blank; somewhat stained, but a sound uncut copy in old (?original) plain wrappers, preserved in a cloth box.* Nykoping, tryckt hos Peter Winge, 1798.

The rare Swedish edition of this mysterious Swedish voyage, camouflaged as an English voyage of exploration. This version, possibly based on a German translation of Mortimer's original, was the work of Carl Fr. Landell who signs the preface "C.F.L.", and it is uniform with his abridgments of Bligh and Forster (both 1795). In his preface Landell broadly reproduces Mortimer's puzzled remarks about the purpose of the voyage, but he does not seem especially conscious that the voyage had anything to do with espionage or clandestine activity against the Russian fur trade; on the other hand, he does not appear at any point to give the ship either of its two names.

In fact the members of the *Mercury* were, though they did not realise it, the first Europeans to hear anything of the course taken by the mutineers. They arrived at Tahiti fifteen days after Christian had left with fresh supplies for Tubuai (and only two days after Bligh's arrival in Timor), and finally left the island eighteen days before the failure of the settlement on Tubuai brought the *Bounty* back to Tahiti for the last time.

They learned from a native that "Titreano, who he said was Captain Bligh's chief officer . . . returned to Otaheite in the Bounty about two months after she had first sailed, without Captain Bligh . . . This story was confirmed by Otoo and several chiefs; who further informed us, that Captain Titreano had sailed but fifteen days before our arrival, and had carried several Otaheitean families with him to Tootate. Where Tootate could be, or who they meant by Titreano, we could not then conjecture . . . ".

There are also many references to Cook, whose path the voyage followed from Tahiti; and on Tahiti, they are shown Webber's portrait of Cook (since lost), with Bligh's note on the back recording the sailing of the *Bounty* with 1015 bread-fruit plants in April 1789.

See also R. Du Rietz, *Gustaf III och Bounty, Tidskrift fur Varnpliktiga Officerare* (Stockholm), 3 (1959), vol. xvii, pp. 2-5. *Kroepelien, 873.*

THE VOYAGE OF THE LADY JULIANA

[223] NICOL, John. THE LIFE AND ADVENTURES of John Nicol, Mariner. *Octavo, with frontispiece portrait; contemporary diced calf, neatly rebacked; an unusually clean and large copy of a book that is usually browned.* Edinburgh, William Blackwood, and T. Cadell, London, 1822.

An important unvarnished account of Pacific voyages made by a common seaman. Nicol, whose naval career spanned 1776 to 1801, first came to the Pacific as a steward with Captain Portlock in 1785-1788. During that voyage he made a brief stay in Hawaii, and his short but interesting observations include a description of the making of knives out of hoop iron for the King of Hawaii.

His account of the voyage of the *Lady Juliana* to New South Wales in 1788, carrying 245 female convicts, is the most important part of the book. Nicol describes nine women on the voyage, including Sarah Sabolah, a Jewess, who disguised as a pious Catholic in South American ports begged birthing linens for the women on board ship. His attraction focused on one Sarah Whitelam "from the moment I knocked the rivet out of her irons"; Sarah bore him a child on the voyage, and when they parted in Sydney in 1790, Nicol promised to return. Much of the narrative then concerns his two attempts to rejoin her. On the second attempt he learned enroute that Sarah had made her escape to Bombay, and a later interview with her parents in Lincoln revealed nothing of her whereabouts.

Nicol's book is virtually the only description of a second fleet voyage. *Ferguson, 875; Hill, p. 211; Lada-Mocarski, 85.*

THE CHALLENGER

[224] SWIRE, Herbert. The Voyage of the Challenger. A personal Narrative of the Historic Circumnavigation of the Globe in the years 1872-1876... [with] Foreword by Major Roger Swire, M.C., R.E. [and] Introduction by G. Herbert Fowler, C.B.E. *2 volumes, small folio, with 10 plates of watercolours in the journal and numerous text illustrations, front endpaper of volume I with map showing the route of the Challenger; original white spines and blue cloth covered boards, deckle edges, boxed; light spotting to endpapers and very occasionally to text; a very good copy.* London, The Golden Cockerel Press, 1938.

One of 300 numbered copies. The *Challenger* voyage — "the inception of modern oceanography as one of the sciences" (Hill) — was the first modern marine investigation of the earth's seas, an expansion of Victorian interest in biological study which had been created by Darwin's *Origin of the Species*. She sailed from Portsmouth on December 21, 1872, and made her leisurely passage around the world by way of Bahia, Cape Town, Melbourne, Sydney, Wellington, the South Sea Islands, the Philippines, Hong Kong, Yokohama, Honolulu, Valparaiso and Monte Video.

This journal was written by a young sub-lieutenant, and is illustrated by some ninety of his sketches. He has a refreshingly irreverent approach to the people and places visited, in considerable contrast to the seriousness of purpose of the voyage itself.

Loosely laid in is a 3 pp. typescript, "A sequel to my father's visit to Fiji in 1874" by Roger Swire, regarding his visit in 1961. *Hill, p. 586; O'Reilly-Reitman, 1307.*

THE EARLIEST KNOWN DRAWING OF PITCAIRN'S ISLAND

[225] TAGUS, H.M.S. Artist unknown. Album of Original Pacific Island Views. *Oblong quarto album (of English paper, watermarked S & C Wise, 1811), containing 30 original drawings, mostly profile views in pencil and watercolour, unsigned, but identified and dated in a contemporary hand; original grey-green boards, corners frayed; occasional spotting to a few leaves, a few folds and margins tender; recent blue leather spine.* At sea, various dates during 1814.

A fine album of coastal profiles: the drawings are almost all dated, enabling full identification of the voyage as that of the *Briton* and the *Tagus*. The ships sailed from England in 1813, visited Valparaiso, Peru, the Galapagos Islands, the Marquesas, and Pitcairn's Island, where members of the voyage (including Shillibeer, who wrote an account of the voyage as *A Narrative of the Briton's Voyage to Pitcairn's Island*, Taunton, 1817) met John Adams, the last survivor of the mutiny on the *Bounty*.

The *Bounty* mutineers were said to have chosen Pitcairn's Island as their refuge as it was one of the most isolated islands in the Pacific. Their luck was also that the only charting of it available at the time of the mutiny was Carteret's, published in Hawkesworth (see items 50-53). Carteret had seen the island in July 1767, but did not go ashore, and as it turned out, his charting was considerably in error, meaning that the island virtually disappeared for later navigators.

Captain Folger accidentally rediscovered the island in 1808 (though his description was not published until Delano included it with other material on the mutiny on the *Bounty* as part of his *Narrative of Voyages*

225: TAGUS. *Kicker Rock drawn from HMS* Tagus, *standing off half a mile; one of 30 original Pacific island views.*

225: TAGUS. *Bell Mountain, near Valparaiso. This fine watercolour view was drawn by the unknown artist aboard HMS* Tagus *in May 1814.*

and Travels, 1817 — see item 151), and the next visitors to the island, only the second since its settlement by the mutineers, were the crews of the *Briton* and the *Tagus* in September 1814.

Carteret's chart of the island as published by Hawkesworth also contained small profiles of the coast from the north-west; the original drawings for those profiles are not known, so that the larger profile of the island contained here, seen from the south-west, and showing signs of cultivation, appears to be the earliest surviving original view of Pitcairn's Island.

The identity of the artist is uncertain, although the precise dating of his landfalls identifies him as a member of the crew of the *Tagus* rather than the *Briton*. Captain Pipon of the *Tagus* sent several surveys back to the Admiralty which are now held in the Hydrographic Department of the Navy at Taunton; they include charts of the Galapagos Islands with views that on grounds of handwriting are almost certainly not by Pipon himself but appear to be by the present artist, agreeing generally in style.

The views are as follows:

1. Bell Mountain near Valparaiso Chilli. 31 May, 1814. *(22 x 27.5 cm.).*

2. Point of Invisible Bay. Rooahouagah 7 or 8 miles. 20th August, 1814. *(8.5 x 24 cm.).*

3. Island of Rooahaoagah 7 or 8 Leagues. One of the Marquesas. 20th August, 1814. *(8.5 x 24 cm.).*

4. Lobus de Mer 7 miles-near Lima. 28th June, 1814. *(18.5 x 24.5 cm.).*

5. Craggy Cliff, 6 Leagues. Isle Noaheawah. 21st August, 1814. *(10 x 27 cm.).*

6. Inside of craggy cliff forming one part of Comptrolers Bay in the Island of Novaheava. 21st August, 1814. *(7.5 x 27 cm.).*

7. Lobus de Turre. 28th June, 1814. *(21.5 x 27.5 cm.).*

8. Outside View of the Island San Lorenzo near Lima. 18th June, 1814. *(double page view-22 x 55 cm.).*

9. Entrance of Anna Maria Bay Nuahevah. 21st August, 1814. *(pencil sketch-19 x 27 cm.).*

10. Nooahavah *(sic)* Island. 30th August, 1814. *(pencil sketch-9.5 x 27 cm.).*

11. Point de los Picos. 28th June, 1814. *(11 x 17.5 cm.).*

12. Isle of Lobus off Sylla de Payta. 29th June, 1814. *(10 x 27.5 cm.).*

13. Pitcairns Island. 17th September, 1814. *(pencil sketch-9 x 27.5 cm.).*

14. Small bay Island of Santa Christiana. 31st August 1814. *(pencil sketch-9 x 27.5 cm.).*

15. Cape St. Elena, 2 miles. 9th July, 1814. *(10.5 x 27.5 cm.).*

16. Island de la Plata, 3 leagues. 11th July, 1814. *(10.5 x 28 cm.).*

17. Enchanted Island. 30th July, 1814. *(10.5 x 27.5 cm.).*

18. Cape Berkley, Albermarle. 3rd August, 1814. *(10.5 x 28 cm.).*

19. Isle Salango. 12th July, 1814. *(double page view-10 x 56 cm.).*

20. Point Salango. 12th July, 1814. *(double page view-21.5 x 56 cm.).*

21. Albermarle Isle. 4 or 5 leagues, Gallapagos. 20th July, 1814. *(double page view-10.5 x 56 cm.).*

22. Charles Island. 5 leagues Gallapagos. 23rd July, 1814. *(double page view-10.5 x 56 cm.).*

23. Charles Island 7 or 8 miles. 25th July, 1814. *(double page view-10 x 56 cm.).*

24. Barrington Isld. 7 or 8 miles. 26th July, 1814. *(10.5 x 26 cm.).*

25. Kicker Rock 12 miles. Chatham Isld. 8 or 9 miles. Dalrymple Rock. 27th July, 1814. *(double page view-10 x 56 cm.).*

26. Rodondo Rock. 1st August, 1814. *(10 x 14.5 cm.).*

27. Isle of Albany. James (?) Island 1/2 mile from the Anchorage. 29th July, 1814. *(double page view-10 x*

80.5 cm.).

28. Kicker Rock. North 1/2 mile. 26th July, 1814. *(16 x 21.5 cm.).*

29. Cape Marshall SE 1/2 E. Albermarle Island. Albermarle Pt. 4th August, 1814. *(double page view-10.5 x 56 cm.).*

30. Narborough Island. 4th August, 1814. *(double page view-10.5 x 56 cm.).*

Some manuscript notes on a blank leaf at the end, and on the blank verso of a folding drawing, record observations made, on one of the Pacific islands visited, of the catching of animals, the preparation of kava, the use of oily nuts as candles, and clothing and sleeping habits.

With the label of Dymocks' Book Arcade, 428 George St., Sydney, and a pencil note which apparently refers to an auction at Hodgson's Rooms, London (30 July 1914, lot 548).

We thank D.M. Mann, Curator of the Hydrographic Department, for information summarised above.

BEST EDITION OF A CLASSIC ACCOUNT

[226] TURNBULL, John. A VOYAGE ROUND THE WORLD, in the years 1800, 1801, 1802, 1803, and 1804; In which the author visited Madeira, the Brazils, Cape of Good Hope, the English Settlements of Botany Bay and Norfolk island, and the principal Islands in the Pacific Ocean. *Quarto, with engraved view of Cairo after Luigi Mayer; contemporary half crimson morocco, spine extra gilt; title and frontispiece view foxed, and occasional spotting of text; bookplate of Lord Egremont; a very attractive copy.* London, Published by A. Maxwell, 1813.

Second and best edition. The author and his partner John Buyers, attracted by lucrative profits of American traders, purchased and fitted out the *Margaret* for a speculative trading venture. They arrived in Sydney via the Cape of Good Hope in February 1801, and the author describes the town, trading activities and agricultural prospects on more than 98 pages. They made similar stays at both the Society and Hawaiian Islands, and while in Hawaii they learned of Kamehameha's planned invasion of the Island of Kauai. In Tahiti, the author set up business curing hogs with salt obtained in Hawaii. He discovered three islands in the Tuamotus.

This edition is the most desirable in that it contains substantial additions to all chapters, revising and expanding each by eight years. An additional chapter on New South Wales, an account of New Zealand, a narrative of Baudin's voyage on the *Geographe* and *Naturaliste*, the destruction of the ship *Boyd* and a description of the Fiji Islands appear here for the first time. *Ferguson, 570; Hill, p. 295; O'Reilly-Reitman, 718.*

[227] TURNBULL, John. A VOYAGE ROUND THE WORLD, in the years 1800, 1801, 1802, 1803 and 1804; in which the author visited Madeira, the Brazils, Cape of Good Hope, the English Settlements of Botany Bay and Norfolk Island, and the principal Islands in the Pacific Ocean. *Quarto; contemporary speckled calf, rebacked but preserving all original spine and*

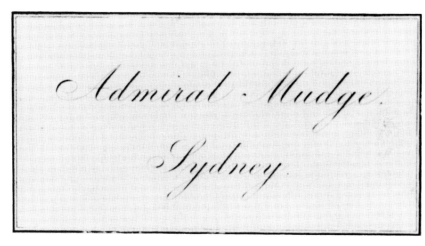

black title label, hinges a little weak, green endpapers; light occasional spotting of text, but a very good copy. London, Published by A. Maxwell, 1813.

Second and best edition. *Ferguson, 570; Hill, p. 295; O'Reilly-Reitman, 718.*

FIRST EDITION IN FRENCH

[228] TURNBULL, John. VOYAGE FAIT AUTOUR DU MONDE, en 1800, 1801, 1802, 1803 et 1804. . . Dans lequel l'auteur a visité les Iles principales de l'Ocean Pacifique et les Etablissements des Anglais dans la Nouvelle-Galle meridionale; Suivi d'un extrait du Voyage de James Grant, à la Nouvelle-Hollande. . . 1800. . . 1802. *Octavo, contemporary quarter calf, French armorial bookplate "Roquencourt", slight wear to top of spine and hinges.* Paris, chez Xhrouet, 1807.

First French edition. Very good copy. *Ferguson, 453; O'Reilly-Reitman, 713.*

OWNED BY VANCOUVER'S LIEUTENANT

[229] VANCOUVER, George. A VOYAGE OF DISCOVERY TO THE NORTH PACIFIC OCEAN, and round the world: in which the Coast of North-West America has been carefully examined and accurately surveyed. Undertaken by His Majesty's command, principally with a view to ascertain the existence of any navigable communication between the North Pacific and North Atlantic Oceans; and performed in the years 1790, 1791, 1792, 1793, 1794, and 1795, in the Discovery sloop of war, and armed tender Chatham, under the command of Captain George Vancouver. *3 volumes, quarto, with 17 engraved plates and a chart; contemporary tree calf rebacked, a fine clean copy on thick paper, with half titles to volumes II & III; with the bookplate "Admiral Mudge, Sydney"; lacking the Atlas.* London, Printed for G. G. and J. Robinson. . . and J. Edwards, 1798.

A fine copy of the text of "one of the most important voyages ever made" (Hill), and the only copy known to us to have been owned by an officer on board.

Vancouver, who had served on Cook's second and third voyages, was made commander of an expedition whose express purpose was to reclaim wherever possible British rights to the Northwest coast of America following the Nootka convention of 1790. He was also to re-examine the existence of a navigable passage from the Atlantic to the Pacific, and this

229: VANCOUVER. *Zachariah Mudge was a lieutenant aboard Vancouver's voyage; he probably named his house in Devon "Sydney" after the fine harbour he had seen in 1795.*

227: TURNBULL. *Turnbull's account of his voyage at the beginning of the nineteenth century includes important material on New South Wales, Tahiti and Hawaii.*

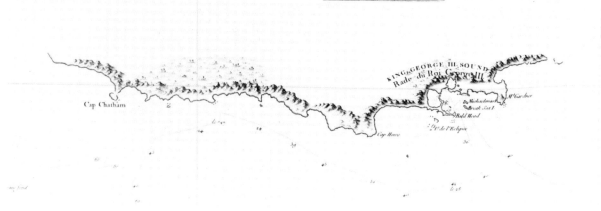

PARTIE DE LA CÔTE SUD-OUEST

DE LA

NOUVELLE HOLLANDE

avec les Routes de la Corvette la Découverte *et sa conserve* le Chatham

commandés par GEORGES VANCOUVER

en l'Année 1791.

230: VANCOUVER. *The fine French edition of Vancouver includes important material on Western Australia.*

voyage permanently laid to rest that theory. He sailed to the Pacific via Australia where he discovered and charted King George's Sound and Cape Hood, passed Van Diemen's Land, then visited New Zealand and Hawaii, and the North West Coast. During the course of three seasons, he surveyed Alaska, the North West Coast, investigated the Straits of Juan de Fuca, discovered the Strait of Georgia, and circumnavigated Vancouver Island. He visited San Francisco, Monterey and other Spanish Settlements in Alta California, and made three visits to the Hawaiian Islands where he introduced cattle from Monterey. A substantial portion of the text relates to these visits.

This copy was owned and annotated by Zachariah Mudge (1770-1852), one of three lieutenants aboard the *Discovery* on this voyage. Mudge, who first was entered on the naval books at age ten, sailed with Vancouver, and "Point Mudge" in the Gulf of Georgia was named by Vancouver in his honour in July 1792. In 1794 Mudge was aboard William Broughton's ship the *Providence* on its voyage through the Pacific (see no. 168). The *Providence*, Bligh's old ship, sailed to Nootka Sound via Rio de Janeiro, Australia, Tahiti and the Hawaiian Islands. Their stop in Australia included a visit to Sydney and a one-week stay at Port Stephens.

Volume II of this work contains short but pungent pencil annotations by Mudge. He identifies one of the Hawaiians (Tymarrow) whom they had met in Nootka in 1792 and returned to the Islands, as "Mrs.

Vancouver". Later, regarding the comment that one of the native women going up and down the ladders took "as much care not to expose her ancles, as if she had been educated by the most rigid governess", Mudge comments "how the world is given to lying".

Mudge saw service in the West Indies and the Mediterranean, and was made a rear-Admiral in 1830. Perhaps as a tribute to the harbour he had seen in 1795, he named his home at Plympton in Devon, "Sydney", and his bookplate is so inscribed. *Ferguson, 281; Hill, p. 304; Lada-Mocarski, 55; Wantrup, 63a.*

THE FINE FRENCH EDITION

[230] VANCOUVER, George. VOYAGE DE DECOUVERTES, à l'ocean Pacifique du Nord, et Autour du Monde, dans lequel la côte Nord-Ouest de l'Amerique a été soigneusement reconnue et exactement relevée ... et executé en 1790, 1791, 1792, 1793, 1794 et 1795. *3 volumes, quarto; nineteenth century black calf spines, and marble paper covered boards, spines extra gilt, marble endpapers and edges, joints a little weak, slight splitting to spines of volume I, text clean and bright; [with] Atlas, containing 16 maps, charts and elevations; folio, original pink mottled paper covered boards, some wear to spine and boards, all maps and plates fine and clean. Paris, de l'Imprimerie de la République, An VIII.*

A particularly good copy of the first French edition, with the atlas a good, large and unfolded example. *Ferguson, 320b; this edition not in Hill.*

XII
French Voyages after La Pérouse

LES CORVETTES LE GÉOGRAPHE, LE NATURALISTE
ET LA GOÉLETTE LE CASUARINA.

The late eighteenth and early nineteenth centuries introduced a new style of explorer. The well fitted vessels of the nineteenth century French explorers were essentially floating research laboratories, attended by qualified and trained personnel. Advances in astronomy, mathematics and optics made it possible to chart positions with accuracy, whilst in the field of species classification, precise scientific methods were employed.

The French were leaders in the appreciation of visual documentation and skilled artists and draughtsmen accompanied every expedition. They recorded objects, peoples, animals, fishes and lands discovered, making it possible to communicate to the European public the beauty and curious richness of the South Seas.

The voyage books published in this period in France are of outstanding quality, distinguished by the exceptional quality of artistic vision coupled with the fullest command to date of the printing processes. The French colour-plate "atlases" to their voyage accounts are among the most beautiful books ever published.

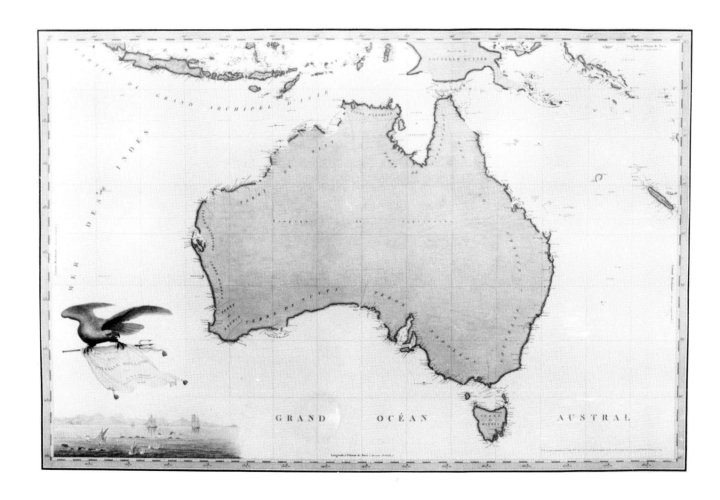

THE BAUDIN VOYAGE

[231] [BAUDIN] PERON, F. A. and L. de FREYCINET. VOYAGE DE DECOUVERTES AUX TERRES AUSTRALES, executé par ordre de Sa Majesté l'Empereur et Roi, sur les corvettes Le Geographe, Le Naturaliste, et la goelette Le Casuarina. *Two volumes, quarto, text, and a two-part large quarto atlas bound in one volume.* Paris, 1807-11-16.

[*and*]

FREYCINET, Louis. VOYAGE DE DECOUVERTES AUX TERRES AUSTRALES... Navigation et Géographie. *Quarto, with its accompanying folio atlas dated 1812, containing engraved title, leaf of contents, and 32 finely engraved charts, each mounted on a stub; an occasional leaf with some foxing or discolouration; an excellent set.* Paris, 1815.

Altogether 4 volumes quarto, and an atlas folio; an excellent set in later half morocco. Paris, 1807-1816.

The full official account of the Baudin-Freycinet voyage, not often found complete; the navigational text and its accompanying atlas were for sale separately, and since their contents were relatively technical, they were not often added to copies of the narrative section, and are now very much rarer.

Baudin died in the course of the voyage: the narrative was begun by Peron, the naturalist, and completed by Freycinet after Peron had also died. The celebrated voyage took back to France the most important collection of natural history specimens in the history of the French Museum, as well as a mass of geographical information.

The French expedition made significant visits to western Australia and Tasmania as well as to Sydney: their interest in the continent was more than that of tourists, and it was with an eye to the military main chance that they looked so carefully at Sydney especially.

The French and English had completed their circumnavigations of the Australian continent at approximately the same time — indeed, they had come across each other in the consequently named

Encounter Bay — but because of Flinders' imprisonment by the French on Mauritius, it was in this account that the first complete and detailed map of the Australian continent appeared. The French map of the continent is one of the most beautiful as well as one of the most famous of all maps of Australia.

A number of the admirable coloured plates which occur in the *Atlas Historique* — many of them a result of the important French visit to Tasmania — have been often reproduced, and thus have become very familiar. *Ferguson, 536 & 603; Wantrup, 78a, 79a, 80a and 81; only the narrative portion is held in the Hill collection — catalogue pp. 229-230.*

FIRST GERMAN EDITION

[232] BAUDIN. PERON, Francois. ENTDECKUNGSREISE NACH AUSTRALIEN... Aus dem Franzosischen uberfest. . . *Octavo, with a folding map and a folding panorama of Port Jackson; original plain grey boards, spine a little worn but a good copy.* Weimar, im Verlage des Landes-Industrie-Comptoirs, 1808.

First German edition of the Baudin expedition: this volume gives the narrative of the voyage up to the stay in Sydney. A second volume continued the account, but did not appear until 11 years later. *Ferguson, 471.*

FIRST ENGLISH EDITION OF FREYCINET'S COMPLETION

[233] BAUDIN. FREYCINET, Louis Claude de. ACCOUNT OF THE BRITISH COLONIES IN N.S. WALES. [On pp. 23-6, 111-116 and 217-221 of The New Monthly Magazine, and Universal Register, Vol. IX] *Octavo, half calf, joints wearing but a good copy.* London, Printed by J. Gillet, 1818.

The first appearance in English of the completion of the Baudin account. Peron had died after finishing the first volume and the second volume was prepared by Freycinet. The editor of *The New Monthly Magazine* explains that "this account, written by a man of superior talents, who resided five months on the

231: BAUDIN. *Lesueur's magnificent view of the new settlement at Sydney, showing present-day Circular Quay, with the mouth of the Parramatta River on the right, was engraved in Paris from a drawing made in 1803.*

spot. . . absolutely contradicts the facts and arguments contained in the justly esteemed works of Colquhoun and Bentham, concerning the British colonies in New South Wales. . .".

BOUGAINVILLE'S SON — THE VOYAGE OF THE THETIS

[234] BOUGAINVILLE, Hyacinthe Yves Philippe Potentin de. JOURNAL DE LA NAVIGATION AUTOUR DU GLOBE de la frégate La Thétis et de la corvette l'Espérance, pendant les années 1824, 1825, et 1826. *Two volumes, quarto, text, with folio atlas; 56 engraved or lithograph plates and maps in the atlas, many coloured by hand; an excellent set in old calf.* Paris, Arthus Bertrand, 1837.

Hyacinthe de Bougainville, son of Louis de Bougainville, sailed as an ensign at the age of 18 on the Baudin voyage. His own expedition of 1826 has continued to be overshadowed by such circumnavigators as Dumont d'Urville. After distinguished service in the Napoleonic Wars, Bougainville was promoted post-captain and given command of the *Thétis*. She was only the second French frigate to be commissioned for a circumnavigation, the first having been his father's vessel the *Boudeuse*.

The voyage took 28 months, visiting amongst other places Pondicherry, Manila, Macao, Surabaya, Sydney (a stay of almost three months), Valparaiso and Rio. Bougainville returned to France with a fine collection of natural history specimens, and the official account of the voyage was handsomely published after a delay of some 11 years.

The major purpose of the expedition was political and strategic, and de Bougainville's first report of 1826 gave the French government a survey of colonial possessions in Asia, of the military strength of Manila, and accounts of Singapore, the Australian colonies and Spanish America. His advice was taken into account in the development of French strategy and diplomacy in the Pacific during the nineteenth century. *Ferguson, 2236; Hill, p. 31.*

VIEWS OF THE THETIS EXPEDITION

[235] BOUGAINVILLE, Hyacinthe Yves Philippe Potentin de. DE LA TOUANNE, Vicomte, *editor.* ALBUM PITTORESQUE DE LA FREGATE LA THETIS ET DE LA CORVETTE L'ESPERANCE. Collection de dessins relatifs à leur voyage autour du monde en 1824, 1825 et 1826, sous les ordres de M. le Baron de Bougainville. *Folio, with 35 uncoloured lithographic plates, of which seven are inserted in the text; all but one of the plates are impressions on India paper, laid down; 2 or 3 leaves with some foxing, and a small number of clean marginal tears, but an excellent copy in the original quarter cloth and marbled boards.* Paris, Bulla, 1828.

A fine series of views, separately issued nine years before the official account of the voyage (see above).

Edmond de la Touanne, a friend and protegé of Bougainville (and referred to in Bougainville's journal as "faithful companion of my travels"), sailed on the expedition as lieutenant de vaisseau. Because of the haste with which the expedition was manned, no

official artist was sent; as Bougainville remarks, no pictorial record of the expedition would have survived but for de la Touanne's sketches.

Rare; not recorded by Ferguson despite considerable Australian content. *Hill, pp. 30-31.*

MARION DU FRESNE'S EXPEDITION

[236] [CROZET] ROCHON, Alexis. VOYAGES AUX INDES ORIENTALES ET EN AFRIQUE, pour l'observation des Longitudes en mer, avec une dissertation interessante sur les îles celebres de Salomon et sur les voyages de Marion, de Surville, de la Peyrouse et de d'Antrecasteau [sic]. . . *Octavo, with a folding map and several folding tables; a fine copy in contemporary sprinkled calf, double labels, spine slightly rubbed.* Paris, chez l'Huillier, 1807.

Second and best edition: Rochon's account of his voyage to Madagascar had first appeared in 1803, but this second edition contains accounts of the expeditions of Marion du Fresne and Crozet — generally known as the Crozet expedition, as well as that of de Surville, and some material on La Pérouse and the voyage in search of him under d'Entrecasteaux.

An astronomer and traveller, Rochon was born at Brest; in 1767 he travelled to Morocco to test theories on the reckoning of longitude, and 2 years later he travelled to the Indian Ocean, at first attached to Kerguelen's first expedition; he had hoped to sail into the Pacific with Marion du Fresne, but "being refused permission to do so, he consoled himself by publishing the account of the expedition, to which he added one of de Surville's. . .".

Marion du Fresne's expedition left Mauritius in 1771, and sailed via the Cape, Crozet Islands, Tasmania, New Zealand, Guam and Manila. A month was spent at the Bay of Islands where Marion and 26 of his crew were massacred by the New Zealanders and Crozet took over the command of the expedition.

Scarce; not in the catalogue of the Hill collection. *Ferguson, 451.*

236: ROCHON. *Rochon's work includes material on the Crozet, de Surville, La Perouse and d'Entrecasteaux expeditions.*

234: BOUGAINVILLE. *The monument to La Perouse erected by the French at Botany Bay (above) and Government House Sydney (below) drawn by de la Touanne on the Bougainville expedition's visit to Sydney in 1825.*

237: DUMONT D'URVILLE.
Chinese stores in Amboina; detail from a coloured plate in the Atlas Historique *of Dumont d'Urville's voyage, based on an original drawing by de Sainson.*

237: DUMONT D'URVILLE.
Detail from the Mollusques *Atlas.*

A MAGNIFICENT SET: WITH THE PLATES IN TWO STATES

[237] DUMONT D'URVILLE, Jules Sebastien. VOYAGE DE LA CORVETTE L'ASTROLABE executé par ordre du Roi pendant les années 1826, 1827, 1828, 1829. . . sous le commandement de M. J. Dumont d'Urville, capitaine de Vaisseau. *Together 15 text volumes (bound in 13), octavo and quarto, and 9 folio atlases; the texts in half blue morocco by Sangorski, the atlases in contemporary half blue morocco, gilt panelled spines; a few corners of atlases bumped, occasional foxing, and a few plates browned as usual, lower margin of part of Hydrographie atlas dampstained, but an extremely attractive set with plates very clean and bright.* Paris, J. Tastu, 1833.

A superb set — the finest that we have seen — of one of the most important French voyages to the Pacific, rarely found complete, with plates magnificently coloured by hand or printed on india paper, and with many duplicated both in coloured and plain states. Perhaps fifty sets were so issued. The set is composed as follows:

TEXTS:

HISTOIRE DU VOYAGE. By Dumont d'Urville. *5 volumes, octavo, with 9 engraved plates and more than 100 text woodcuts.* Paris, 1830-1833.

BOTANIE. By Lesson & Richard. I. Essai d'une Flore de la Nouvelle Zelande. II. Sertum Astrolabianum. *Octavo, two parts in one volume.* Paris, 1832-1834.

ZOOLOGIE. By Quoy & Gaimard. *4 volumes, octavo, with 8 lithograph plates.* Paris, 1830, 1832, 1834, 1832.

ENTOMOLOGIE. By Boisduval. I. Lepidoptères. II. Coleptères. *2 volumes (in 1), octavo.* Paris, 1832, 1835.

PHILOLOGIE. By Dumont d'Urville. *2 volumes (in 1), octavo.* Paris, 1833, 1834.

OBSERVATIONS NAUTIQUES, METEOROLOGIQUES, HYDROGRAPHIQUES ET DE PHYSIQUE. By Dumont d'Urville. *Quarto, with 2 engraved folding tables.* Paris, 1834, 1833.

ATLASES:

ATLAS HISTORIQUE. *3 volumes, folio, engraved titles to each part, with lithograph portrait of Dumont d'Urville and 4 pp. list of plates, 8 maps (6 folding, 1 part coloured); with 237 plates numbered 1-243 (the numbering includes 9 plates which were never published); 84 plates are present in both coloured (on heavy wove) and uncoloured (on India paper) states; 3 plates are in colour only, and 1 plate is in both forms, uncoloured.* Paris, 1833.

MOLLUSQUES. *2 volumes, folio, engraved titles to each part; with 95 plates numbered 1-93 + 'bis' plates 47 & 66 (plate 67 misnumbered 65); all plates present in both coloured and plain states.* Paris, 1832.

BOTANIQUE. *Folio, engraved title and explanation leaf, 2 parts in 1. I. Flore de la Nouvelle Zealande, II. Sertum Astrolabianum; with 84 engraved plates (39 in each part + 2 'bis' plates), part printed in sepia, with 4 plates in first part here in both coloured and plain states.* Paris, 1834.

POISSONS, ZOOPHYTES, ENTOMOLOGIE. *Folio, engraved title; with 50 plates; 12 fish plates (numbered 1-20, but including 8 plates never published) present in both coloured and plain states; 38 zoophyte plates present in both coloured and plain states.* Paris, 1832.

ZOOLOGIE. *Folio, engraved title, with 8 pp. list of plates dated Paris 30 December, 1834; with 59 plates, 28 of mammals (23 here in both coloured and plain states) and plate 3 in both states, both uncoloured; 31 bird plates, all in coloured and plain states.* Paris, 1833.

HYDROGRAPHIE. *Double folio; with engraved title, 25 text pp., 42 engraved maps, charts and plans (19 folding or double page) and 3 plates of New Zealand coastal views (coloured) and folding engraved table.* Paris, 1833.

The *Astrolabe* (Duperrey's old ship the *Coquille*, renamed in honour of La Pérouse), sailed from Toulon in April 1826. Dumont d'Urville was instructed to explore the principal island groups in the South Pacific, completing the work of the Duperrey voyage, on which the commander himself had been a naturalist. Because of his great interest in natural history, huge amounts of scientific data and specimens were collected, described and illustrated in sumptuous folio atlases. The expedition sailed via the Cape of Good Hope, through Bass Straits, stopped at Port Phillip, and arrived at Sydney on December 1, 1828.

Both Sydney and Parramatta (where Dumont d'Urville visited Samuel Marsden) are described and illustrated in the *Atlas Historique*, and the illustrations of Port Phillip are the first of today's Melbourne. The expedition sailed for New Zealand in January 1827, explored Tasman Bay, found a pass between an island in Cook Strait and the northern shore of South Island (the island consequently named d'Urville and the strait "French Strait") and worked up the coast of North Island, completing the "most comprehensive exploration of the islands since Cook's death". They made Tonga in April 1827, explored the Fiji archipelago, New Britain and New Guinea. In

November, after a stop at Amboina, they coasted along the northwest coast of Australia and reached Tasmania. In 1828 they continued to Vanikoro in search of traces of La Pérouse, and stopped at Guam in the Marianas, before returning via the Cape of Good Hope, reaching Marseilles on March 25, 1829.

The plates in the *Atlas Historique* include 26 of New Holland, 14 of Van Diemans Land, 31 of New Zealand, 29 of Tonga, 6 of Fiji, 7 of Guam and 17 of New Guinea. The *Hydrographie* atlas is notable for its extraordinary coloured profile views of the New Zealand coastline, and some of the finest Pacific maps ever produced. *Ferguson, 1341 (not noting any copies with plates in both states); Hill, p. 88.*

UN PETIT SOUVENIR DE L'ASTROLABE

[238] DUMONT D'URVILLE, Jules Sebastien. FINE AUTOGRAPH LETTER SIGNED, to Mme. la Baronne Hyde de Neuville, written shortly after the return of the Astrolabe expedition to France. *Single leaf, quarto, neatly written on recto only, signed "J. Dumont D'Urville"* Paris, 12th May 1829.

A very fine letter by the great navigator, written about 2 months after the return of the *Astrolabe* expedition. Dumont d'Urville writes that the Baroness, he is told, has "deigned to express an interest in the outcome of the *Astrolabe* expedition. . . Among the objects that we have brought back with us is one of those brilliant birds from New Guinea — practically the only object [from the expedition] that a woman could contemplate with any pleasure. . .".

The bird has therefore been sent to her, as "une legère marque de ma gratitude et en même temps comme un petit souvenir de l'Astrolabe. . .".

237: DUMONT D'URVILLE. Otarie cendree, *drawing by Pretre of a young specimen found in Australia, from the* Zoologie *atlas of the Dumont d'Urville expedition.*

237: DUMONT D'URVILLE. *The* Poissons, Zoophytes, Entomologie *atlas includes a series of twelve magnificent plates of fish, present in both coloured and plain states.*

239: DUMONT D'URVILLE. *The* Astrolabe *in the ice; from the* Atlas Pittoresque *of Dumont d'Urville's second, Antarctic voyage.*

238: DUMONT D'URVILLE. *Detail from the explorer's letter sending an ornithological specimen from his recent expedition.*

Original letters by Dumont d'Urville, or indeed by any of the great navigators, discussing their expeditions are very rare, as most are permanently housed in official archives.

DUMONT D'URVILLE'S ANTARCTIC VOYAGE

[239] DUMONT D'URVILLE, Jules Sebastien. VOYAGE AU POLE SUD ET DANS L'OCEANIE sur les corvettes l'Astrolabe et la Zélée. . . pendant les années 1837, 1838, 1839, 1840. *23 volumes bound in 21, octavo, and 6 folio atlases bound in 9 volumes, a little light spotting to text volumes and to a few plates in the Atlas Historique, but overall in excellent condition, in the original half red morocco, a fine set.* Paris, Gide, 1841-1854.

The full official account of Dumont d'Urville's second expedition, a fine set, absolutely complete and comprising the following:

TEXTS:

HISTOIRE DU VOYAGE. *10 volumes.* Paris, 1841-46.

PHYSIQUE. Paris, 1842.

HYDROGRAPHIE. *2 volumes.* Paris, 1843-1851.

BOTANIQUE. *2 volumes in 1.* Paris, 1845-1853.

ZOOLOGIE. *5 volumes in 4.* Paris, 1846-1854.

GEOLOGIE ET MINERALOGIE. *2 volumes.* Paris, 1848-1854.

ANTHROPOLOGIE. Paris, 1854.

ATLASES:

PITTORESQUE. *2 volumes, with 2 frontispieces, 2 double-page maps and 198 plates, mostly on papier de Chine and mounted; some spotting affecting the plates on ordinary paper.* Paris, 1854.

HYDROGRAPHIQUE. *57 maps, mostly double-page.* Paris, 1851.

BOTANIQUE. *66 plates, 20 of which are coloured.* Paris, 1853.

ZOOLOGIQUE. *3 volumes, 140 plates, 36 of which are finely coloured plates of birds.* Paris, 1854.

GEOLOGIQUE. *4 coloured maps and 9 plates.* Paris, 1854.

ANTHROPOLOGIQUE. *50 plates on papier de Chine, mounted.* Paris, 1854.

"The aims of this expedition were to explore the south polar regions and various island groups in the Pacific. The expedition reached the ice pack in January 1838, but failed to penetrate it or get south of the 64th parallel. Returning eastward they visited the South Orkney and South Shetland Islands, and discovered Joinville Island and Louis Philippe Land. Then they proceeded to Valparaiso and Juan Fernandez Island and landed at Mangareva, the Marquesas, Tahiti, Samoa, and Tonga. Proceeding to Fiji, Guam, and Palau, the ships afterwards coasted along New Guinea and circumnavigated Borneo. In 1840, from Tasmania, they returned to the Antarctic region where Adelie Land was discovered. An extensive visit was made to New Zealand. The return voyage took them through Torres Strait to Timor, La Reunion and St. Helena. . ." (Hill).

The last, and one of the most successful, of the great French scientific expeditions. *Hill, p. 89 (Historique section only).*

THE SERIES OF COLOURED BIRD PLATES

[240] DUMONT D'URVILLE, Jules Sebastien. VOYAGE AU POLE SUD ET DANS L'OCEANIE sur les corvettes l'Astrolabe et la Zélée. . . Natural History atlas only. *Folio, with a total of 61 plates, mostly coloured; 7 plates uniformly browned, otherwise in excellent condition, in the original quarter blue morocco, spine worn at base.* Paris, 1842.

One of three natural history atlases from Dumont d'Urville's second expedition (see above), containing the spectacular series of finely coloured bird plates, 36 in all, followed by 25 plates of insects. A number of the birds are Australian species.

ORIGINAL JOURNAL FROM THE ANTARCTIC VOYAGE

[241] DUMONT D'URVILLE, Jules Sebastien. VINCENDON-DUMOULIN, Adrien. VOYAGE DES CORVETTES DE L'ETAT L'ASTROLABE ET LA ZELEE AU POLE AUSTRAL ET AUTOUR DU MONDE. Journal particulier. *2 volumes, folio; autograph manuscript journal; the first volume containing 125 unnumbered leaves, the second the same number but with 25 leaves blank; original*

half cloth and marbled boards, rather worn; considerable damp-staining throughout and parts of the second volume severely affected; preserved in a half green morocco bookform case. At sea, 1837-1840.

The original manuscript journal kept by Adrien Vincendon-Dumoulin during the Dumont d'Urville expedition to the South Pole. Vincendon-Dumoulin not only travelled as official hydrographer on the great expedition to the Antarctic, but he was also, after the death of Dumont d'Urville, given the task of completing the official narrative of the expedition.

His own journal remains quite unpublished, except for some quotation made from it in the official account. It allows us to follow the exact course of the 38 months that the ships spent on the voyage; it gives exact details of the progress of the expedition and of the discoveries made. It is particularly interesting in light of the fact that Vincendon-Dumoulin, as official hydrographer, was always at the centre of activity. His maps and charts were one of the great results of the expedition, many of them being of such high quality that they were still in use at the beginning of this century.

The first volume records the voyage from the departure from Toulon in September 1837, through stops at the Canaries, Brazil and Valparaiso, to their arrival at Raffles Bay and Port Essington in Australia in March 1839.

The second volume deals with the remainder of the voyage, in the far south and far east, and tracks the return, including the stop at St. Helena to see Napoleon's tomb. At the end of the second volume, Vincendon-Dumoulin gives precise tables of latitude and longitude, in keeping with his role as official hydrographer, for the course of the whole voyage.

The manuscript offers an extraordinary insight into Dumont d'Urville's second voyage, as much in the realm of scientific discoveries, often using new techniques, as in the business of topographical discovery and the great successes made in the Antarctic.

The first volume of the manuscript is in good unsophisticated condition; the second volume has been exposed to considerable damp (?sea water), which has affected the ink on a large portion of a number of pages. However only in the first 15 leaves is the legibility of the manuscript seriously affected.

Original manuscript journals deriving from any of the *grands voyages* are very rarely offered for sale.

For a full account of the voyage, see Sharp, *French Explorers in the Pacific*, II, pp. 341-383.

MEDAL FROM THE ANTARCTIC EXPEDITION

[242] DUMONT D'URVILLE, Jules Sebastien. ORIGINAL BRONZE COMMEMORATIVE MEDALLION, ISSUED ON THE RETURN OF THE ASTROLABE AND ZELEE TO FRANCE. Relief portrait (by Barre) of Louis Philippe I and inscription "Louis Philippe I. Roi des Francais" on recto; on verso a long inscription (see below). *51 mm. diameter, bronze medallion, pierced, in good condition.* Paris, 1837.

A rare relic of the second Dumont d'Urville expedition, in which the *Astrolabe* and the *Zélée* explored the Antarctic and named Adelie Land.

The recto of the medal has a portrait of Louis Philippe I; the verso is inscribed "Voyage Autour Du Monde. Exploration Du Pole Austral. Corvettes L'Astrolabe et La Zélée. Mr. Ducampe de Rosamel Vice-Amiral Ministre de la Marine. Mr. Dumont D'Urville Cape. de Vu. Commt. L'Expédition. Mr. Jacquinot Commt. La Zélée. 1857.".

Both rare and desirable: such medals would have been issued only to participants in the expedition. *Marquess of Milford Haven, "British and Foreign Naval Medals", London 1919-1928.*

THE ORIGINAL PROSPECTUS

[243] DUPERREY, Louis-Isidore. VOYAGE AUTOUR DU MONDE, executé par ordre du Roi. . . Prospectus. *Quarto, 12 pp., in fine condition; marbled boards.* Paris, Arthus Bertrand, March 1826.

Very scarce: an original prospectus for the publication of Duperrey's voyage, describing the publication at some length and detailing the various issues available to subscribers. *Not in the catalogue of the Hill collection.*

241: DUMONT D'URVILLE.
Vincendon-Dumoulin was the official hydrographer on Dumont d'Urville's second expedition, to the Antarctic. His original manuscript journal details the progress of the expedition.

242: DUMONT D'URVILLE.
Original medallion from the Dumont d'Urville Antarctic expedition.

THE FULL SET, AS ORIGINALLY ISSUED

[244] DUPERREY, Louis-Isidore. VOYAGE AUTOUR DU MONDE, exécuté par Ordre du Roi sur la Corvette de Sa Majeste, La Coquille, pendant les années 1822, 1823, 1824 et 1825, sous le Ministère et conformément aux Instructions de S.E.M. le Marquis de Clermont-Tonnerre, Ministre de la Marine. *Nine volumes in seven, quarto, text, and four folio atlases; all parts composed of loose leaves and unstitched, as issued; mostly in original wrappers or boards with the exception of the Hydrographical atlas which is in a boards binding of the period, its spine partly defective.* Paris, 1826-1830.

A full set of this magnificent work, publication of which was never completed; in original unsewn sheets, as issued. The set is composed of the following:

HISTORIQUE. *One volume, quarto, and folio atlas containing 60 coloured plates in their 15 original fascicules.*

ZOOLOGIE. *Four volumes in two, quarto, and thick folio atlas containing 157 coloured plates in their 27 original fascicules.*

BOTANIQUE. *Two volumes quarto, and folio atlas containing 106 plates (25 in colour) in their 15 original fascicules.*

HYDROGRAPHIE. *Two volumes, quarto, and folio atlas containing 55 maps and charts.*

The chief purposes of this great expedition were scientific, and they were well achieved by Duperrey. The Museum of Natural History had its collections enriched by specimens of about 1200 insects (some 450 being new), mostly collected on the voyage by Dumont D'Urville, later to make two famous voyages of his own. In addition there were 264 birds and quadrupeds, 63 reptiles, and 288 fishes, more than 80 of these being new species.

Lesson (who published the only full narrative account of this voyage, as Duperrey's own was not completed) was responsible for taking back 300 geological samples. There were also reports on Polynesian languages, costumes, weapons and artefacts, many of these being illustrated in the *Atlas Historique*.

The expedition discovered new islands (for instance in the Gilbert and Caroline groups), corrected errors in existing maps and charts, especially of the Society Islands, and collated valuable meteorological data from an extensive 31-month series of observations of sea temperature and air pressure and temperature, during which six observations were made daily. *Ferguson, 1069; Hill, p. 90.*

BOTANICAL ATLAS: MAGNIFICENT SEAWEED PLATES

[245] DUPERREY, Louis-Isidore. VOYAGE AUTOUR DU MONDE... Histoire naturelle, Botanique. Atlas. *Folio, with 25 coloured plates of seaweed and 14 uncoloured plates numbered 1 to 38, and 51 [of 61 or 67] uncoloured botanical plates numbered 1 to 52; a little light spotting or soiling, but overall in excellent condition and the coloured plates very clean and bright; original front wrapper preserved; old half dark brown morocco, spine gilt with raised bands, a good copy.* Paris, Arthus Bertrand, 1826.

Voy. de la Coquille.   Pl. 5.

LESSONIE NOIRCISSANTE
Lessonia Nigrescens, B

Although the botanical plates by Bessa include 8 of orchids and 11 of ferns, and are drawn from places visited as far apart as the plains of Bathurst and the islands of Polynesia, it is the series of 25 coloured plates of seaweed in this atlas which are the most striking aspect of the book. They have an extraordinary beauty.

The Atlas was never properly finished: the full series of coloured plates is present, but a number of the uncoloured plates were never issued, and the atlas is probably complete as up to a certain date in the form seen here with a total of 90 plates, although either 100 or 106 were eventually issued (according to different authorities) and 117 had originally been intended. *Ferguson, 1069 (noting that the National Library set does not contain the present volume); O'Reilly-Reitman, 822; Hill, p. 90.*

THE VOYAGE OF THE URANIE

[246] FREYCINET, Louis Claude Desaulces de. VOYAGE AUTOUR DU MONDE, enterpris par ordre du Roi... exécuté sur les corvettes de S. M. l'Uranie et la Physicienne, pendant les annees 1817, 1818, 1819 et 1820. *Together 9 volumes, quarto and 4 folio atlases; very occasional spotting to part of text, all plates very clean and bright and the whole set in fine condition; half purple morocco by Niedrée, slightly rubbed.* Paris, chez Pillet ainé & Imprimerie Royale, 1824-1844.

244-245: DUPERREY. *The botanical atlas of Duperrey's voyage includes a striking series of coloured plates of seaweed.*

OPPOSITE:
239-240: DUMONT D'URVILLE. *The official account of Dumont d'Urville's Antarctic voyage includes a magnificent series of coloured plates of birds.*

243: DUPERREY. *Prospectus for the official account of Duperrey's voyage.*

VOYAGE
AUTOUR DU MONDE,
Exécuté par ordre du Roi.

246: FREYCINET. *Dance of the Caroline Islanders; engraving after an original drawing by Jacques Arago, from the official account of the Uranie voyage.*

A fine set of one of the most important of all voyages to the Pacific. It is composed as follows:

TEXTS:

HISTORIQUE. By Freycinet. *2 volumes in 3; with colour printed engraved plate of Chinese tomb stones at Timor in Vol. I Pt. II (1828).* Paris, chez Pillet ainé, 1827-28, 1829, 1839.

OBSERVATIONS DU PENDULE. By Freycinet. Paris, chez Pillet ainé, 1826.

MAGNETISME TERRESTRE. By Freycinet. *With folding engraved chart.* Paris, Imprimerie Royale, 1842.

ZOOLOGIE. By Quoy & Gaimard. Paris, chez Pillet ainé, 1824.

METEOROLOGIE. By Freycinet. Paris, Imprimerie Royale, 1844.

BOTANIQUE. By Charles Gaudichaud. Paris, chez Pillet ainé, 1826.

NAVIGATION ET HYDROGRAPHIE. By Freycinet. *2 volumes in 1, with 3 engraved plates in Vol. II.* Paris, chez Pillet ainé, 1826.

ATLASES:

HISTORIQUE. *Folio; with engraved title, 10 + 2 blank pp. list of plates; 112 plates comprising 13 maps and plans (2 folding) and 99 engraved plates (41 printed in colour and finished by hand).* Paris, chez Pillet ainé, 1825.

NAVIGATION & HYDROGRAPHIE. *Folio, with 22 engraved sheets of maps and charts (10 of which are folding).* Paris, 1826.

ZOOLOGIE. *Folio; with engraved title, and 15 + 1 blank*

pp. *list of plates; with 96 engraved plates (all but 19 printed in colour and finished by hand).* Paris, 1824.

BOTANIQUE. *Folio; with engraved title, and 22 + 2 blank pp. list of plates; with 120 engraved plates.* Paris, chez Pillet ainé, 1824.

Freycinet's major Pacific expedition, noted for its scientific discoveries, was organised by the French government primarily to make observations on geography, magnetism and meteorology, though its natural history discoveries were to prove of equal value. In command was Louis Desaulces de Freycinet, who had previously sailed to the Pacific with Baudin, and Jacques Arago, the official artist.

The *Uranie* sailed from Toulon in September 1817, proceeded via the Cape of Good Hope, and called at the Ile de France in May, 1818. At all points Freycinet compared and corrected the maps of d'Entrecasteaux and Baudin. At Shark's Bay, Western Australia, where he had previously been with Baudin, he more accurately surveyed the bay, discovering a potentially treacherous sand bar. Proceeding through Timor and Waigiou to the Marianas, they spent three months at Guam provisioning, restoring the health of the crew, and conducting the most important charting of the voyage. Guam was surveyed in its whole circumference by canoe.

The expedition arrived at Hawaii on August 8, 1819, visiting Maui, Hawaii and Oahu, and their visit was the last careful examination of the native culture before it was dismantled by western influences.

At Port Jackson, they conducted important experiments at Sydney, visited Parramatta, botanized in the Blue Mountains and examined aboriginal culture.

On their way back to Europe they struck a rock and were shipwrecked at French Bay, Falkland Islands in February 1820, eventually returning to France on an American vessel which Freycinet purchased at the Falklands and renamed the *Physicienne.*

Despite the shipwreck losses, they transported literally masses of natural history specimens, of which 45 of the birds (among which were three new genera), more than 30 reptiles and perhaps 120 fishes were entirely new to science. Of the approximately 3000 plant specimens (largely from Australia, the Mariannas and Hawaii) some 1,200 were hitherto unknown.

The rarely seen *Atlas Hydrographique* contains 7 maps of Guam, 4 of Hawaii (including Kealakekua Bay, Lahaina, Maui and Honolulu), 1 of Australia and 4 of New Guinea. The *Atlas Historique*, with plates by Arago, Pellion and others, contains 16 views and plates of Australia, 32 of Guam and the Mariannas, 9 of Hawaii and 16 of Timor.

Freycinet, in advance of modern scientific method, passed out standardised questionnaires among his staff, requesting them to particularly examine everything which "embraced the physical, moral, and political condition of man". The voyage has also become famous from the fact that Freycinet, contravening orders, was clandestinely accompanied by his wife, who thereby became the first white woman to land in Western Australia and to see many Pacific Islands, including Hawaii. *Ferguson, 941; Hill, p. 425 (Historique only).*

THE EDGE-PARTINGTON COPY

[247] [FREYCINET EXPEDITION] ARAGO, Jacques. NARRATIVE OF A VOYAGE ROUND THE WORLD, in the Uranie and Physicienne Corvettes, commanded by Captain Freycinet, during the years 1817, 1818, 1819 and 1820. *Quarto, 2 parts in 1, folding frontispiece map (mounted on linen) and 25 lithograph plates; modern three-quarter tan morocco, raised panelled spine, top edges gilt; occasional spotting of plates and slight offsetting to a few pages, but an attractive copy; with the bookplate of the noted Pacific collector, James Edge-Partington.* London, Treuttel and Wurtz, 1823.

First edition in English with an important report on the voyage made to the Academy of Sciences in Paris, not in the French edition. An informal account by the official artist of the expedition, written in the form of letters to a friend, deliberately omitting the "eternal repetition of winds, currents, longitude and lattitude". Extensive portions relate to Australia, with descriptions of Sydney, the Blue Mountains, and of meetings with Governor Macquarie and John Oxley. The Hawaii portion comprises more than 95 pages; that of Guam and the Mariannas 104 pages. An early owner has inserted at page 162 an article "The Uranie at Sydney" from *The Gentleman's Magazine* for April 1820.

Arago's introduction sets the tone of the book: "During our long voyage I became acquainted with the numerous tribes; hunted with the Brasilian and the Guanche, danced with the negroes of Africa, and slept

under the hut of the Sandwich Islander. . . I sat at their hospitable tables; and everywhere welcomed, I everywhere contributed my share by a cheerful gaiety, or the present of some European trifles". *Ferguson, 570; Hill, p. 295; Judd, 4.*

WITH THE SERIES OF LITHOGRAPH PLATES BY ARAGO

[248] [FREYCINET EXPEDITION] ARAGO, Jacques Etienne Victor. PROMENADE AUTOUR DU MONDE pendant les années 1817, 1818, 1819 et 1820, sur les corvettes du Roi l'Uranie et la Physicienne, commandées par M. Freycinet. *2 volumes, octavo, modern half calf; with Atlas, small folio, with separate title, table and 23 lithograph plates; paper covered boards, light foxing and some damp stains throughout; occasional spotting mainly to blank leaves of text; a fine entirely uncut copy.* Paris, Leblanc, 1822.

First edition. The list of officers and crew, with interesting biographical details (here in the first volume), does not appear in the English edition. *Ferguson, 850; Hill, p. 7.*

[249] [FREYCINET EXPEDITION] ARAGO, Jacques Etienne Victor. PROMENADE AUTOUR DU MONDE... Atlas of plates only, *small folio, comprising a map and 25 lithograph views, some foxing, generally to margins of plates; old cloth spine and marbled boards.* Paris, Leblanc, 1822.

The full series of lithographs published by Jacques Arago (the official artist to the Freycinet expedition) on his own account. *Ferguson, 850; Hill, p. 7.*

THE BOTANICAL ATLAS

[250] [FREYCINET EXPEDITION] GAUDICHAUD, Charles. VOYAGE AUTOUR DU· MONDE. Botanique. *Quarto, modern three-quarter tan morocco, green cloth boards; moderate foxing of text; with Atlas folio, separate*

VOYAGE AUTOUR DU MONDE,

Sur les Corvettes de S. M. l'Uranie et la Physicienne,

M. LOUIS DE FREYCINET,

Navigation et Hydrographie.

(ATLAS.)

PARIS,

1826.

246: FREYCINET. *The hydrographical atlas to Freycinet's* Voyage autour du Monde *contains a highly important series of Pacific maps.*

246: FREYCINET. *The encampment at Shark Bay on the Peron Peninsula; this view, one of the earliest of any settlement in Western Australia, shows the members of the Freycinet expedition setting up camp ashore.*

title and list of plates, containing 120 engraved plates, some foxing as usual, uniformly bound to match text volume; Bodleian Library duplicate with their release stamp. Paris, Chez Pillet ainé, 1826.

The very scarce botanical results — forming part of the full official account — of the Freycinet expedition. The text begins with general remarks on areas visited, including Brazil, the Cape of Good Hope, New Guinea, the Marianas (17 pp.) Hawaii (20 pp.) and New Holland (18 pp.). The 32 plates of Hawaiian plants include the Sandalwood (Pl. 45), and there are 20 plates of newly described plants from New Holland, "a charming country" ('ce charmant pays') and the only place visited on the voyage which reminded Gaudichaud of "notre belle France". *Ferguson, 850; Hill, p.7.*

ORIGINAL MANUSCRIPT JOURNAL OF THE URANIE EXPEDITION

[251] [FREYCINET EXPEDITION] GAIMARD, Joseph Paul. JOURNAL DU VOYAGE DE CIRCUMNAVIGATION, tenu par Mr. Gaimard Chirurgien à Bord de la Corvette L'Uranie. *Large folio, 489 numbered pages, manuscript in ink on paper, some material at the beginning of the manuscript written by a clerk, otherwise entirely autograph, well written in a legible, cursive hand; some marginal illustrations and separate drawings by Jacques Arago; in very fine condition, contemporary calf binding, spine renewed.* Written at sea,

on board the *Uranie*, between September 1817 and June 1819.

The splendid autograph manuscript journal of surgeon Gaimard of the *Uranie*, recording Louis de Freycinet's voyage to Australia and the Pacific.

A highly literate and informative journal, lengthy and wide-ranging, of the Freycinet expedition to Australia, with fine marginal and other illustrations by the official artist Jacques Arago. Gaimard shows himself throughout to be a perceptive and informed observer, and covers almost every aspect of the countries visited.

The Western Australian material is of particular interest, and includes Gaimard's first-hand account of his expedition on the Peron Peninsula, in which he hoped to prove his theory that the Australian aborigine drank sea water.

Apart from some use, including direct quotation, by Freycinet for his published account of the voyage, Gaimard's manuscript remains unpublished.

The manuscript is written on one stock of French paper, and bound from bifolia; the alternating watermarks are a bunch of grapes and "Blanchet à Rives".

The journal covers the period September 1817 to June 1819. A note by Gaimard on p. 461, dated 8 November 1820, reads "La suite de ce journal, tenu à la mer, se trouve dans les autres cahiers que je remets en même temps que celui-ci à Mr. De Freycinet, Chef

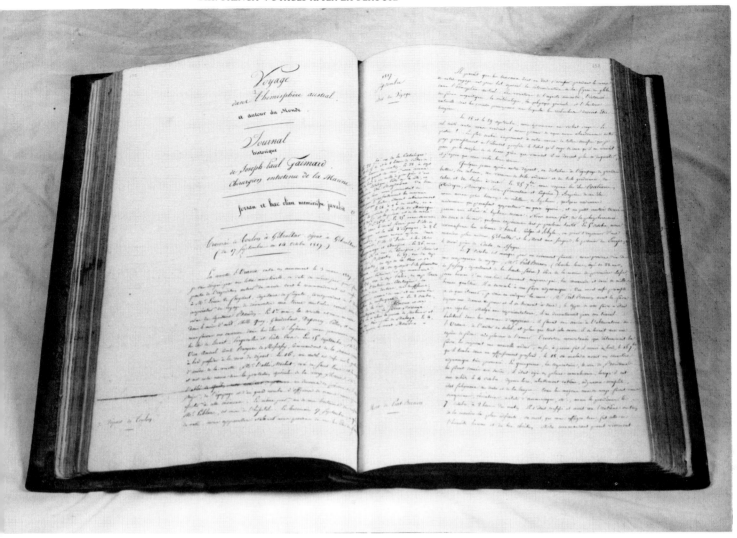

251: GAIMARD. *The beginning of the narrative section of Gaimard journal.*

de l'Expédition, d'après la demande qu'il nous a faite." This implies that Gaimard continued his journal in the form of loose notebooks. What has happened to the remainder is unknown, but it is not beyond possibility that the continuation, whatever the exact form it took, was among the 'many papers' lost in the wreck of the *Uranie* off the Falklands.

The first 60 pages of the journal were written for Gaimard by a clerk, and contain his record of instructions for the voyage, both general and those specific to his role as surgeon. The remainder of the manuscript is in Gaimard's hand.

A note by Gaimard (p. 65) acknowleges that the drawings in the margins were executed for him by Jacques Arago, the expedition's official artist: "Je dois à la complaisance de Mr. Arago la plupart des dessins que l'on voit sur quelques marges de mon journal. P. Gaimard."

These marginal drawings comprise:

(a) 2 ink drawings of Canary Islands spiders (p. 146).

(b) "Cabanes des naturels de la presqu'île Peron". 2 ink and wash drawings of Western Australian aboriginal shelters seen on the Peron Peninsula (p. 278).

(c) "Costume des Guerriers Ombayens". Wash portrait of an armed Ombay native (p. 296).

(d) "Bouclier des Guerriers Ombayens". Wash drawing of Ombay native's shield hanging from a tree (p. 298).

(e) Fine wash portrait of a Timor native (p. 310).

(f) "Tombeau de Van Taybeno". Pen-and-ink drawing of a Dutch tomb in Coupang (p. 326).

(g) "Cabanes de Rawak". Wash drawing of native cabin on stilts in water, Rawak. (p. 358).

(h) "Entrevue avec les Carolins". Wash portrait of tattooed Caroline islander (p. 380).

(i) Outline ink drawing of a fish from a native drawing, Caroline Islands (p. 381).

(j) "Costume actuel des Mariannaises". Wash portrait of two women of the Marianne islands (p. 420).

(k) "Costume actuel des Mariannais". Wash portrait of Marianne islander (p. 424).

(l) "Le Capitaine Martinez avait donne au Tamor Carolin la feuille de papier sur laquelle cette lettre fut ecrite". Pen and wash drawing (p. 455).

(m) "Lepre". Wash drawing of Marianne islander affected by leprosy (p. 468).

(n) "Elephantiasia". Wash drawing (p. 470).

(o) "Lian des Iles Mariannes". Wash double portrait of leprosy sufferers, Marianne islands (p. 472).

(p) "Lepre tuberculeuse". Pencil outline portrait, partly completed in wash, of leprosy victim, Marianne islands (p. 474).

In addition there are 3 larger drawings by Jacques Arago, on separate sheets, not belonging integrally to the original manuscript in a technical sense, but

possibly added to it during the voyage. They are as follows:

1. VUE DE LA CHAPELLE DITE N. D. DE BON VOYAGE à Rio Janeiro. *8 x 10 inches, pencil drawing within ink border; signed. Opposite p. 150.* View of the chapel of Our Lady, on an island in Rio harbour.

2. NATUREL D'OMBAY. *10 x 8 inches, ink and pencil drawing within ink border; signed and dated. Opposite p. 294.* Head and shoulders portrait of an Ombay native.

3. ARMES DES HABITANS D'OMBAY. *8 x 10 inches, pen-and-ink drawing within ink border; extensive captions; signed. Opposite p. 296.* Weapons of the Ombay natives.

A major narrative manuscript, of great Australian and Pacific significance; photographs and a full catalogue are available on request.

VOYAGES AND SHIPWRECKS

[252] LAFOND DE LURCY, Gabriel. VOYAGES AUTOUR DU MONDE et Naufrages Celebres. *8 volumes, octavo, with frontispiece portrait in volume 1, and 76 engraved plates (including 31 hand coloured) and vignette views on title pages; contemporary half dark blue morocco, gilt raised spines; a very attractive set.* Paris, Administration de Librairie, 1843-1844.

An elaborate collection of voyages, including those of the author, in the Pacific. Lafond visited Tahiti on the *Estrella* in 1822 and was in Hawaii in April 1828 on the *Alzire*. Volume 8 includes his account of the voyage of the *Candide* to Australia, New Zealand, Tonga, Fiji and the Mariannas.

Voyages to Mexico and South America are in volumes 1-3; to Hawaii, the Philippines and China in volume 4; South-East Asia in volumes 5-6; Africa, volumes 7-8. *Hill, p. 170; Judd, 99; O'Reilly-Reitman, 805.*

FRENCH INTERESTS IN THE PACIFIC

[253] LAPLACE, Cyrille Pierre Theodore. CAMPAGNE DE CIRCUMNAVIGATION DE LA FREGATE L'ARTEMISE, pendant les Années 1837, 1838, 1839 et 1840. *6 volumes, octavo, with 31 engraved plates, 2 folding coloured maps; original green publishers boards as issued, some wear to corners, text uncut and partially unopened, light spotting of text and plates in volume V, browned as usual; a fine set.* Paris, Arthus Bertrand, 1841-1854.

Laplace's second voyage of circumnavigation, and of the greatest importance in the consolidation of French interests in the Pacific. Begun five years after his earlier voyage in the *Favorite*, the objectives here were to advance wherever possible French political and commercial interests in the Pacific, particularly with respect to Tahiti and Hawaii. The map of the voyage shows the route travelled by both this and Laplace's earlier voyage on the *Favorite* 1830-1832.

John Dunmore, in *French Exploration in the Pacific* (pp. 317-340), discusses this voyage at length and concludes: "The importance of the expeditions of the Venus, the Artemise and the Heroine in laying the foundations for the subsequent sharing-out of Oceania should never be overlooked. . .".

Her visit to Hawaii in July 1839 was one of

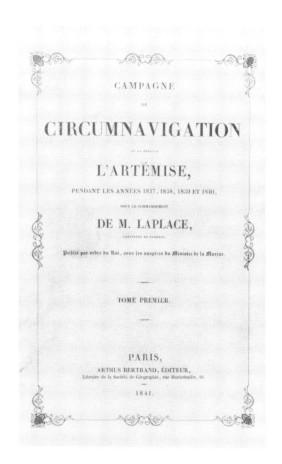

"avowed hostility" (Judd), forcing the government to sign a treaty granting freedom of worship by Catholics, the introduction of French priests, wines and brandies and the trial of French nationals by foreign juries only, backed up by a $20,000 guarantee, which emptied the treasury.

A visit was made to Tasmania where the captain, who had been instructed to look for possible sites for a penal colony, examined the prison system. A lengthy account is included of the stop at Sydney, where he was viewed with some suspicion by the government.

The account of the *Artemise*'s visit to California includes stops at San Francisco and Monterey, and includes a fine view of the mission of San Carlos at Monterey.

Other engraved views include Port Arthur, Tasmania, Honolulu, Manilla, Macao, Calcutta, Bombay and various places in Indo-China. *Not in Ferguson; Judd, 105; O'Reilly-Reitman, 984.*

THE FULL SET OF VAILLANT

[254] VAILLANT, Auguste Nicholas. VOYAGE AUTOUR DU MONDE Execute pendant les années 1836 et 1837 sur la corvette La Bonite, commandée par M. Vaillant, capitaine de vaisseau. *Together 15 volumes of text (in 13), octavo, and 3 folio atlases; uniformly bound in modern half vellum, green morocco labels; title page of Album Historique and list of plates repaired at an early date, light foxing to title and margins of a few plates, but all images clean and bright, preliminary leaves of natural history atlases foxed, but all plates generally very fresh.* Paris, Arthus Bertrand, 1840-1866.

253: LA PLACE. La Place's expedition was of great importance for the consolidation of French interests in the Pacific.

OPPOSITE:
254: VAILLANT. The official account of Vaillant's voyage includes a fine series of 100 topographical plates.

NYCTOCLEPTE DEKAN, Temminck.

254: VAILLANT. *"Nyctoclepte Dekan": hand coloured engraving after a drawing by Meunier in the Zoologie Atlas.*

254: VAILLANT. *Detail from the Zoologie Atlas.*

A fine set of this voyage, very rarely found complete. The set consists of the following:

TEXTS:

RELATION DU VOYAGE. By De La Salle. *3 volumes, with 4 engraved views in volume I.* Paris, 1845, 1851, 1852.

ZOOLOGIE. By Eydoux & Souleyet. *2 volumes.* Paris, 1841, 1852.

PHYSIQUE. By Darondeau & E. Chevalier. *4 volumes (in 3), with 1 plate in volume III.* Paris, 1842, 1846, 1840, 1841.

BOTANIQUE. INTRODUCTION. By Gaudichaud. *2 volumes.* BOTANIQUE I. CRYPTOGAMES. By Montagne, Leveille and Spring. Paris, 1844-1846. BOTANIQUE II. EXPLICATION ET DESCRIPTION DES PLANCHES DES ATLAS. By Charles d'Alleizette. Paris, 1866.

GEOLOGIE ET MINERALOGIE. By E. Chevalier. *Octavo, with 5 engraved plates.* Paris, 1844.

ZOOPHYLOLOGIE. By Laurent. *Octavo.* Paris, 1844.

ATLASES:

ALBUM HISTORIQUE. *With title and 2 pp. list of plates; with 100 lithographs by Bichebois after the drawings of Lauvergne, Touchard and Fisquet, printed on India paper and laid down, some with an added tone plate.* Paris, Arthus Bertrand.

HISTOIRE NATURELLE. BOTANIQUE. By Gaudichaud. *With title and 2 index pp.; with 150 engraved plates (including the double plate numbered 39-40) and 6 coloured engraved plates of sponges and polyps.* Paris, Arthus Bertrand.

HISTOIRE NATURELLE. ZOOLOGIE. By Eydoux and Souleyet. *With title and 8 index pp; with 201 engraved plates (all but 4 coloured).* Paris, Arthus Bertrand.

Though the purpose of this voyage was to expand French interests in South America, the Pacific and the Far East wherever possible, the commander was requested to draw up comprehensive reports on countries visited, with particular attention paid to the natural history of each area. The published results of both the narrative and the scientific investigations are of continuing value.

The ship sailed via Cape Horn, visiting Brazil, Chile, Bolivia, Peru and Columbia. They stayed a month in Hawaii, September-October 1836, visiting both Kealakekua Bay and Honolulu, then continued on to the Philippines and to Canton. Cochin China, Singapore and India were also visited, and the final port of call was St. Helena.

The *Atlas Historique* plates include 6 each of Brazil, Chile, Hawaii and the Philippines, 14 of Macao and Canton, 4 of Singapore, 7 of Pulopenang and 12 of India.

The botanical plates include ferns (12), Bromeliads (19), Pandanus (21), and Lobelioids (7). The Zoology atlas contains plates of Mammals (12), fish (10), Insects (102), and molluscs (52), all but one of which are beautifully coloured.

This set includes the very rare and important botanical volume published in 1866, which describes the plates in the atlas and contains significant revision to the main text. It is not in the Hill collection and does not appear in any set offered at auction for many years. *Hill, p. 303; Borba de Moraes II, 319.*

XIII
Russian Voyages of the Nineteenth Century

Russian voyages into the Pacific began as a direct result of the expanding fur trade with Alaska and the Northwest coast. In 1728 Bering, sent to Kamchatka by orders of Peter the Great, proved the separation of the two continents by the straits which bear his name.

The Russian American Company was formed in 1779, the year of Cook's death; and in 1799 they received a monoply charter from Tsar Paul, and Baranov established his headquarters at New Archangel, Sitka Sound. Russia then entered upon her golden age of maritime achievement, with an outstanding group of naval officers, and executed a series of "Grands Voyages" which were the envy of Europe.

Krusenstern was in charge of the first voyage, and with him served Lisianski, Langsdorff and Kotzebue. Kotzebue was in charge of the second circumnavigation, and with him sailed the artist Choris and von Chamisso, all of whom wrote extensively and well. Kotzebue made a further voyage to the Pacific some five years later.

The Russian vision of the Pacific, although in the same tradition as the European explorers, was distinctively different, as can particularly be seen in the work of the artist Choris.

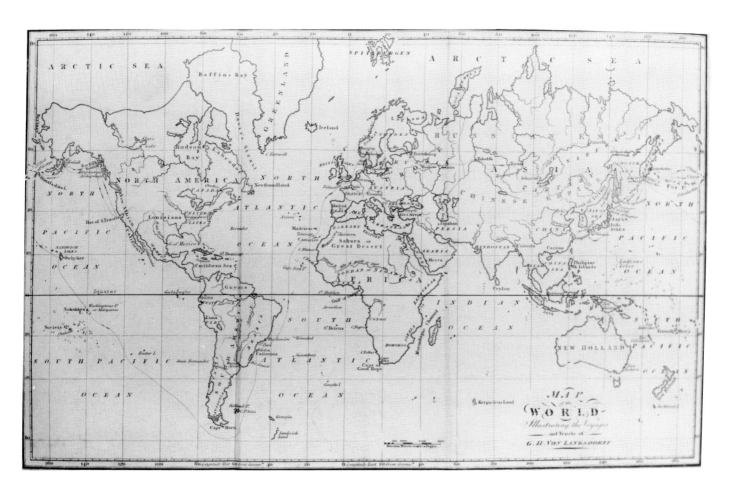

EXPLORATION OF THE NORTHERN PACIFIC

[255] COXE, William. ACCOUNT OF THE RUSSIAN DISCOVERIES BETWEEN ASIA AND AMERICA. To which are added, the Conquest of Siberia, and the History of the Transactions and Commerce between Russia and China. *Quarto, with 3 folding maps and a folding plate; some foxing of text; contemporary tortoise calf rebacked.* London, Printed by J. Nicols, for T. Cadell, 1780.

Second edition, revised and corrected. An important source on Russian exploration and expansion into the Northern Pacific, and their attempt to open trade with Alaska and the Aleutian Islands. Coxe, who travelled to Russia as tutor to the Earl of Pembroke's son, took advantage of his stay to collect, compare and translate journals and voyages subsequent to that of Bering and Tschirikoff in 1741. He collected maps at St. Petersburg, consulted with authorities and included several journals "never before given to the public", directing the "curious and inquisitive reader" to compare them to Cook's then unpublished journals.

The second part, on Siberia, largely taken from works by Muller and Pallas, includes an interesting account of a Russian-Chinese frontier town in Mongolia (illustrated by a large folding plate) and important notes on Chinese-Russian trade.

With the Emo library book plate and ticket of "Sonners, Bookseller, Blandford" at end. *Hill, p.71; Lada-Mocarski, 29.*

[256] SARYCHEW, Gavrila A. ACCOUNT OF A VOYAGE OF DISCOVERY TO THE NORTH-EAST OF SIBERIA, the Frozen Ocean, and the North-East Sea. *Octavo, with 3 folding (& 2 coloured) plates; original cloth; a good modern facsimile.* "London, Printed for Richard Phillips, 1806" [Amsterdam, Nico Israel, 1969].

"Sarychev's journal of the Russian expedition, commanded by the Englishman Captain Joseph Billings, to explore the Arctic and North Pacific Ocean. This official expedition was sent out by Catherine II from 1785 to 1793, during which Alaska and the Aleutians, especially Unalaska, were first carefully charted... Sarychev was an assistant (to Martin Sauer) and this work is an abridged translation of the Russian original of 1802". (Hill). *Hill, p.267.*

THE FIRST RUSSIAN CIRCUMNAVIGATION

[257] KRUSENSTERN, Ivan Fedorovich. VOYAGE ROUND THE WORLD, in the years 1803, 1804, 1805, & 1806, by order of His Imperial Majesty Alexander the First, on board the ships Nadeshda and Neva... translated from the original German by Richard Belgrave Hoppner... *2 volumes, quarto, with folding map of the voyage and two hand coloured aquatint frontispieces; contemporary dark green quarter morocco, spines extra gilt; light occasional foxing.* London, Printed by C. Roworth for John Murray, 1813.

The first Russian circumnavigation, written by its commander, and of great importance to Pacific history for his account of the attempt to open Japan to commerce, and for his notes on the Russian-Chinese trade. The work was of great interest to the west as the

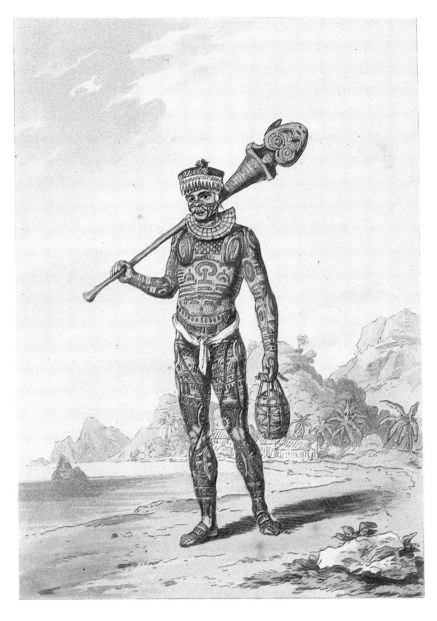

257: KRUSENSTERN. *The tattooed native of Nukahiva, encountered on the Krusenstern voyage.*

ships had been purchased in England, and Krusenstern had served in the British navy. The *Nadeshda* and the *Neva* (with Lisianski in command) sailed from Kronstadt on July 19, 1803, and were together at the Marquesas and Hawaii; there they separated and from this point on Krusenstern's narrative concerns the western Pacific.

After a stop at Kamschatka, they sailed for Japan, arriving at Nagasaki on August 30, with the emissary from the Tsar, and presents, including looking glasses and a portrait of Catherine the Great. Hoping to open a trade mission, and expecting more freedom than the Dutch, they found themselves "greatly mistaken". They were kept in confinement and suspense, and at the audience the following April, the negotiations collapsed. The ships' repairs were put to the Imperial account, all gifts were sent back and they were politely but firmly requested not to return. The narrative contains a detailed account of the negotiations, and includes a view of Nagasaki Harbour, one of the first coloured views of Japan published in the west. Krusenstern charted much of the west coast of Japan, made a short stop at Hokkaido, and at Aniwa Bay, and

257: KRUSENSTERN. *An unusual English binding, for Lord Egremont, on the first English edition of Krusenstern.*

258: KRUSENSTERN. *Lithograph — a proof before letters — from the Parisian atlas to the French edition of Krusenstern: the plates were lithographed by Engelmann from drawings by Tilesius.*

257: KRUSENSTERN. *Lord Egremont's book-plate, which also appears on numbers 202 and 226.*

gives an account of his contact with Ainu people.

At Canton, trade possibilities (particularly in tea) between Russia and China, were investigated, with comparisons between that of England and America. Krusenstern's comments on the Marquesas differ greatly from those of Lisianski.

A fine copy, from the library of George Wyndham, with his signature on the title-page and his bookplate as Lord Egremont. *Hill, p.167; Lada-Mocarski, 61-62 (note).*

WITH THE VERY RARE ATLAS

[258] KRUSENSTERN, Ivan Fedorovich. VOYAGE AUTOUR DU MONDE, fait dans les années 1803, 1804, 1805 et 1806, par les ordres de sa Majesté Impériale Alexandre 1er Empereur de Russie, sur les vaisseaux la Nadiejeda et la Neva. . . *2 volumes, octavo, contemporary quarter calf gilt, tan glazed paper covered boards; [with] Atlas folio, containing separate title, 21 lithograph plates and 9 engraved maps (3 folding); modern quarter red morocco, neat repair to lower corner of title-page and last map; title and all plates in very fine fresh condition.* Paris, Librairie de Gide fils, 1821.

First French edition, with the very rare atlas of plates not published in the English edition. The work was translated and revised by J.B.B. Eyries who also wrote part of the text for Choris' *Voyage Pittoresque.* Though unsigned, O'Reilly says the plates are probably the work of Tilesius, one of the naturalists; they were lithographed by Engelmann in Paris. They include a portrait of Kruzenstern, 4 views of

Nukuhiwa, 8 of Japan (including the Ainus) and one of Aleut Indians. The maps include 3 of the Marquesas and 4 of Japanese interest.

A particularly fine copy of the text, with the plates in the atlas all proofs before letters. "The atlas volume is very important and is difficult to obtain. . ." (Hill). *Hill, pp. 167-8.*

THE FIRST POPULAR ACCOUNT

[259] KRUSENSTERN, Ivan Fedorovich. REISE UM DIE WELT, in den jahren 1803, 1804, 1805 und 1806. . . auf den Schiffen Nadeshda und Newa. *2 volumes (in 3), 16mo; contemporary half calf rebacked, preserving all original spines, red and tan labels with portrait frontispiece of Krusenstern, 12 engraved plates (10 folding and 2 coloured), the Nagasaki plate repaired at an early date, all plates and text clean and bright.* Berlin, bei Haude und Spener, 1811.

The first edition to be printed in Germany (a reprint of the German St. Petersburg edition of 1810-1812) and the first popular account of this important voyage available to the public. The plates include Nukuhiwa (3), Japan (3), Macao, Canton, St. Helena and St. Catherine, Brazil.

An excellent copy of this scarce edition. *Not in Hill; O'Reilly-Reitman, 728; Kroepelien, 691.*

[260] KRUSENSTERN, Ivan Fedorovich. [ATLAS OF THE VOYAGE ROUND THE WORLD] *Large folio, 104 plates on loose sheets, some double-page, a number printed in colour; original blue cloth portfolio.* St. Petersburg,

Engraved by Cooper.

G. V. Langsdorff

Engraved and printed at the Press of the Imperial Navy, 1813. [Amsterdam, Nico Israel, 1973].

Facsimile of the extremely rare Russian-printed atlas to Kotzebue's voyage.

THE FIRST AERIAL ASCENSION IN JAPAN

[261] LANGSDORFF, Georg Heinrich, freihher von. VOYAGES AND TRAVELS IN VARIOUS PARTS OF THE WORLD, during the years 1803, 1804, 1805, 1806 and 1807. *2 volumes (in 1), quarto, with frontispiece portrait and 21 engraved plates, and folding map; contemporary half russia, slight scuffing to spine and joints, some offsetting of plates, stains to a few pages and occasional foxing; a good tall copy.* London, Printed for Henry Colburn, 1813.

First edition in English. Langsdorff was a physician and naturalist on the voyage round the globe on the *Neva* under Krusenstern. He went around Cape Horn to Kamschatka, making stops at the Marquesas and Hawaii. At Kamschatka, he left the expedition and proceeded on the *Maria* with Nicolai Rezanov, a

261: LANGSDORFF. *Langsdorff, who travelled as physician on the* Neva *under Krusenstern, wrote his own account of the expedition.*

262: LISIANSKI. *Northwest coast landscape, from Lisianski's* Voyage.

Russian official who was commissioned to study the Russian American Company in Alaska and to conduct trade negotiations with Japan. Langsdorff states that, though they were politely but firmly refused, their visit was "the most interesting part of our expedition", devoting nearly 100 pages to their stay at Nagasaki. In their spare time they constructed a Mongolfier-type balloon and made the first aerial ascent in Japan.

The narrative contains a lengthy record of their stay in the Marquesas, and a "fuller account of Sitka and the settlement of San Francisco than any other contemporary account" (Sabin). The plates include 8 of the Marquesas, 5 of Japan, 3 of Alaska and 2 of California. *Hill, p. 171.*

KODIAK TO HAWAII

[262] LISIANSKI, Iurii Fedorovich. A VOYAGE ROUND THE WORLD, in the years 1803, 4, 5, & 6; performed, by order of His Imperial Majesty Alexander the First, Emperor of Russia, in the Ship Neva. *Quarto, with frontispiece portrait, 8 coloured charts (including 3 folding), 3 plates and 2 hand coloured aquatint views; modern full diced citron calf, spine extra gilt, red morocco title labels, marble end papers, a.e.g.; occasional very light spotting to text, unobtrusive repair to title page, slight offsetting of some plates as usual, but all plates in very fine condition.* London, Printed for John Booth, 1814.

First English edition. A narrative of the greatest

importance for its account of Russian expansion into Alaska. When the Krusenstern expedition split in Hawaii in 1804, Lisianski proceeded on the *Neva* directly to Kodiak where he confirmed reports of the destruction of the settlement at Sitka by Kolosh Indians, who were determined to prevent any attempts at reoccupation. Lisianski sailed into Baranov, repulsed the Indians, and took possession of a new hill, which he named New Archangel. He spent more than a year at both Sitka and Kodiak, and the narrative of more than 100 pages proves him to have been a keen observer.

Enroute to China with a rich cargo of furs, he struck a reef, thereby discovering the island in the Hawaiian chain which bears his name. Though uninhabited, it was a potential danger to navigators.

His account of the Marquesas differs from that of Krusenstern, and the Hawaii portion is of greater length, including visits to Kealakekua and Waimea Kauai. The Pacific narrative concludes with a generous account of his stay at Canton.

The aquatint views of Alaska are among the most beautiful ever issued of that area. The maps were produced under the direction of Arrowsmith in London, and include profile views.

A most attractive copy of a rare work. *Hill, p. 182; Lada-Mocarski, 68 (describing the Russian edition of 1812, calling this narrative "very important and rare. . . on the history of Alaska in general and Sitka in particular").*

KOTZEBUE'S FIRST VOYAGE

[263] KOTZEBUE, Otto von. ENTDECKUNGS-REISE IN DIE SUD-SEE UND NACH DER BERINGS-STRASSE... Unternommen in den Jahren 1815, 1816, 1817 und 1818... auf dem Schiffe Rurick. *Quarto, with 7 engraved maps and charts (6 folding), 7 hand coloured aquatint plates (3 folding), 1 plain plate and 'monkey skull' plate, and 11 hand coloured plates of butterflies; modern three-quarter tan calf over earlier boards, preserving the original paper title label; frontispiece portrait to Volume II remargined, and plate at page 60 (Vol. II) uncoloured and from another edition; but withal, a remarkably fine clean copy, entirely uncut, printed on Velin paper.* Weimar, Gebruder Hoffmann, 1821.

First, Weimar edition. A celebrated narrative, important for its descriptions of Alaska, California, Hawaii and Micronesia, which contains Kotzebue's acute observations on areas visited, with particular and often critical attention paid to their administration. The *Rurik* sailed from Kronstadt July 30, 1815, for the Pacific via Cape Horn. After making the Chilean coast, they stopped at Easter Island March 1816, sailed through the Tuamotus, and out of Polynesia, discovered Radak and Ralik chains of the Marshall Islands, which are described her in great detail. Later, after a stop at Kamschatka, and in search of a North-East passage, they explored the sound North of Bering Strait now named Kotzebue Sound. Lada-Mocarski calls their account of Alaska "rich in early original source material". The *Rurik* sailed along the California coast, stopped at San Francisco, described the missions, and the work is considered one of the most important early accounts of the state.

Kotzebue made a stop in Hawaii in November-December 1816, revisiting again in September-October 1817, anchoring off Hawaii and Oahu. The Hawaiian portion is extensive with important observations on life and customs during the reign of Kamehameha I, whose famous "red vest" portrait by Choris is one of the illustrations.

The third volume has considerable scientific data on all areas visited, and includes the beautiful coloured butterfly plates omitted from the English and Russian editions. The plates, many of which are very-beautiful hand coloured aquatints, include 2 each of Alaska and Hawaii, and 4 of Micronesia. *Hill, p.164-5; Judd, 904; Lada-Mocarski, 80; Kroepelien, 670.*

[264] KOTZEBUE, Otto von. A VOYAGE OF DISCOVERY, INTO THE SOUTH SEA AND BEERING'S STRAITS, for the purpose of Exploring a North-East Passage, undertaken in the years 1815-1818... in the ship Rurick. *3 volumes, octavo, with 9 engraved plates and portraits (8 coloured), 6 charts (3 folding); half calf antique, original marbled boards, slight wear to a few joints; a fine copy.* London, Printed for Longman, Hurst, Rees, Orme, and Brown... 1821.

First edition in English, translated by Hannibal Evans Lloyd of the Foreign Office, London, and published the same year as the German original. The long introduction by Krusenstern reviews the voyage and stresses the need for subsequent explorations. The attractive plates after watercolours by Choris include a

view of Kailua, Kona, and the famous portrait of Kamehameha I. "A very important and much prized work". (Hill). *Hill, p.165; O'Reilly-Reitman, 776.*

[265] [KOTZEBUE: FIRST VOYAGE] CHAMISSO, Adaelbert von. REISE UM DIE WELT mit der Romanzossischen Entdeckungs-Expedition in den Jahren 1815-18 auf der brigg Rurik, Kapitain Otto V. Kotzebue. [*In:*] Werke. Erste-vierter band. *4 volumes (in 2), duodecimo, with frontispiece portrait of Chamisso, folding table and 2 maps of the Caroline Islands; contemporary half roan, worn, back hinge to first volume broken; with 19th century San Francisco bookseller's label "W. Schleiden's Bookstore, Sacramento 2 doors below Montgomery".* Leipzig... 1842.

Second edition of Chamisso's narrative of the first Kotzebue voyage on the *Rurik* in 1815-1818, containing lengthy accounts of Micronesia, Hawaii and California.

The second volume contains a comparative vocabulary of 4 Mariannas Islands dialects. *This edition not in Kroepelien (see 185-186 for other editions); Hill II, p.373 (first edition).*

VOYAGE PITTORESQUE: 104 HAND-COLOURED LITHOGRAPHS

[266] CHORIS, Louis. VOYAGE PITTORESQUE AUTOUR DU MONDE, avec des Portraits de Sauvages

263: KOTZEBUE. *The first edition of Kotzebue's voyage in the* Rurik *includes a beautiful series of coloured plates of butterflies.*

d'Amerique, d'Asie, d'Afrique, et des îles du Grand Ocean; des paysages, des vues maritimes, et plusieurs objets d'histoire naturelle. *Folio, with lithograph frontispiece portrait of Count Romanzoff, 104 hand coloured lithograph plates, folding map of the voyage and 2 plans (on one sheet); with text in 12 separately paged sections and with plates also separately numbered; contemporary red morocco spine and corners, red glazed paper boards, title in gilt on spine; occasional foxing to text leaves as in nearly all copies, some browning to a few plates. Paris, de l'Imprimerie de Firmin Didot, 1822.*

A fine copy of the most beautiful colour plate book of the North and Central Pacific, containing more early coloured views of Hawaii, Alaska and California than any other.

Choris, a Russian of German stock, was only 20 when he was appointed as official draughtsman on the Kotzebue expedition of 1815-1818. During this voyage he produced a vast number of important sketches and watercolours, and on his return to Paris was encouraged to produce this great work. It was first issued in 22 parts between 1820 and 1822, though only a very few copies today contain the 1820 title page and the portrait of the artist. Most of these views did not appear in the official account of the expedition published in Germany and in Russia. A number of the plates were re-lithographed to suit the artist.

This copy contains the Norblin version of the Queen Kaahumanu portrait, the preferred Langlume lithograph of Kamehameha and the first state of the female dancers (Plate XVI) with the plain background.

The many beautiful plates include views and scenes of native life, artefacts, plants, shells and animals. Twelve relate to California (including several of San Francisco), while nineteen are of Hawaii (with the first view of Honolulu), twenty-three of Alaskan interest, and twenty-one of various parts of Micronesia. Lada-Mocarski calls it "one of the very valuable and fundamental works on Alaska, California and the Hawaiian Islands". The list of subscribers, which accounts for only 188 copies, includes the Emperor of Russia, and the King of France.

This is the Pourtales-Carlsmith copy, with the armorial bookplate of Count Frederic de Pourtales. *Hill, p.51-52; Lada-Mocarski, 84.*

VUES ET PAYSAGES: 24 COLOURED PLATES

[267] CHORIS, Louis. VUES ET PAYSAGES DES REGIONS EQUINOXIALES, recueillis dans un voyage autour du monde. *Folio, with 24 hand coloured lithographs; contemporary red morocco spine, marble paper covered boards, corners bumped and one torn, extremities of spine a little worn, occasional spotting to text and some plates, plate VII and leaf of text repaired at an early date. Paris, Imprimerie Paul Renouard, 1826.*

Choris' handsome sequel to his *Voyage Pittoresque,* this contains hitherto unpublished views taken on the Kotzebue Expedition of 1815-1818. The strikingly beautiful plates emphasise the lush effects of palms and

266: CHORIS. *Queen Kaahumanu; Choris' portrait shows the Rurik at sea in the background.*

OPPOSITE:
266: CHORIS. *King Kamehameha was the last great ruler of the Hawaiian Islands. Choris' famous portrait of him (below) also appeared in several different versions including the so-called "red vest" image published by Kotzebue (opposite number 263).*

267: CHORIS. *Landscape from Choris' second folio.*

other plants in the tropics, contrasted by the stark grandeur of the views of Kamchatka and Chile, which were inspired by von Humboldt's *Tableaux de la Nature*, to whom the work is dedicated. The plates include 5 of Brazil, 3 of Chile, Micronesia (6), Hawaii and Kamchatka with 2 each, and Manilla, the Cape of Good Hope, St. Helena and Easter Island with one each. A Kamchatka plate shows an Aleutian in his baidar approaching a sea-lion covered shore. The most famous and important plate (XVIII) shows the audience of officers of the Kotzebue expedition, with King Kamehameha at Kailua, Kona. *Not in Hill; Lada-Mocarski, 90.*

KOTZEBUE'S SECOND VOYAGE

[268] KOTZEBUE, Otto von. A NEW VOYAGE ROUND THE WORLD, in the years 1823, 24, 25, and 26. *2 volumes, octavo, 2 engraved plates, 1 plan and 2 folding charts; contemporary green calf, gilt panelled spines, red and green title labels, the spines slightly faded, some wear to joints of vol. I; bookplate of Sir Richard Vyvian; a fine copy.* London, Henry Colburn & Richard Bentley, 1830.

First English edition of Kotzebue's second voyage to the Pacific. In 1823, the author was ordered to the Northwest coast on the *Predpriatie* to protect the Russian American Company from foreign fur poachers and to also conduct a scientific voyage. After calling at Kamschatka, they made a stay of several months on Baranov Island (Sitka) during which Kotzebue records much on the Tlingit Indians who had caused so much trouble for the Russians. He then continued down the coast of California to the Russian settlement at Fort Ross, provides a good description of San Francisco and the various missions and includes the prophetic

comment that "how abundantly and happily might thousands of families subsist here".

The long stay at Hawaii is of special interest. The author describes at length the political and social changes that had occurred since his visit on the *Rurik* in 1816, regretting that the people of Oahu had "lost the simplicity and innocence of character which formerly distinguished them". Other places visited include Rio de Janeiro, Micronesia and Tahiti, all of which are described in some detail. Although Pitcairn was not visited, Kotzebue gives a general history including particulars learned in Tahiti from members of Adams' family. *Hill, p.166; Lada-Mocarski, 93 (St. Petersburg edition, 1828).*

[269] LUTKE, Frederic. VOYAGE AUTOUR DU MONDE, executé par ordre de sa majesté l'Empereur Nicolas 1er sur la Corvette Le Seniavine, dans les années 1826, 1827, 1828 et 1829. *3 volumes, octavo; with Atlas folio, containing 3 maps (2 folding) and 64 lithographed views and plates (on 51 sheets); original cloth, a good modern facsimile.* "Paris, Typographie de Firmin Didot Frères, 1835-1836" [Amsterdam, Nico Israel, 1971].

"An outstanding example of Russian explorations in the North and South Pacific". (Lada-Mocarski). The expedition sailed to the Pacific via Cape Horn, made a stop at Sitka, explored the Aleutian Islands and the Bering Sea, and fully explored and mapped the Kamschatka peninsula. Islands in the Caroline group of Micronesia were explored during the winter of 1828, and the voyage collected a vast amount of zoological, botanical, and other natural history specimens which were deposited in the Imperial Academy of Sciences, St. Petersburg. *Hill, p.185-6; Lada-Mocarski, 100.*

XIV
Voyages of Other Nations

アメリカ
ぞうき
蒸氣舩
之圖

While the French, English and Russian expeditions dominated the nineteenth century Pacific, there was still room for other nations. Some of the lesser known but most important printed accounts of the period give us details of Japanese, Swedish, Dutch, German and Spanish voyages.

Eventually the Americans were to launch their own full-scale expedition under Charles Wilkes, but their presence in the Pacific began earlier with the missionaries and the private commercial voyages, and their military presence was strongly felt from the second decade of the century in the form of the predatory frigate the Essex *under her captain David Porter.*

THE DYING WHALE

DUTCH CIRCUMNAVIGATION

[270] BOELEN, Jacobus. REIZE NAAR DE OOOST-EN WESTCUST VAN ZUID-AMERIKA, en, van daar, naar de Sandwichs en Philippinische Eilanden, en China enz., gedaan, in de jaren 1826, 1827, 1828 en 1829, met het koopvaardijschip: Wilhellmina en Maria. *3 volumes, octavo, with chart of the voyage and 4 maps (all folding), 6 coloured engravings and 4 lithograph views (2 folding); original printed wrappers as issued, some foxing and occasional chipping to wrappers, text uncut and partially unopened, and free from foxing; a fine copy of a very scarce voyage.* Te Amsterdam, Ten Brink & De Vries, 1835.

A little known Dutch commercial circumnavigation, important as an extensive portion of the text relates to the author's trading in ports on both sides of the South American Coast including Rio de Janeiro, Montevideo, Valparaiso, Africa and Guyaquil.

The work is important for its narrative of Boelen's 1828 visit to Hawaii in the *Wilhelmina and Maria*; stopping first at Kealakekua Bay, the ship continued on to Honolulu, and the account contains significant descriptions of both ports, with perceptive comments on the King, the various cheifs and foreigners he came into contact with.

At Canton, Boelen reported on Dutch activities in the area, and the voyage continued to the Philippines and Batavia, returning to Europe via the Cape of Good Hope.

The plates, which are rarely found coloured as here, include a view of Rio, 5 costume plates of South American interest, an engraved map of the Hawaiian Islands, a view of the *Wilhelmina and Maria* at Kealakekua Bay, 2 maps of the China coast, a coloured engraving of Canton merchants and a view of the Hongs at Whampoa. *Hill, p. 357; Judd, 23.*

SWEDISH CIRCUMNAVIGATION

[271] [EUGENIE EXPEDITION] ANDERSSON, Nils Johan. EN VERLDSOMSEGLING SKILDRAD I BREF, af N. J. Anderson, naturforskare under expeditionen med fregatten Eugenie aren 1851, 1852 och 1853. *3 volumes in 2, duodecimo, with folding frontispiece map; original brown cloth spines, blue marble paper covered boards, slight scuffing to boards, occasional spotting of text, repaired tear to one leaf affecting a few words; a very good copy.* Stockholm, Samson & Wallin, 1853-54.

First edition: an account of the first Swedish circumnavigation (1851-1853) by the naturalist of the expedition. Andersson, a botanist and professor at Uppsala University, was aboard the frigate *Eugenie* under the command of Capt. C. A. Virgin. They sailed to Rio de Janeiro, Buenos Aires, and around South America to California, with numerous stops en route. The ship anchored in San Francisco Bay and the author made a trip to the Goldfields near Sacramento which he describes at length (60 pp.). The voyage stopped at Hawaii, pp. 33-197, Tahiti, pp. 197-239, New Holland, pp. 1-71 of the 2nd volume and China, pp. 97-173.

Andersson's account was popular in Europe, and several German editions appeared. *Hill, p. 341; Kroepelien, 24.*

THE OFFICIAL ACCOUNT

[272] [EUGENIE EXPEDITION] SKOGMAN, Carl. FREGATTEN EUGENIES RESA OMKRING JORDEN aren 1851-1853, under befal af C. A. Virgin. *2 volumes in 1, octavo, with 3 folding tinted maps, and 20 lithographs (18 coloured) and numerous woodcuts; contemporary black calf spine and corners, gilt spine, embossed paper covered boards with gilt cypher on upper cover, some wear to boards, hinges a trifle weak; a good copy.* Stockholm, Adolf Bonnier, [1854-1855].

First edition. The official account of the first Swedish circumnavigation. Undertaken by order of Oscar I, son of Marshal Bernadotte who had founded the present reigning royal family, the purposes were political, scientific and commercial. The work contains particularly good accounts of their stops in Honolulu, Tahiti, San Francisco, Sydney and Manilla, with shorter notices on various South American ports, the Galapagos, Hong Kong, Singapore and the Cape of Good Hope. The chromolithograph plates include 4 of Tahiti, 3 of Hawaii, 2 of Manilla and a view of Mission Dolores, San Francisco. *Not in Ferguson; Hill, p. 573; Kroepelien, 1196.*

THE EUGENIE IN HONOLULU

[273] [EUGENIE EXPEDITION] [SKOGMAN]. DUTTON, Meiric K. *Translator.* HIS SWEDISH MAJESTY'S FRIGATE EUGENIE AT HONOLULU... 22 June-July 2, 1852. *Octavo, with folding frontispiece map; printed blue wrappers.* Honolulu, Loomis House Press, 1954.

A translation with an introduction of the Hawaiian portion of Skogman's account, and the only portion available in English. *Judd, 163a.*

272: EUGENIE. *Skogman's account of the* Eugenie *expedition contains lithographs after his own drawings.*

An Account of a recent discovery *of* seven Islands *in the South Pacific Ocean, by* JOSEPH INGRAHAM, *Citizen of Boston, and Commander of the brigantine* Hope, *of seventy Tons burthen ; of, and from this Port, bound to the N. W. Coast of America. By permission of the Owners, copied from the Journal of said* Ingraham, *and communicated to the Public, by the* HISTORICAL SOCIETY.

AFTER passing Cape Horn, on the 26th of January, 1791, Capt. Ingraham saw the islands of St. Ambrose and Felix, on the 9th of March—and on the 14th of April, touched at *Port Madre de Dios* in the island of *Dominica*, one of the cluster called the *Marquesas* lying in lat. 9° 58′ S. Having procured such refreshments as the place afforded, he sailed thence, on the 18th of April ; and here the extract from his Journal begins.

"*April* 19. [a day ever memorable to Americans.] We steered N. N. W. from the island of Dominica, and at 4, P. M. saw *two islands* under our lee ; one bore N. W. by N. from us, and N. N. W. distant 35 leagues from the N. W. end of Dominica ; the other bore W. of us. This sight was unexpected, as I knew we had seen and passed all the group called the Marquesas. On this I examined Capt. Cook's chart of the world, his voyages, Quiros's voyage, who was with the Spanish Admiral, that discovered the Marquesas in 1595, M. Bougainville's account of circumnavigators and lands discovered by them, all my charts and globes of modern date ; but could find no account of but five islands in the group, called Marquesas de Mendoça, or any land laid down where these islands we then saw were. Of course I had reason to conclude ourselves the first discoverers. On which I named the first WASHINGTON's *island*, in honour to the illustrious President of the United States of America. The other I called ADAMS's

274: INGRAHAM. *The American discoveries in the Marquesas are now known to have preceded those of Marchand.*

DISCOVERY OF THE NORTHERN MARQUESAS

[274] INGRAHAM, Joseph. AN ACCOUNT OF A RECENT DISCOVERY OF SEVEN ISLANDS IN THE SOUTH PACIFIC OCEAN... [Pp 20-24 of] Collections of the Massachusetts Historical Society, No. 1, January 1793. *Octavo, 24 pp., light water-stain but an excellent unsophisticated copy in the original printed wrappers, uncut, spine torn, unstitched as issued, held at spine with original pin.* Printed at the Apollo Press in Boston by Belknap and Hall, 1793.

The only contemporary account of the discovery of the northern Marquesan Islands, including Nukuhiva — the setting for Herman Melville's *Typee*.

Ingraham traversed the Marquesas in 1791; Mendana had already discovered the four southernmost islands, and Cook had added Fatu Huku, but it was Ingraham who discovered Ua Pou (which he named Adams Island), Ua Huka (Washington Island), Nukuhiva (Federal Island), Motuoa (Lincoln Island), Motuiti (Franklin Island), Eiao (Knox Island) and Hatutu (Hancock Island).

Information about these discoveries appeared only in this scarce publication of the Massachusetts Historical Society, which did not circulate widely. As a result it was thought for a long time that the islands had in fact been discovered by the French voyager Etienne Marchand a few months later. Percy Buck proved Ingraham's prior claims, working from a photostat of Ingraham's journal of the voyage. This

publication, which is taken directly from Ingraham's journal on his return to his home port of Boston, was not known to Buck, but is used by Sharp to demonstrate the same argument.

Ingraham's original journal is now in the Library of Congress. The Hawaiian Historical Society published a section from it, describing Hawaii, in 1918, and Bjarne Kroepelien of Oslo published the Marquesas section, in French, in 1937. Both these slight publications are now rare, and no full text of the log appeared until the Imprint Society of Barre, Massachusetts, published a limited edition in 1971.

This is therefore the single contemporary printed source for the discovery of the northern Marquesas, as well as the only contemporary printed account of any part of this important early American voyage to the Pacific. *Sharp, Discovery of the Pacific Islands, pp. 166-8; Buck, Explorers of the Pacific, Honolulu, 1953, pp. 63-4; not in the catalogue of the Hill Collection (but referred to in notes to the 20th century publications, pp. 443 & 456).*

VIANA: A PRESENTATION COPY

[275] [MALASPINA] VIANA, Francisco Xavier de. DIARIO DEL VIAGE EXPLORADOR DE LAS CORBETAS ESPANOLAS "DESCUBIERTA" Y "ATREVIDA" en los anos de 1789 a 1794. . . *Octavo, with two title-pages (as issued, confusing Ferguson); in fine condition in original quarter calf.* Montevideo, Cerrito de la Victoria, Imprenta del Ejercito, 1849.

One of the rarest voyage books relating to Australia and the Pacific: a particularly fine presentation copy with an inscription on the title-page from Viana. The first publication of a crucial Spanish world voyage made at the end of the eighteenth century and including an important visit to Port Jackson in 1793.

Malaspina's voyage was the major Spanish circumnavigation of the eighteenth century. An official publication was intended, and the artists and scientists of the expedition worked towards its production, but Malaspina became a victim of Spanish court intrigues and ended up in prison; his narrative of the voyage was suppressed (eventually being published in Madrid in 1885) and the full official account was completely abandoned.

Not until 1849 was any account of the voyage published, when this narrative by an ensign on the voyage, Francisco Viana, who settled in Uruguay towards the beginning of the nineteenth century, was published by his sons in Montevideo. The book is extremely rare, and was not republished until 1967 when the Australian Documentary Facsimile Society reprinted the Port Jackson section with a preface and translation by A. Grove and Virginia M. Day in an edition limited to 275 copies.

Its importance to Australian history is considerable; the visit to Port Jackson took place barely five years after the first settlement — indeed it is described at some length in Collins' *Account of the English Colony* — and the visitors were welcomed by Grose (in the governor's absence) and entertained by Collins, White, Prentice and Johnston.

Ferguson's entry for the book is very confused (he

DIARIO

DEL

VIAGE EXPLORADOR

DE LAS

CORBETAS ESPAÑOLAS

"DESCUBIERTA" Y "ATREVIDA,"

EN LOS AÑOS DE 1789 á 1794,

LLEVADO POR EL TENIENTE DE NAVIO D. FRANCISCO JAVIER DE VIANA,
Y OFRECIDO PARA SU PUBLICACION, EN SU ORIGINAL INEDITO, POR
EL Sr. D. FRANCISCO JAVIER DE VIANA, Y DEMAS HIJOS DEL AUTOR.

CERRITO DE LA VICTORIA.
IMPRENTA DEL EJÉRCITO.
1849.

describes it under two separate numbers, 5100 and 5228). He records a copy at the National Library of Australia and another at the Mitchell Library in Sydney; in fact the Mitchell copy, as Grove Day pointed out, lacked the crucial Port Jackson section itself, but the Library has recently acquired a perfect copy. Grove Day also records copies of the book at the Museo Naval in Madrid and in the Library of Congress, but notes that it is not held by the British Library. No copy is recorded in the catalogue of the Hill Collection.

For modern treatments of the expedition see particularly *The Spanish at Port Jackson* (Sydney, 1967) and *Voyages of Enlightenment: Malaspina on the Northwest Coast 1791-2* (Oregon Historical Society, 1977). For Malaspina's own account see *Viaje Politico-Cientifico alrededor del Mundo. . .* (Madrid, 1885).

MALASPINA'S ARTISTS

[276] [MALASPINA] SERRANO, Carmen Sotos. LOS PINTORES DE LA EXPEDICION DE ALEJANDRO MALASPINA. *2 volumes, quarto, with over 800 photographic illustrations, some in colour; a fine copy in the original pictorial wrappers.* Madrid, Real Academia de la Historia, 1982.

The standard work on the artists of the Malaspina expedition. The reproductions of the original pictorial materials held in Madrid show quite how grand an account would have been published of this important expedition if circumstances had not intervened.

THE SPANISH AT PORT JACKSON

[277] [MALASPINA] GROVE DAY, Dr. A. & Virginia M. THE SPANISH AT PORT JACKSON. The visit of the corvettes Descubierta & Atrevida, 1793. *Quarto, with a frontispiece, 9 pages of tipped-in facsimiles, and 2 other facsimiles; a good copy in original printed boards, slightly soiled.* Sydney, Australian Documentary Facsimile Society, 1967.

One of only 275 copies: the first appearance in English of Viana's description of the visit of the Malaspina expedition to Sydney in 1793.

RARE JAPANESE PACIFIC NARRATIVE

[278] [MANJIRO NAKAHAMA] A RECORD OF DRIFTING (title in Japanese). By "Dontsushi". *16 double leaves, contemporary Japanese binding, in a folding cloth case; a few worm holes neatly repaired at an early date; a particularly fine copy.* Nagasaki, 1852.

275: MALASPINA. *No account of Malaspina's eighteenth century expedition was published until this very rare Montevideo printing of the ensign Viana's narrative.*

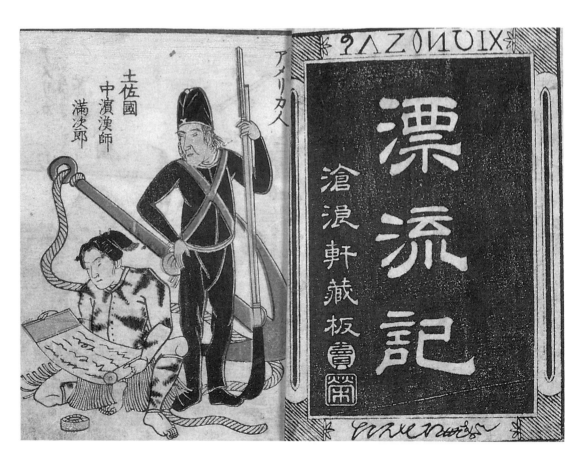

278: MANJIRO. *One of very few Japanese narratives of Pacific exploration.*

An extremely rare Pacific narrative (virtually the first by an Asian) Manjiro Nakahama played a major part in opening of Japan to the Western world. His account was written while the Japanese exclusions edict was still in effect, which forbade travel out of the country as well as the dissemination of any knowledge of foreign lands; it is signed with the pseudonym "Dontsushi". In the preface Manjiro explains: "I recorded this for the purpose of distributing among my friends. It is kept in secret so I am prohibited to sell this book".

Manjiro and four companions were shipwrecked in 1841 on the island of Torijima, where they existed for six months by eating albatross, until rescued by Captain Whitfield of the *John Howland.* Manjiro (better known at this time as "John Mung") accompanied Whitfield to New England where he became a member of his household and was given a sound New England education. He later went on several whaling voyages, eventually becoming first mate of the *Franklin.*

His later career included gold prospecting in California (1850) and translating Bowditch's *Practical Navigator* into Japanese. An accomplished seaman, he was the first Japanese to navigate a ship using Western scientific instruments.

On his return to Japan he was closely questioned regarding his extensive knowledge of America, and during Perry's visits in 1853 and 1854 served as translator and advisor. He was also official translator on two important expeditions from Japan to the West (the signing of the Commercial Treaty in Washington, 1860 and the observation of the Franco-Prussian War of 1870).

Elevated from the status of a common fisherman to that of low Samurai rank, and probably the first commoner to be allowed a given name, he was a legend both in Japan and in Fairhaven, Massachusetts. President Franklin D. Roosevelt once told Manjiro's biographer, Miss Emily Warinner that Manjiro was a "fabulous character of my boyhood".

The *Record of Drifting* contains the following woodcut illustrations of Manjiro's adventures:

1. Portrait of the author in his Western clothes; 2. Ship; 3. Hawaiian birds; 4. Taro of Oahu; 5. Shipwreck on Torijima; 6. Catching Albatross for food; 7. Manjiro's rescue by the *John Howland*; 8. Honolulu Harbour.

PRUSSIAN CIRCUMNAVIGATION

[279] MEYEN, F[ranz] J[ohann] F[riedrich]. REISE UM DIE ERDE ausgefurt auf dem konglich preussischen seehandlungs-schiffe Prinzess Louise, commandirt von Capitain W. Wendt, in den jahren 1830, 1831 und 1832. *2 volumes, quarto, with 2 folding maps (part coloured), lithograph view of Chile, and 2 plates; original printed boards, light dampstaining to lower fore-edge, affecting last portion of text only, but generally a fine uncut copy.* Berlin, In der Sander'schen Buchhandlung, 1834, 1835.

A very scarce Prussian circumnavigation, by a young naturalist who had joined the ship at the suggestion of Von Humboldt. Meyen's travels about South America are recorded in some detail: the Chile narrative on more than 200 pages, and that of Peru with more than 135 pages, and he includes a map of his travels. The *Princess Louise* stopped at Hawaii in

June 1832, where the author made a natural history tour about Oahu, stopping at Pearl Harbour. He includes a description of the town of Honolulu, a shipboard visit by Kamehameha III, notes on other members of the royal family and foreign residents including Don Marin. China was reached via Luzon, and Meyen devotes more than 100 pages to his stay at Canton, includes a detailed map of the factories, and an appendix which includes a chapter on chess and the game of "Go" with two explanatory plates.

The ship returned via the Cape of Good Hope, stopping at St. Helena long enough to make the obligatory visit to Napoleon's Tomb. *Not in Hill; Judd, 126; Not in Kroepelien; Borba de Moraes II, 570.*

THE CRUISE OF THE CYANE

[280] MEYERS, William H. JOURNAL OF A CRUISE TO CALIFORNIA AND THE SANDWICH ISLANDS in the United States Sloop-of-War Cyane, 1841-1844. Edited by John Haskell Kemble. *Folio, with frontispiece map and 10 coloured plates, red morocco spine, linen covered boards.* San Francisco, The Grabhorn Press for the Book Club of California, 1955.

In 1842, anticipating a war with Mexico over the question of Texas independence and fearing that Mexico might cede California to Britain, the *Cyane*, part of the U.S. Pacific Squadron, proceeded to Monterey California, where Capt. Thomas Catesby Jones marched ashore on October 20th, took possession and raised the American flag. It was hurriedly lowered the next day when it was learned that no such war had occurred. Later in August 1843, the ship visited Hawaii just after their sovereignty had been restored after a provisional cession to Britain. The author was a gunner aboard and the short but pithy entries in his journal are supplemented by his watercolours. The seven of California include San Francisco, Santa Barbara and San Diego, and one of the 3 views of Hawaii is a panoramic view of Honolulu.

A finely printed book — one of 400 copies — by the pre-eminent private press in California.

WHALING

[281] OLMSTED, Francis Allyn. INCIDENTS OF A WHALING VOYAGE. To which are added some observations on the Scenery, Manners and Customs, and Missionary Stations, of the Sandwich and Society Islands. *Octavo, with 12 lithograph plates from drawings by the author; original olive cloth, rebacked, preserving part of original spine, text foxed, plates inserted from another copy; very scarce in any condition.* New York, Published by D. Appleton and Co., 1841.

A valuable and much quoted work. Olmsted was advised to take a sea voyage for his health soon after graduation from Yale. He left New Haven on the whaler *North America* in 1839, and the text includes lively descriptions of whaling, illustrated with his sketches, which are considered among the best whaling scenes ever made. Olmsted was in Hawaii from May to August 1840, and provides a lengthy and fresh account including travels about the island of Hawaii, local chiefs, missionaries and customs. He left

282: PORTER. *Captain David Porter of the* Essex.

for Tahiti on the Bark *Flora* on August 3rd, curiously the first ship to export sugar from Hawaii to any American port. The Rev. Hiram Bingham and family were fellow passengers. He made a long stay in Tahiti which he describes in an attractive manner.

The views include the ship *North America*, three of Hawaiian churches, and a rare view of Hawaiians surfing. *Hill, p. 218; Judd, 138.*

THE CRUISE OF THE ESSEX

[282] PORTER, David. JOURNAL OF A CRUISE MADE TO THE PACIFIC OCEAN, by Captain David Porter, in the United States Frigate Essex, in the years 1812, 1813, and 1814. . . *Octavo, 2 volumes in 1 with a folding map (repaired) and 13 engraved plates, somewhat spotted and browned as is usual with American books of this period and particularly this title, overall an excellent copy in the original marbled sheep, neatly rebacked preserving old red label; with the ownership inscription in several places of Samuel Wetherill Junior.* Philadelphia, Published by Bradford and Inskeep, 1815.

The rare first edition of Porter's account of the first American naval expedition to the Pacific Ocean in 1813.

TORREY'S NARRATIVE:

OR, THE

LIFE AND ADVENTURES

OF

WILLIAM TORREY.

WHO FOR THE SPACE OF 25 MONTHS, WITHIN THE YEARS 1835, '36 AND '37, WAS HELD A CAPTIVE BY THE CANNIBALS OF THE MARQUESAS, (A GROUP OF ISLANDS IN THE SOUTH SEA,) AMONG WHOM HE WAS CAST FROM THE WRECK OF THE BRIG DOLL, CAPT. ———, OF OTAHEITE, OF WHICH WRECK HIMSELF, AND ONE SHIPMATE, CAN ALONE TELL THE SAD TALE. ALSO, FOR MANY YEARS SERVED IN THE SEVERAL CAPACITIES REQUISITE FOR SEAMEN, ON BOTH ENGLISH AND AMERICAN MERCHANTS' SHIPS.

WRITTEN BY HIMSELF.

Illustrated with Engravings of his own Sketching.

" 'Tis mine to tell a tale of grief,
Of constant peril, and of scant relief;
Of days of danger, and of nights of pain.''

BOSTON:
PRESS OF A. J. WRIGHT, 3 WATER STREET.
1848.

283: TORREY. *The memoirs of a runaway seaman.*

"Captain David Porter of the U.S. Navy was the only American commander to sail against the British in the Pacific Ocean during the War of 1812. In the Atlantic, the frigate Essex under Porter captured seven brigs, one ship, and the British sloop Alert. Sailing into the Pacific, around Cape Horn, without authority, he took many British whalers, doing British shipping damage to the extent of half a million pounds. Porter's step-son, David G. Farragut, sailed with him on this voyage. Porter annexed Nuku Hiva, the largest of the Marquesas or Washington Islands, but the government never asserted any claim. He also visited the Galapagos Islands. In March 1814, the Essex was captured off Valparaiso by the British warships Cherub and Phoebe. When Porter returned home, he was hailed as a hero. Porter, later, was involved in the Fajardo affair of 1824 on Puerto Rico and was found guilty by a court-martial for his role. He resigned from the U.S. Navy in anger and from 1826 to 1829 served as an admiral in the Mexican Navy. He ended his life as an American diplomat in Turkey." (Hill).

A particularly attractive copy of this rare narrative, which was several times reprinted: the Hill collection, at the time of their first catalogue in 1974, had only the second and third editions and described the first edition as "suppressed and a very rare book". The first edition was only added to the Library in time for their 1982 volume. *Hill, p. 540.*

"A SUCCESSFUL BOLT"

[283] TORREY, William. TORREY'S NARRATIVE: or the Life and Adventures of William Torrey. . . written by himself. *Duodecimo, frontispiece portrait, numerous text woodcuts; original olive cloth, rebacked, gilt ornament on upper cover, extremities worn, occasional spotting of text, recased with later endpapers; very scarce.* Boston, Press of A. J. Wright, 1848.

The Pacific adventures of a common seaman. Torrey, born of "poor but respectable parents" was several times a runaway from factory employment before making a "successful bolt" at age 18. He shipped for the Pacific on the *Huntress* at New Bedford in 1832, and was variously employed on sealing and whaling ships. He visited the Society Islands, Pitcairn, Tonga, the Galapagos (hunting for turtles), the coast of South America and the Northwest Coast. He went hunting at Drakes Bay California, and was in Hawaii in 1833 and 1837.

On the English ship the *Doll* he was shipwrecked at the Marquesas February 2, 1835, remaining there for 25 months in the course of which he took part in one of the incessant tribal wars, and was tattooed (as shown in his portrait). After his escape, he continued a nautical career in the Atlantic, but made a visit to Canton via the Cape of Good Hope. *Forster, The South Sea Whaler, 96; not in Hill; Judd, 173.*

XV
The United States Exploring Expedition

The United States Exploring Expedition, comprising the Sloops of War Vincennes *and* Peacock, *the
brig* Porpoise, *a store ship and two tenders, under the command of Charles Wilkes, sailed from Norfolk,
Virginia, on 18th August 1838. It was the first American scientific expedition, charged to "extend the
bounds of Science and promote the acquisition of knowledge", and was one of the most important and
ambitious Pacific expeditions ever attempted.*

*The expedition visited and explored the coast of South America, over 200 Pacific Islands, Australia and
New Zealand (1839-1840), the Hawaiian Islands (1840-41), the Northwest coast of America and
California (1841) and the South Pacific again in 1841. The ships returned home via the Philippines,
Singapore and the Cape of Good Hope, reaching New York in June 1842. The scientists collected
specimens wherever they went and, when possible, explored the interiors of the regions they visited —
notably Hawaii, the Oregon territory, California and Australia. Although many specimens were lost in
the wreck of the* Peacock *at the Columbia River in July 1840, an astonishing quantity of material was
brought back, the botanical specimens alone numbering 50,000 items.*

*The great achievement of the voyage, of course, was the expedition into the Antarctic in the winter of
1839-1840. Leaving Sydney in the last week of December, Wilkes spent January and February 1840
following the coastline of Antarctica long enough to prove its continental character. He turned back to
Sydney on the 22nd February, and published the first news of his discovery in the* Sydney Morning
Herald *of 13th March 1840, thus beginning a controversy over its discovery which still rages, as the
French explorer Dumont d'Urville had made a landfall at the same time. Recent work by Australian
cartographers tends to vindicate his discovery, but, says his biographer, "whoever first saw it, it was the*
Vincennes *train of successive land falls that won the prize by showing that a continent and not so many
islands lay within the ice".*

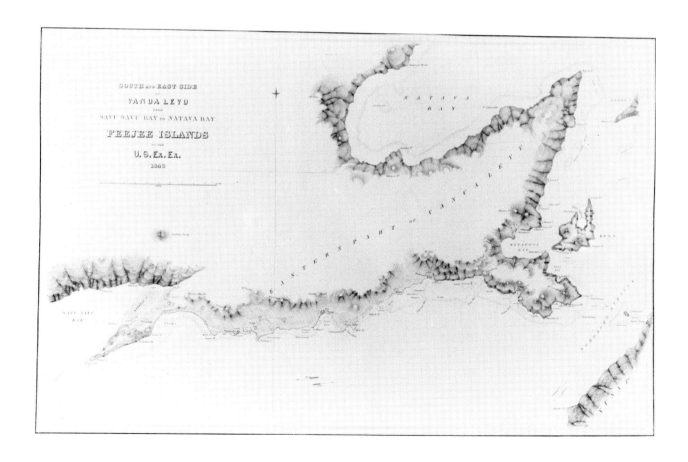

THE VERY RARE OFFICIAL ISSUE

[284] WILKES, Charles. NARRATIVE OF THE UNITED STATES EXPLORING EXPEDITION, during the years 1838, 1839, 1840, 1841, 1842. *All texts quarto, bound in original black morocco, gilt eagle devices on covers, expertly and sympathetically rebacked in black morocco by Sangorski; the atlases in original half black morocco and grey-green cloth, rebacked; texts good to fine, with coloured plates fresh and, apart from the occasional spot, very clean.* Philadelphia, 1844-1874.

A remarkable set of the extremely rare official issues of the formal account of the United States Exploring Expedition, issued over 30 years. Containing altogether 19 volumes of various sizes, this splendid set lacks only the following parts: Pickering, *Races of Man* (1848); Dana, *Geology text and atlas* (1849); Wilkes, *Meterology* (1851); Gould, *Mollusca text* (1852); Dana, *Crustacea text and atlas* (1852-55); Brackenridge, *Botany text and atlas* (1854-55); Wilkes, *Hydrography Atlas vol. I* (1850).

It should be emphasised that even single volumes from this voyage are rare, and a substantially complete set like this is almost unknown in private hands. This is probably the only set containing as many of the natural history texts and atlases that has been on the market in over 30 years, and it is highly unlikely that another will become available.

For a full bibliographical description and history of the publication, Daniel C. Haskell's *The United States Exploring Expedition, 1838-1842 and its Publications 1844-1874* (New York Public Library, 1942) should be consulted. The set comprises the following:

TEXTS:

NARRATIVE. By Charles Wilkes. *5 volumes, quarto, and an atlas, quarto with 5 folding maps (2 coloured).* Philadelphia, C. Sherman, 1844.

The official issue, of which 100 copies were printed, issued in 1845. (Note: the maps are never coloured in the regular issue). *Haskell, 16.*

ETHNOLOGY & PHILOLOGY. By Horatio Hale. *Quarto. With 2 charts (1 folding), and a folding map, coloured in part.* Philadelphia, C. Sherman, 1846.

The offical issue: 100 copies were printed but 25 were destroyed by fire. *Haskell, 19.*

ZOOPHYTES. By James D. Dana. *Quarto.* Philadelphia, C. Sherman, 1846.

The official issue: 100 copies were printed but 25 were destroyed by fire. This is the first state with the very rare preface known in only a few copies (here bound upside down). *Haskell, 21-a.*

MAMMALOGY & ORNITHOLOGY. By John Cassin. *Quarto.* Philadelphia, C. Sherman, 1858.

The official issue, of which 100 copies were printed, as a replacement to the Peale text which Wilkes had found objectionable (see Haskell no. 27). *Haskell, 28.*

BOTANY. PART I. PHANEROGAMIA. By Asa Grey. *Quarto.* Philadelphia, C. Sherman, 1854.

The official issue: 100 copies were printed but 21 were destroyed by fire and not replaced. *Haskell, 60.*

BOTANY. CRYPTOGAMIA. By William S. Sullivant (& five others). Phanerogamia. By John Torrey. *Quarto.* Philadelphia, Sherman & Co., 1874.

The official issue, of which 100 copies were printed, but few actually distributed. *Haskell, 68.*

HERPETOLOGY. By S. F. Baird. *Quarto.* Philadelphia, C. Sherman, 1858.

The official issue, of which 100 copies were printed (the actual author was Dr. Charles Girard — see Haskell, 76, pp. 99-100). *Haskell, 76.*

HYDROGRAPHY. By Charles Wilkes. *Quarto. With 3*

284: WILKES. *Coloured plate, after a drawing by Peale, from the Mammalogy Atlas of the Wilkes voyage.*

folding maps and 2 plates. Philadelphia, C. Sherman, 1861.

The official issue: 100 copies were printed, but it was not actually issued until 1873. *Haskell, 80.*

ATLASES:

ZOOPHYTES. By James D. Dana. *Folio, with 61 hand coloured engraved plates.* Philadelphia, C. Sherman, 1849.

The official issue: 100 copies were printed but 25 were destroyed by fire and later replaced; plate number 27 is misnumbered '30'. *Haskell, 25.*

MAMMALOGY & ORNITHOLOGY. By John Cassin. *Folio, with 53 hand coloured engraved plates.* Philadelphia, C. Sherman 1858.

The official issue, of which 100 copies were printed; with plate 42 "procellaria invea" in the second state as in all copies of the official issue. *Haskell, 30.*

MOLLUSCA & SHELLS. By Augustus Gould. *Folio, with 52 hand coloured engraved plates.* Philadelphia, C. Sherman 1856.

The official issue, of which 100 copies were printed, although it was not issued until 1860. *Haskell, 52.*

BOTANY. PHANEROGAMIA. By Asa Grey. *Folio, with 100 engraved plates.* Philadelphia, C. Sherman 1856.

The official issue, of which 100 copies were printed, although it was not issued until 1858. *Haskell, 62.*

HERPETOLOGY. By S. F. Baird (i.e. Dr. Charles Girard). *Folio, with 23 hand coloured engraved plates.* Philadelphia, C. Sherman 1858

The official issue, of which 100 copies were printed. This was all that was issued of this section, although the text lists and describes 32 plates. *Haskell, 78.*

ATLAS OF CHARTS. Vol. II. *Elephant folio, with engraved charts and maps.* Philadelphia, C. Sherman 1858.

The official issue, of which 100 copies were printed, issued in 1859. *Haskell, 85.*

On August 26th, 1842, shortly after the return of the exploring expedition, Congress passed an Act providing for a publication ". . . with illustrations and published in a form similar to the voyage of the Astrolabe, lately published by the Government of France". It was determined that "nothing should be printed except what was new" and that the work should be an American production. The scientists were instructed to surrender all journals and records to the Captain, and to furnish no information to outsiders. The narrative appeared first, and was lavishly illustrated by more than 350 views and vignettes by the artists Agate and Peale. The scope of the publication increased even as official indifference mounted. The 15 volumes of text and 9 atlases planned by Wilkes in 1845, had increased by 1848 to 18 text and 11 atlases, though many of these had to be abandoned. That anything at all appeared was due to the determination of Wilkes himself, who year after year bullied the Congress for appropriations and wrote that ". . . in Science as in Law you must expect to pay well for talent". One senator compared the publication to the famous and long standing chancery suit "Jarndyce vs. Jarndyce" in Dickens' *Bleak House*, while another suggested that the solution was to throw the whole thing into the Potomac. By 1872, the total appropriations amounted to approximately $369,000 and there were (and still are) unfinished parts.

One hundred copies of each part were printed, but a fire in the printers' warehouse destroyed 25 copies of many of the parts, some of which were replaced by unofficial issues. Sixty-three copies were immediately distributed on publication, one to each state, and designated countries, with 2 each to France, Great Britain and Russia. Copies were kept in reserve for future states. Only three copies were issued to private citizens — William C. Hudson, Cadwallader Ringgold, and Captain Wilkes himself. *Hill, pp. 600-602 and passim (only 10 volumes of the official issue held in the collection); Ferguson, 3954.*

THE ZOOPHYTE ATLAS

[285] [WILKES]. DANA, James D. ZOOPHYTE ATLAS. *Folio, with 61 engraved plates (part coloured), with plate 27 misnumbered 30 as in almost all copies; original half black publishers morocco, title in gilt and gilt eagle at top of panelled spine, slight cracking of joints, some browning to explanation leaves as usual, plates in fine condition and free*

284: WILKES. *One of a series of engravings of snakes from the* Herpetology Atlas *of the Wilkes expedition.*

286: WILKES. *Studio portrait of Commander Wilkes.*

from spotting; a fine copy. Philadelphia, [C. Sherman], 1849.

Official issue, one of 100 copies printed, of which 25 were destroyed by fire but later replaced. The 61 plates contain 1008 figures, and illustrate the text of Dana's important work on Corals, which he planned as the "most complete work on the subject ever published". Very rare. *Haskell, 25.*

THE STORMY PETREL

[286] [WILKES]. Commander Charles Wilkes. CARTE DE VISITE PHOTOGRAPH, mounted on card reading "Brady's National Portrait Gallery, Washington". *Fine image, top corners clipped, and very slight spotting to top, with retail label of Selby & McCauley, Baltimore Street, on verso.* Washington, circa 1860.

An attractive three-quarter portrait of the Commander of the United States Exploring

Expedition, taken in the most famous photograph studio in America. Although it is often dangerous to deduce character from a photograph, one can here clearly see the determination that earned him the title of "the stormy petrel".

WILKES' THEORY OF THE WINDS

[287] WILKES, Commander Charles. THEORY OF THE WINDS... To which is added Sailing Directions for a Voyage around the World... *Large octavo, with a large folding map and two other charts; front flyleaf missing, otherwise a near-fine copy in the original black cloth, gilt.* Philadelphia, 1856.

Wilkes' article on the theory of the winds was intended for the official volume of Hydrography, which did not actually appear until 1861 (see above). He explains here that "many delays incident to the publication of such an extensive work have taken place, both in the preparation, engraving and printing, which have been beyond the control of those engaged in its superintendence. But, even the part that has been printed is, as it were, a sealed book — for there are only one hundred copies ordered by the Government for the use of the world!"

Haskell describes an original binding of brown paper wrappers, but not the black cloth binding seen here, which may indicate a special issue. *Haskell, 81.*

LIGHTS AND SHADOWS

[288] CLARK, Joseph G. LIGHTS AND SHADOWS OF SAILOR LIFE, as exemplified in fifteen years' experience, including the more thrilling events of the U.S. Exploring Expedition. *Octavo; original dark green cloth, front hinge tender, light foxing to text, slight wear to head and toe of spine.* Boston, John Putnam, 1847.

Presentation copy from the author to Revd. Thomas Dawes of Fair Haven, Nov. 22, 1847. This is a narrative of the Wilkes expedition by a seaman aboard the *Vincennes*, in which the author, following the official narrative, describes various Pacific islands, Australia, the North West Coast and California, from a personal viewpoint. At Fiji, during a confrontation with the natives, his companions Emmons and Henry were killed and he narrowly escaped. *Hill, p. 53; not in Ferguson.*

FIRST ILLUSTRATED EDITION

[289] [WILKES] CLARK, Joseph G. LIGHTS AND SHADOWS OF SAILOR LIFE... including the more thrilling events of the U.S. Exploring Expedition. *Duodecimo, with 6 woodcut illustrations; original brown blind stamped cloth, gilt ship ornament on upper cover, gilt spine; slight wear to covers and spine; a good copy.* Boston, Benjamin B. Mussey, 1848.

Second edition; the woodcut illustrations appear here for the first time. Despite some 5 pages on Australia, this was not known to Ferguson, and only a single copy of this edition (Sydney University), and none of the first edition (see above), is recorded in the Addenda volume. *Ferguson, 4735a; Hill, p. 53 (first edition only); Judd, 34; Haskell, 113 (not noting this edition).*

Books Consulted

General Index

Index of Ships' Names

Books Consulted

ABBEY, J. R. *Travel in Aquatint and Lithography . . . from the Library of J. R. Abbey*, 1956-57.

BEAGLEHOLE, J. C. *The Journals of Captain James Cook, edited by J. C. Beaglehole.* Hakluyt Society, 1955-67; *The Life of Captain James Cook*, 1974.

BEDDIE, M.K. *Bibliography of Captain James Cook.* Sydney, 1970.

BORBA DE MORAES, R. *Bibliographia Brasiliana.* Revised edition, Los Angeles, 1983.

BUCK, Peter H. *Explorers of the Pacific.* Bernice P. Bishop Museum, special publication 43. Honolulu, The Museum, 1953.

DAVIDSON, Rodney. *A Book Collector's Notes on Items relating to the Discovery of Australia.* Melbourne, 1970.

DAY, A. Grove. *Books about Hawaii.* Honolulu, 1977.

DNB. *Dictionary of National Biography.* 1908-1986.

DUNMORE, John. *French Explorers in the Pacific. Vol. I. The Eighteenth Century. Vol. II. The Nineteenth Century.* Oxford, 1965-1969.

DUNN, F. M. *A Catalogue of Memorials by Pedro Fernandez de Quiros . . . in the Dixson and Mitchell Libraries.* Sydney, 1974.

FERGUSON. *Bibliography of Australia.* Sydney, 1941-1986.

FORSTER, Honore. *The South Sea Whaler.* Sharon, Massachusetts, The Kendall Whaling Museum, 1985.

HASKELL, Daniel C. *The United States Exploring Expedition, 1838-1842, and its publications.* New York Public Library, 1942.

HILL. *The Hill Collection of Pacific Voyages, edited by Ronald L. S. De Braganze (and others).* San Diego, University of California, 1974, 1982, 1983.

HOCKEN, T. M. *A Bibliography of New Zealand.* Wellington, 1909.

HOLMES, Sir Maurice. *Captain James Cook, R.N., F.R.S. A Bibliographical Excursion.* London, 1952.

HUNNEWELL, James F. *Bibliography of the Hawaiian Islands.* Boston, 1869.

JUDD, Bernice & LIND, Helen Yonge. *Voyages to Hawaii before 1860.* Honolulu, 1974.

JOPPIEN, Rudiger & SMITH, Bernard. *The Art of Captain Cook's Voyages,* Vols. I & II. Oxford, 1985.

KROEPELIEN. Bibliotheca Polynesiana. *A Catalogue of some of the books in the Polynesiana Collection formed by the late Bjarne Kroepelien, by Rolf du Rietz.* Oslo, privately published, 1969.

LADA-MOCARSKI, Valerian. *Bibliography of books on Alaska published before 1868.* New Haven, Yale University Press, 1969.

MARCHANT, Leslie. *France Australe.* Perth, 1982.

MOOREHEAD, Alan. *The Fatal Impact. An Account of the Invasion of the South Pacific 1767-1840.* 1966.

NAN KIVELL, R. and S. SPENCE. *Portraits of the Famous and Infamous.* 1970.

NMM. *National Maritime Museum Catalogue of the Library.* 5 volumes. 1968-1976.

O'REILLY, Patrick & Edouard REITMAN. *Bibliographie de Tahiti et de la Polynesie Francaise.* Paris, Musée de l'Homme, 1967.

POLAK, Jean. *Bibliographie Maritime Francaise.* Grenoble, 1976-83.

PRINTING AND THE MIND OF MAN. *A Descriptive Catalogue illustrating the Impact of Print on the Evolution of Western Civilisation, by John Carter and Percy H. Muir.* 1967.

ROBERT, Willem C. H. *Contributions to a Bibliography of Australia and the South Sea Islands.* 4 volumes. Amsterdam, 1969.

SABIN, Joseph. *Dictionary of Books relating to America.* New York, 1868-1936.

SHARP, Andrew. *The Discovery of the Pacific Islands.* Oxford, The Clarendon Press, 1960.

SCHILDER, Gunter. *Australia Unveiled.* Amsterdam, 1975.

SMITH, Bernard. *European Vision and the South Pacific*. Second (revised) edition. Sydney, 1984.

SPATE, O.H.K. *The Pacific Since Magellan*. 2 volumes. Canberra, 1979-1983.

STC. *Short-Title Catalogue of Books Printed in England, Scotland & Ireland . . . 1475-1640*. 1976-1980.

TIELE, P. A. *Memoire Bibliographique sur les Journaux des Navigateurs Neerlandais . . . la plupart en la possession de Frederik Muller*. Amsterdam, 1867.

TOOLEY, R. V. *English Books with Coloured Plates 1790 to 1860*. Revised edition, Folkestone, 1979.

TOOLEY, R. V. *The Mapping of Australia*. 1979.

TOOLEY, R. V. *The Mapping of America*. 1980.

WANTRUP, Jonathan. *Australian Rare Books 1788-1900*. Sydney, Hordern House, 1987.

WING, Ronald. *Short Title Catalogue of English Books 1641-1700*. New York, 1972-82-51.

General Index

Index of Ships' Names